Ignoring Poverty in the U.S.

The Corporate Takeover of Public Education

Ignoring Poverty in the U.S.

The Corporate Takeover of Public Education

by

P. L. Thomas
Furman University

Information Age Publishing, Inc.
Charlotte, North Carolina • www.infoagepub.com

Library of Congress Cataloging-in-Publication Data

Thomas, P. L. (Paul Lee), 1961-
Ignoring poverty in the U.S. : the corporate takeover of public education
/ by P. L. Thomas.
p. cm.
Includes bibliographical references.
ISBN 978-1-61735-783-1 (pbk.) -- ISBN 978-1-61735-784-8 (hc) --
ISBN 978-1-61735-785-5 (ebk) 1. Business and education--United States.
2. Education--Economic aspects--United States. 3. Poor
children--Education--United States. 4. Education and state--United States.
5. Public schools--United States. 6. Educational equalization--United
States. I. Title.
LC1085.2.T53 2011
379.1'11--dc23

                                            2012003206

Printed in the United States of America

CONTENTS

ACKNOWLEDGMENTS

While drafting this book on ignoring poverty, I experienced a resurgence in my life as a poet; much of the drafting was tinted and seemingly bogged down by hours spent on poems instead of drafting this book. One poem that emerged is:

"poverty and poetry"

poverty turns to *poetry*
just drop the "v"

po erty
   v

and swap the "r" and "t"

poetry

playing with words
becomes obscene
when we believe
words matter more
than what they mean

As I write this brief acknowledgment, poetry, being a writer, and being a scholar remind me again and again about the collaborative and communal nature of expression that tends to get lost and marginalized in academia and the public sphere. In short, this book, like all of my writing, would never exist without countless others who contribute directly and indirectly to the work. Although this will be incomplete, I would like to acknowledge some of those influences:

Ignoring Poverty in the U.S.: The Corporate Takeover of Public Education, pp. vii–viii

- Beth Day, former Furman student and beginning teacher, who read, copy-edited, and offered insight during the drafting of this book. Her contribution is transparent to the reader, but invaluable to me.

- Information Age Publishing, George Johnson (president and publisher, IAP), and Curry Mallott, the confluence of faith and support that has welcomed my work at IAP.

- Nita Schmidt, former colleague at Furman University and brilliant scholar, who contributes to my scholarly life perpetually.

- Furman University and Woodruff High, the places of my career that have been the workshops for my coming to know better teaching, learning, and the powerful influence of privilege and poverty.

- A wide range of fellow scholars who have come more directly into my life as a scholar in recent years—Adam Bessie, Stephen Krashen, Susan Ohanian, Diane Ravitch, Walt Gardner, Randy Bomer, Paul Gorski, Stephanie Jones, Valerie Strauss, and the National Education Policy Center.

- All the teachers and students of my life and career, too many to name but too important not to acknowledge.

- The touchstones for my place in the universe—Kurt Vonnegut, Margaret Atwood, e. e. cummings, George Carlin, Howard Zinn, Paulo Freire, bell hooks.... It is art and activism that celebrate and seek human dignity and social justice in ways that politics and the market never will....

- Portions of this book have been adapted from commentaries/Op-Eds and scholarly articles (2010b, 2010c, 2010d, 2010e, 2010f,

- 2010g, 2010h, 2010i, 2010j, 2010k, 2010l, 2010m, 2010n, 2010o,

- 2010p, 2010q, 2010r, 2010s, 2010t, 2010u, 2010v, 2010w, 2010x,

- 2010y, 2010z, 2010aa, 2011a, 2011b, 2011b, 2011d, 2011e, 2011f, 2011g, 2011h, 2011j, 2011k, 2011n, 2011o, 2011p, 2011q, 2011s, 2011t, 2011u, 2011v, 2011w, 2001y, 2011aa).

PREFACE

Adam Bessie

We've all heard the "F" word, that unspeakable expletive that everyone knows, but no one is supposed to say in polite company. Now, we have another such unmentionable: the "P" word. And Paul Thomas hasn't been afraid to spell it out, especially in polite company: P-O-V-E-R-T-Y.

In 2010, as nearly 1/6 of the country found itself below the poverty threshold in the Great Recession, the "P" word could not be found, lost from our national discourse (Mulady, 2011). Most likely, you'll find poverty cloaked in Orwellian euphemism, hidden under opaque doublespeak like "jobless recovery," which permits us to discuss our vast, persistent unemployment without actually having to think about our neighbors struggling to make ends meet. Similarly, the reams of statistics and reports on the Great Recession—filled with numbers so vast and arcane—sterilize poverty, cleansing it from any human experience. And when the "P" word absolutely must be used, it's most likely to be placed inside sarcastic quote marks, as a Fox News segment did, pointing out that nearly all "poor" Americans have modern "luxuries," like the refrigerator (Cavuto, 2011).

During the time we have needed to talk about poverty most directly, when we have had the most poor Americans in over 50 years of recorded history (United States Census Bureau, 2011), the "P" word was not casually misplaced, lost like an errant bottle of ketchup in the back of the fridge; rather, as Thomas has passionately argued in *The New York Times*, *The Washington Post*, and pretty much everywhere he can, it has been ignored, minimized, and actively maligned—especially in the dramatic, highly publicized national debates on education reform. Rather than dis-

Ignoring Poverty in the U.S.: The Corporate Takeover of Public Education, pp. ix–xv
Copyright © 2012 by Information Age Publishing

cuss how the vast foreclosures and unemployment affect our children, rather than acknowledge the 20% childhood poverty rate which plagues us, rather than face the reality that 1 in 10 children find themselves mired in "deep poverty," surviving on half the poverty threshold (Gould, 2011), we hear repeated, over and again:

Poverty doesn't exist.

Poverty doesn't matter.

And Thomas, a veteran educator and prolific scholar, has been an almost singular voice of dissent against this powerful tide, tirelessly reminding us of a simple truth:

Poverty does exist.

Poverty does matter.

Thomas has not made a revolutionary discovery. But when first reading his passionate posts last year at the *Daily Censored* (an independent blog at which I write as well), it certainly felt to me like a revelation—finally, somebody had the temerity to say aloud my truth, what I see every day as a community college English professor in the San Francisco Bay Area, dealing with many teens and adults fighting for their education against incredible odds.

In Thomas's pugnacious prose, I see my student Cecilia. We are meeting in my office to discuss the first essay, which she has not passed. As we are studying the sentences on the page, as we look at her verb tense and her thesis statement, we start to talk about life, about the circumstances in which she wrote the paper. To answer, Cecilia pulls out another paper—the local newspaper, dated the previous day—in which she was just featured on the front page. In 2008, she had full-time work and had a place of her own, raising her two young sons; today, at 27, Cecilia now lives in "deep poverty," which means that she has less than $11,000 a year to run the house and take care of her boys. She has been out of work for a year, and has had to move in with her grandmother—to a house that is in foreclosure.

"I'm pretty much homeless," Cecilia told the reporter (O'Brien, 2011, n.p.). While she has earned a medical assistant certificate, she elaborated to me, she hasn't been able to find an open position, and has been cleaning houses whenever she can. "I never thought it would be this bad," Cecilia said in the newspaper, which we read together in my office, her essay pushed to the side for a moment. "My situation is pretty scary, in terms of housing, kids and being able to provide for them" (n.p.).

And Cecilia is not alone. She may be the most recent (I talked to her hours before writing these words), but she is just one in a seemingly endless line of real, living people, sitting in my office, essay trembling in hand, struggling with all their might for their educations, for their futures, for their family's future, against the terrible gravity of poverty, pulling them away from school, away from their dreams, away from security and safety.

Cecilia does exist.

She does matter.

Besides Thomas's posts, however, Cecelia doesn't seem to exist. My students are unmentionables, like the "P" word; they aren't discussed, are not really "poor," or they deserve their poverty.

And when my students do exist, they are held aloft as icons of failure—but not the failure of the speculative, deregulated corporatism that blew the housing bubble until it burst our economy, leaving a trail of foreclosures, decimated communities, lost pensions, and poverty in its wake. And certainly, their struggles do not represent the moral failure of the richest nation in the history of the world to invest in the welfare of all its citizens, especially its most vulnerable.

No, in the widely disseminated and largely unchallenged script of the "'no excuses' reformers"—as Thomas has dubbed billionaire Bill Gates, celebrity superintendent Michelle Rhee, and their followers—the struggles of students like Cecilia represent the failure of public education, and, in particular, the teachers themselves. Yes, the Bad Teacher now infests our schools, sleeping through class wearing the same stained shirt he had on the night before, waiting down the clock for the school day to end and a fat, unearned pension check to roll in (Bessie, 2010).

The documentary *Waiting for "Superman"* introduced the public to the Bad Teacher, who, along with the Evil Union, has left us with Broken Schools, in a state of crisis that threatens to destroy the very fabric of the nation. The Bad Teacher—and public education in general—is the villain du jour, the lazy fat cat at which the American public can project its considerable frustration and anger about the Great Recession. And these poor, marginalized students—and the future of our nation in general—can only be saved by a vigorous "free-market," by deregulation, by privatization, by "productivity" and "accountability." In *Waiting for "Superman"*—and the script of the new reformers performed by countless pundits and unwitting reporters across the media—our students can only be saved by the very same cutthroat corporate culture that busted and bankrupted the country (see Huff & Bessie, 2011, for a thorough discussion of this education reform narrative).

Talk about suspension of disbelief.

Less than a decade ago, this corporate reform script—based on loathing of "big government" and blind faith in the goodness of the "free-market"—was discussed exclusively by conservative think tanks like the American Enterprise Institute (AEI) without currency nor popular sway. Now, these formerly marginal ideas enjoy "the status of conventional wisdom," as Richard Rothstein (2011) of the Economic Policy Institute commented on Court-TV founder Steve Brill's union-bashing book *Class Warfare*.

Conservative education scholars at *Education Next* cite the success of their ideas with *Waiting for "Superman"*—not just because of its popularity, but because it was directed by a "liberal," Davis Guggenheim, best known for his global warming documentary with former Democratic Vice President Al Gore, *An Inconvenient Truth* (Peterson, Kanstoroom, & Finn, Jr., 2011). Indeed, President Barack Obama—labeled a socialist for the first half of his presidency—"seemed to be channeling a generation of conservative education analysts in stating bluntly that more money absent reform won't do much to improve public schools" when Obama appeared on *The Today Show* (Hess, West, & Petrelli, 2011, n.p.). And President Obama's education policies also follow the same corporate reform script, one which gave President George W. Bush a "third term in office," according to distinguished education historian Diane Ravitch (2009), by essentially rubber stamping the same failed free-market reforms of his conservative predecessor.

This "new normal" is best defined by another "P" word: Productivity. Secretary of Education Arne Duncan (2010) presented at AEI alongside the neoconservative think tank's resident education scholar Frederick Hess, in a session entitled "The New Normal: Doing More With Less." Rather than discuss the consequences of "less" on students, rather than discussing how poverty has affected learning, Duncan sounds more like a CEO selling widgets: during the course of the speech, Duncan said "productivity" 17 times, and "learning" five times. He did not mention "poverty" once during the speech, a pattern which Thomas shows has been normal for Duncan—and the Obama administration in general.

Not only did the corporate message of the new reformers enjoy bipartisan support at the highest levels of our government, but also the Fourth Estate was caught up in the hype, unwilling or unable to seriously question the "miracle cure" (Ravitch, 2011) they pitched, even though there is ample evidence that these reforms are questionable at best—evidence Thomas provides in this book. Rather, as Thomas has shown us time and again—and does in this book, damningly—the media has willingly participated in the corporate reform narrative, providing new reformers without education experience, like Bill Gates and musician John Legend, expert status, allowing them a platform to broadcast their claims without the annoying interference of questions. While the new reformers cry for accountability, they themselves have not been held accountable by the press, as Thomas shows us here, and as new reformer Hess himself found in a study of corporate news from 1995 through 2005: reporters were loathe to write critical accounts of the education philanthropists funding the reform movement, finding there to be 13 positive accounts to each critical one (Ravitch, 2010). More recently, Hess said in a *New York Times* report, "everyone is implicated" in supporting Gates' efforts to reform education—including Hess himself, whose organization received $500,000 from The Gates Foundation for advocacy. Overall, The Gates Foundation invested nearly eighty million dollars in such public relations efforts, including two million to promote *Waiting for "Superman"* (Dillon, 2011)—and thus, it should be of little surprise that the Myth of Bad Teacher, the Evil Union, the Broken School, and the Miracle Cure of the Free Market have become "conventional wisdom."

Welcome to the new normal—the education reform bubble, a powerful consensus between the government, corporate America, and the media, filled with hype and unjustified, unproven optimism in the power of the free market, one that sounds frighteningly similar to the real estate bubble, as veteran educator Anthony Cody (2011) observed. "Cut off from dissenters, the [echo] chambers fill with an unjustified sense of certainty" (Gladstone, 2011, p. 130), NPR media critic Brooke Gladstone observes in *The Influencing Machine*, in what could well describe the current education reform discussion. Gladstone calls this phenomenon "incestuous amplification," in which the "like-minded," isolated or insulated from critique, grow increasingly extreme in their beliefs, "marginaliz[ing] the moderates and demonize[ing] dissenters" (p. 130). The education reform bubble amplifies the chorus, it encourages ideological harmony, and it won't let anyone on stage who refuses to sing along (Bessie, 2011).

And with this book, Paul Thomas has climbed on stage and refuses to sing along. Instead, he has created his own harmony, composed of Thomas Jefferson, Diane Ravitch, Kurt Vonnegut, Paulo Friere, James Baldwin, Henry Giroux and Martin Luther King, powerful and diverse voices that tell an entirely different tale of what public education is—and can be—in America. And in this song, we can hear Cecilia, her life the chorus, the center of his verse: she exists, she matters. And where the new reformers sing a tragedy of impending educational apocalypse, Thomas sings of promise, of a truly public educational system, of a nation that no longer ignores poverty, that no longer marginalizes nor maligns those mired in it, but rather, of one that refuses to tolerate poverty, that strives to fulfill Cecilia's promise, and that of her boys, just entering school.

Cecilia's promise, Thomas believes, can be fulfilled if we can start to sing along, and create a harmony of our own:

Poverty does exist.

Poverty does matter.

REFERENCES

Bessie, A. (2010, October 8). The myth of the bad teacher. *The Daily Censored.* Retrieved from http://dailycensored.com/2010/10/08/the-myth-of-the-bad-teacher/

Bessie, A. (2011, July 4). Indestructible! Nothing can stop it! The "Education Reform" bubble. *Common Dreams.* Retrieved from http://www.commondreams.org/view/2011/07/04-0

Cavuto, N. (2011, July 19). Your World with Neil Cavuto [Television series episode]. New York, NY: Fox News Network.

Cody, A. (2011, April 28). When will the testing bubble burst? *Education Week.* Living in Dialogue [Web log post]. Retrieved from http://blogs.edweek.org/teachers/living-in-dialogue/2011/04/when_will_the_testing_bubble_b.html

Dillon, S. (2011, May 21). Behind grass-roots advocacy, Bill Gates. *The New York Times.* Retrieved from http://www.nytimes.com/2011/05/22/education/22gates.html?_r=2&ref=todayspaper

Duncan, A. (2010, November 17). The new normal: Doing more with less. Presented at the *American Enterprise Institute* panel "Bang for the Buck in Schooling." Washington, D.C. Retrieved from http://www.aei.org/docLib/20101117-Arne-Duncan-Remarks.pdf

Gladstone, B. (2011). *The influencing machine.* New York, NY: W. W. Norton.

Gould, E. (2011, September 13). Deep poverty at all time high. *Economic Policy Institute* [Web log post]. Retrieved from http://www.epi.org/blog/deep-poverty-time-high/

Hess, F., West, M., & Petrelli, M. (Spring 2011). Pyrrhic victories. *Education Next: A Journal of Opinion and Research.* Retrieved from http://educationnext.org/pyrrhic-victories/

Huff, M., & Bessie, A. (with Martin, A. Higdon, N., & Damiens, C. R.) (2011). Framing the messengers: Junk food news and news abuse for dummies. In M. Huff (Ed.), *Censored 2012: Sourcebook for the Media Revolution* (pp. 183-228). New York, NY: Seven Stories Press.

Mulady, K. (2011, August 21). Poverty. Just say it. *truthout.* Retrieved from http://www.truth-out.org/poverty-just-say-it/1313932122

O'Brien, M. (2011, Sept. 13). Young people hit hard as U.S. poverty rate increases to 15.1 percent. *Contra Costa Times.* Retrieved from http://www.contracostatimes.com/news/ci_18884838?nclick_check=1

Peterson, P., Kanstoroom, M., & Finn, C., Jr. (2011, Spring). A battle begun, not won. *Education Next: A Journal of Opinion and Research.* Retrieved from http://educationnext.org/a-battle-begun-not-won/

Ravitch, D. (2009, June 13). Obama gives Bush a 3rd term in office. *The Huffington Post.* Retrieved from http://www.huffingtonpost.com/diane-ravitch/obama-gives-bush-a-3rd-te_b_215277.html

Ravitch, D. (2010). *The death and life of the great American school system.* New York, NY: Basic Books.

Ravitch, D. (2011, May 31). Waiting for the miracle school. *The New York Times.* Retrieved from http://www.nytimes.com/2011/06/01/opinion/01ravitch.html

Rothstein, R. (2011, September 1). Grading the education reformers: Steven Brill gives them much too easy a ride. *Education Review.* Retrieved from http://www.edrev.info/essays/v14n8.pdf

United States Census Bureau. (2011, September 13). *Income, poverty and health insurance in the United States: 2010—Highlights.* Retrieved from http://www.census.gov/hhes/www/poverty/data/incpovhlth/2010/highlights.html

INTRODUCTION

Thomas Friedman carries authority as a columnist for *The New York Times* and as a winner of the Pulitzer Prize for best-selling books such as *The World Is Flat*. And when he writes to endorse the U.S. Secretary of Education, the authority is magnified exponentially.

At the end of the first decade of the twenty-first century, Friedman's (2010) "Teaching for America" is a stark snapshot of the popular and political view of poverty and education in the U.S. But that snapshot isn't pretty or flattering. And it is significant for what is left out more so than for what is captured.

Friedman's (2010) commentary on Secretary of Education Arne Duncan's November 4, 2010 speech reveals an ironic lesson that many people have failed to learn from Mark Twain's apt quip from the turn of the twentieth century: "Figures often beguile me, particularly when I have the arranging of them myself; in which case the remark attributed to Disraeli would often apply with justice and force: 'There are three kinds of lies: lies, damned lies and statistics'" (Twain, 2000, p. 195).[1]

Friedman (2010) proceeds to reinforce Duncan's claims about education in the U.S. without mentioning poverty a single time (just as Duncan mentioned teachers over four dozen times in an August 25, 2010, speech in Little Rock, Arkansas, also without mentioning poverty). As well, Friedman emphasizes a "few data points" offered by Duncan as evidence.

While Duncan's November speech, noted earlier, being lauded by Friedman does mention poverty, Duncan does so only to reinforce that education somehow has the power alone to produce something just shy of miracles:

> Education is still the key to eliminating gender inequities, to reducing poverty, to creating a sustainable planet, and to fostering peace. And in a

Ignoring Poverty in the U.S.: The Corporate Takeover of Public Education, pp. xvii–xxviii
Copyright © 2012 by Information Age Publishing

knowledge economy, education is the new currency by which nations maintain economic competitiveness and global prosperity. (Duncan, 2010c)

This idealism is powerful in the U.S., where many are committed to the cultural myths that guide and deform us (Freire, 1998)—rugged individualism, pulling one's self up by the boot straps, a rising tide lifting all boats.

The possibilities inherent in education as a process and the influence of poverty as a reality in the lives of millions of people (including children) are addressed as *both* myths and facts any time the power elites address either education or poverty—directly and by omission. Education suffers a dual fate that is contradictory (education can cure all ills, *but* our public education system is now and always has been a failure), while poverty is seen as a phenomenon without any *cause*—other than the not-so-subtle American charge that people living in poverty have failed the consumer culture and the rights to life, liberty, and the pursuit of happiness bestowed upon all in the greatest country ever to exist.

Education and poverty, if one listens only to the surface of what political and media elites say, exist in vacuums.

A "FEW DATA POINTS"—STATISTICS AS DECEPTION

Before examining the claims about education offered (in the chasm left by ignoring or distorting poverty) from both Friedman and Duncan, let's look briefly at a state-to-state comparison here in the U.S. to illustrate the folly of making sweeping claims about educational quality with a "few data points" (Thomas, 2010w, 2010z), especially when those data points are crafted to paint an incomplete picture.

Two southern states, Mississippi and South Carolina, share both a long history of high poverty rates (Mississippi at over 30% and South Carolina at over 25%, the first and tenth most impoverished states in the union in 2010) and reputations for failing schools systems. Yet, when comparing the 2010 SAT scores from Mississippi (CR 566, M 548, W 552 for a 1666 total) to scores in South Carolina (CR 484, 495, 468 for a 1447 total), we may be compelled to conclude that, through their education system, Mississippi has overcome a higher poverty rate than South Carolina to achieve, on average, 219 points greater.

This conclusion, based on a "few data points," is factually accurate, but ultimately false once we add just one more data point, the percentage of students taking the exam: 3% of Mississippi seniors took the exam compared to 66% in South Carolina. A fact of statistics tells us that South Carolina's larger percentage taking the exam is much closer to the normal distribution of all seniors in that state; thus the average must be lower than a uniquely elite population, such as the 3% population of test takers in Mississippi. Here, the data point of populations taking the exam trumps the raw data of test averages even when placed in the context of poverty.

In short, the SAT averages used to compare Mississippi and South Carolina tell us little of value—except that statistics, a "few data points," are powerful when carefully selected to match the assumptions already existing in a culture eager to have those assumptions reinforced but unwilling to confront them even when presented with data. This is how many are apt to offer numbers without ever uttering the word "poverty."

And thus, the claims made by Friedman based on the speech by Duncan.

In his Op-Ed, Friedman (2010) raises education to a similar miracle status found in Duncan's speeches, suggesting that education is "the epicenter of national security" (n.p.). Friedman first confirms Duncan's position that economic health is directly related to educational health in any country. Of course, any good journalist knows that claims are not enough; we need evidence.

The "few data points" praised by Friedman (2010) and used by Duncan—drop-out rates, the relationship between education and economic success, and the comparison of teacher pools among countries—appear, like SAT scores, to be valid data points to draw conclusions about the quality of nations' schools. But the full picture proves that assumption to be misleading.

One of the most damning failures of the claim is that rigorous research by Gerald Bracey (2004) has shown us few positive correlations between measured educational quality and the strength of any nation's economy. Claiming good schools are essential for economic strength is good political discourse, but the evidence isn't there. Next, the call to recruit the best and brightest students (as other top countries do, they always add) is also a compelling charge that falls apart when placed against evidence. Studies, again, have failed to show that such a simple process in fact achieves what we would expect (Sears, Marshall, & Otis-Wilborn, 1994).

Finally, the persistent refrain praising Finland and Denmark as "countries leading the pack in the tests that measure these skills" (Friedman, 2010, n.p.) offers yet another simplistic conclusion (such as the one above about Mississippi) that is compelling but incomplete. Finland and Denmark, according to studies from UNICEF (Adamson, 2005, 2007), have childhood poverty rates of 2.8% and 2.4% respectively, while the U.S. childhood poverty rate is 21.9%.

Further, Finland's entire population is only 5 million people, while the U.S. school system educates 50 million children with 3.2 million teachers.

In short, as with Mississippi and South Carolina, the full picture about populations reveals a "few data points" as being more misleading than illuminating.

Does the U.S. need better schools and do all children deserve the best teachers in every classroom possible? Of course. No one refutes either of these statements. But these valid goals cannot be attained as long as we refuse to acknowledge the historical pattern of social failures that are reflected in (and too often exacerbated by) our schools, such as high drop-out rates for racial minorities and children living in poverty.

Throughout the world, the full picture of any nation's schools reflects the social realities of that country; when schools appear to be failures, the facts show that social failures (the conditions of children's lives outside of school) are driving the educational outcomes. And we certainly will never address these social failures reflected in U.S. public schools if our political leaders and media voices refuse even to say the word "poverty" while languishing in the simplistic manipulation of data that condemns statistics to Twain's bitter assessment over a century ago.

BRAVE WORDS? NO, BUT STARTLING OCCASION(S)

"America is said to be the arena on which the battle of freedom is to be fought; but surely it cannot be freedom in a merely political sense that is meant. Even if we grant that the American has freed himself from a political tyrant, he is still the slave of an economical and moral tyrant," wrote Henry David Thoreau (1863) in "Life without Principle." Thoreau, I believe, was being appropriately skeptical about the fate of America, a fate we are now living. But I believe his comment is even more chilling when we consider the lives of children in our free nation, especially when we consider children in the context of the plight of poverty and the promise of universal public education.

In June of 2010, the news was bleak for children living in the United States:

> The rate of children living in poverty this year will climb to nearly 22%, the highest rate in two decades, according to an analysis by the non-profit Foundation for Child Development. Nearly 17% of children were living in poverty in 2006, before the recession began. (Szabo, 2010; see also Land, 2010)

And throughout the first decade of the twenty-first century, the U.S. stands as one of the richest and most powerful countries in the world that also has one of the highest rates of childhood poverty among other affluent and powerful countries. A UNICEF report, in fact, detailed that "the

United Kingdom and the United States find themselves in the bottom
third of the rankings for five of the six dimensions reviewed" (Adamson,
2007) concerning childhood poverty.

As the evidence grew about the disproportionately impoverished conditions of children's lives in the United States, simultaneously throughout
that decade, the federal government pursued the most aggressive over-
haul of the public education system in its history with the passing and
implementation of No Child Left Behind (NCLB). Under President
George W. Bush and two education secretaries, Rob Paige and Margaret
Spellings, the Department of Education promoted messages that didn't
correspond with the evidence, messages that portrayed the power of the
federal government to change through accountability the course of an
education system mislabeled as a failure for a century (Bracey, 2003;
Holton, 2003; Krashen, 2001, 2006, 2007, 2008). With the election of
Barak Obama, however, many believed the refrain of hope and change,
especially members of the educational community. But within a month of
the reports of childhood poverty rates rising, President Obama and Secretary of Education Arne Duncan stood before the rising tide of critics and
defended their educational policies that stand on an essential claim that
teachers and schools are at the heart of what we need to change in order
to improve educational success.

"Of all the work that occurs at every level of our education system, the
interaction between teacher and student is the primary determinant of
student success" (U.S. Department of Education, 2010, n.p.) represents
the central message coming from the Obama administration that now
pursues a policy built on competition, Race to the Top, and both direct
and indirect endorsements of charter schools, despite the evidence that
neither accountability nor charter schools address the central problems
facing public education (CREDO, 2009; Mathis, 2010; Welner, 2010). The
criticism of the Obama administration's education policy has increased
from the left (National Opportunity to Learn Campaign, 2010; The
National Council of the Churches of Christ in the USA, 2010) while the
right has begun to embrace what is being called brave and powerful messages and actions taken against teachers' unions and the central code
word of those supporting Obama and Duncan, the "status quo."

To the critics, Obama sent this message on July 29, 2010:

> But I know there's also been some controversy about the initiative [Race to
> the Top]. Part of it, I believe, reflects a general resistance to change; a com-
> fort with the *status quo* [emphasis added]. But there have also been criti-
> cisms, including from some folks in the civil rights community, about
> particular elements of Race to the Top. (Sweet, 2010, n.p.)

Just two days before, Secretary Duncan (2010a) offered a similar refrain: "We have to challenge the *status quo* [emphasis added]—because the status quo in public education is not nearly good enough—not with a quarter of all students and, almost half, 50% of African-American and Latino young men and women dropping out of high school" (n.p.).

School reform advocates from the right, those supporting school choice and even dismantling public education, see a much different Obama than the critics from the left. Consider this blog post from Rick Hess (2010) at *Education Week*: "Good for Obama. These are hard things to say, especially for a Democratic President facing a challenging fall, and he deserves much credit for hanging tough" (n.p.).

Good for Obama? These are *hard things* to say? Hanging tough?

In January 1953, Ralph Ellison (2003) gave an address for the National Book Award; the speech carries the title "Brave Words for a Startling Occasion." Then, Ellison said about his *Invisible Man* that its strength came from "its experimental attitude, and its attempt to return to the mood of personal moral responsibility for democracy which typified the best of our nineteenth-century fiction" (p. 151). Further, Ellison built to this: "On its profoundest level American experience is of a whole. Its truth lies in its diversity and swiftness of change" (p. 154). When I read Obama's and Duncan's defenses of their policies by charging those opposing them as defenders of the status quo, and when I read people *praising* Obama for his bravery in the face of that status quo, I thought of Ellison, and the nature of brave words.

It is no brave thing said or done, the education policies of the Obama administration, because the words and ideals are built on cultural mythologies and ideologies that we dare not question or speak against. The truth, the complicated truth that we can face if we pull aside our rose-colored glasses, is that neither democracy nor capitalism will ever address the plight of children in poverty. Children have no political power since they cannot vote, and children have no capital with which to sway the market (except for their proxy roles spending the disposable capital of relatively affluent parents).

Brave words would include recognizing the "moral responsibility" noted by Ellison (2003). Brave words would acknowledge what we know to be *social* failures that are reflected in our schools, not caused by our schools. Brave words would speak to the following:

- School and teacher quality matter but are dwarfed by the power of poverty (Berliner, 2009; Hirsch, 2007; Traub, 2000). To scapegoat schools as a *cause* of an achievement gap, instead of admitting that the achievement gap is a reflection of a larger equity gap in the lives of children, is to perpetuate a social status quo that protects the interests of those already in power. Our ruling and economic elite will continue to point their fingers at public education so that few will ever look at the larger social dynamics that keep the power status intact.

- Teacher quality is important, but holding teachers accountable for student achievement and firing teachers deemed weak mask the real inequities with teacher *assignments*. One direct and significant failure of public schools is that teacher assignments perpetuate the social inequities children suffer in their lives (Peske & Haycock, 2006).

Speaking to teachers in 1963, Ralph Ellison (2003) addressed then the exact concerns we have today (the inordinate failure rate of African American males), and he challenged his audience: "Let's not play these kids cheap; let's find out what they have" (p. 548). And instead of blaming teachers, schools, or the children themselves, Ellison believed, "As we approach the dropouts, let us identify who *we* [emphasis in original] are and where we are" (p. 550).

Brave words.

REFORMING EDUCATION TO MAINTAIN THE STATUS QUO

U.S. public education has suffered a long history of being simultaneously championed as *the* path to all sorts of social ideals and demonized for an equally staggering list of failures. Secretary of Education Arne Duncan (2010c) spoke to the view of education as savior—"the key to eliminating gender inequities, to reducing poverty, to creating a sustainable planet, and to fostering peace"(n.p.). But this idealism, often framed as if education exists in a social vacuum (Duncan's speeches remain largely absent of references to poverty), is typically balanced against proclaiming public education a failure, with such charges of failure reaching back into the mid-1800s.

The discordant political and popular messages about education as well as the silence concerning poverty and social inequity prove to be powerful messages themselves about where U.S. commitments lie—not in social justice or the promise of universal public education, but in cultural mythologies (rugged individualism, pulling oneself up by the bootstraps, a rising tide lifting all boats), corporatism, and consumerism. Kohn (2010a) unpacks how the political dynamic manipulates messages and agendas to perpetuate these commitments and mythologies while claiming reform:

But conservatives have gone a step further. They've figured out how to take policies that actually represent an *intensification* [emphasis in original] of the status quo and dress them up as something that's long overdue. In many cases the values and practices they endorse have already been accepted, but they try to convince us they've lost so they can win even more. (n.p.)

Unlike Kohn, I would eschew the narrow charge against "conservatives" because this tactic—maintaining the status quo by calling it reform—is the tool of the political, economic, and cultural elite of the U.S. This is not about claimed partisan political affiliations (President Obama and Secretary Duncan are as committed to anything Kohn or others may label "conservative"); this is about maintaining the balance (or rightly *imbalance*) of power couched in access to wealth, voice, and knowledge.

Cody (2010), in his *Education Week* blog, captures how the political discourse fails to face the realities about American society while it distorts our view of schools:

The intense discomfort the "school reformers" have with our low-performing schools may reflect our unwillingness to recognize that yes, we have a growing underclass in the United States. Yes, we have a burgeoning strata of society that no longer can even grasp the bottom rung of the economic ladder. We can blame the schools for this, but the schools did not create this situation, and getting everyone ready for college and careers will not fix it. Only when we get our economy back onto firm ground and restore some balance, so the wealthy are paying their fair share of taxes, and the middle class can survive and prosper, and the poor can truly access the ladder to success, only then will we see hope return to our students and see the gaps in achievement really begin to close. (n.p.)

In that context, I will examine in the following pages the anemic commitment in the U.S. to public education and our inability as a culture to see (and thus to speak about) poverty as a mirror of social inequity—in short, how it is part of the American ethos to ignore poverty.

IGNORING POVERTY IN THE U.S.: THE CORPORATE TAKEOVER OF PUBLIC EDUCATION

Paulo Freire represents both the voice about education reform and cultural poverty that the U.S. needs and the exact voice that is being muted by the political and media discourse about schools and silence about poverty:

At a time when memory is being erased and the political relevance of education is dismissed in the language of measurement and quantification, it is all the more important to remember the legacy and work of Paulo Freire. Freire is one of the most important educators of the 20th century and is considered one of the most important theorists of "critical pedagogy"—the educational movement guided by both passion and principle to help students develop a consciousness of freedom, recognize authoritarian tendencies, empower the imagination, connect knowledge and truth to power and learn to read both the word and the world as part of a broader struggle for agency, justice and democracy. (Giroux, 2010a, n.p.)

Freire (2005) offers a counterbalance to the corporate ideology and behavioral grounding of running U.S. public education and education reform:

[A]s we put into practice an education that critically provokes the learner's consciousness, we are necessarily working against myths that deform us. As we confront such myths, we also face the dominant power because those myths are nothing but the expression of this power, of its ideology. (p. 75)

For Freire and critical educators, the purpose of education is to confront, unpack, and even replace cultural norms and assumptions. But the critical promise of education is not an ideal: "If education cannot do everything," Freire (1998) explains, "there is something fundamental that it can do. In other words, if education is not the key to social transformation, neither is it simply meant to reproduce the dominant ideology" (p. 110). But this admission about the power of education within the much more powerful norms of any culture works against what many in the U.S. believe, a belief system that political and media leaders speak to in order to maintain the consumer dynamic that feeds their elite status.

The unsettling irony of how we view education and ignore poverty within our cultural norms and our political leadership is that these "myths that deform" work against the exact individual freedoms and social equity that we claim *are* our cultural myths:

The freedom that moves us, that makes us take risks, is being subjugated to a process of standardization of formulas, models against which we are evaluated.... We are speaking of that invisible power of alienating domestication, which attains a degree of extraordinary efficiency in what I have been calling the bureaucratizing of the mind. (Freire, 1998, p. 111)

Within Freire's call for critical pedagogy, I will examine the complex dynamic that entangles universal public education, economic systems, and cultural norms.

In Chapter 1, "Universal Public Education: Two Possible—and Contradictory—Missions," I examine how many different stakeholders in public education view the purposes of education. Further, I consider here that we often fail to identify exactly what purposes we are addressing in the political and popular discourse about schools. The inherent contradictions in many of the purposes of schooling are exposed by identifying the contrast between "indoctrination" and "teaching," especially in the context of social inequities and the systemic stratification of children in formal schooling. The importance of critical pedagogy for the pursuit of human agency and empowerment is presented before moving to the next chapter.

Chapter 2, "Politicians Who Cry 'Crisis': Education Accountability as Masking," details the era of accountability that runs from 1983 with the publication of A Nation at Risk under President Ronald Reagan through the passing of No Child Left Behind (NCLB) in 2001 and up to the consideration of reauthorizing NCLB under the Obama administration. Here, I explore the inherent flaws in high accountability reform measures based on high-stakes testing; labeling students, teachers, and schools; and corporate views of running and reforming public education. The political commitment to crisis discourse and utopian goals represents the political manipulation of education as an avenue to insuring political success.

Politicians, however, are not alone in misrepresenting education. Chapter 3, "Legend of the Fall: Snapshots of What's Wrong in the Education Debate," examines the role of the media in promoting distorted political messages and speaking to social norms instead of exposing the complexity of education and education reform. The 2010 release of the documentary Waiting for "Superman" provides the basis for the discussion of the failures of media in education reform as well as confronting the failures of corporate and consumer America. The role of poverty in the media messages reveals the mixed claims of that media and the failure of the general public to look critically at media assertions.

School choice, specifically in the form of vouchers, gained political momentum under President Reagan along with the genesis of the current accountability era. But for the past 30 years, school choice has floundered in many forms, never quite finding the widespread support that political and ideological supporters envisioned. Chapter 4, "The Great Charter Compromise: Masking Corporate Commitments in Educational Reform," presents the rise of charter schools as the newest version of school choice, buoyed by the endorsement of President Obama (along with Michele Obama). The political Right and Left appear poised to join forces behind the so-called "miracle" charter schools that target children living in poverty—specifically the Harlem Children's Zone (HCZ) and Knowledge Is Power Program (KIPP). Here, however, I expose the flaws in supporting charter schools (the research finds no difference for charters compared to traditional public schools) as well as detailing the fixed ideological agendas of those seeking corporate schools to replace U.S. public education.

Along with President Obama endorsing charter schools, a unique attack on teacher quality (along with teachers' unions) characterizes the U.S. Department of Education led by Secretary Duncan. Chapter 5, "The

Teaching Profession as a Service Industry," challenges the claims that teachers are the most important element of student achievement since all evidence points overwhelmingly to out-of-school factors dwarfing both teacher and school quality. Despite the political and popular messages to the contrary, social inequity drives down student achievement, and while schools do not cause poverty (and cannot eradicate that poverty either), public education is guilty of perpetuating social stratification through teacher quality and teacher assignment—details omitted in the attacks on teacher quality coming from the White House.

Chapter 6, "'If Education Cannot Do Everything...': Education as Communal Praxis," builds an argument for what education can do—if the U.S. makes a renewed commitment to social justice. School reform, then, must occur within larger social reform. But there are many reforms public schools need and can achieve. Here, I present universal public education as Adrienne Rich (2001) envisions—"the development of a literate, articulate, and well-informed citizenry so that the democratic process can continue to evolve and the promise of radical equality can be brought closer to realization" (p. 162).

The cultural myth in the U.S. that honors the rugged individual fuels a distorted view of people who live in poverty—poverty is the result of laziness, a flaw inherent in the people who are poor. This deficit view of people living in poverty is perpetuated in the deficit views of poverty and learning dominant in our schools. Chapter 7, "Confronting Poverty Again for the First Time: Rising above Deficit Perspectives," rejects deficit views of poverty as well as deficit practices in teaching and learning. This final chapter calls for a renewed and evidence-based understanding of poverty that honors the dignity of all people and doesn't blame people living in poverty for their circumstances. Here, I argue that seeking blame is nonproductive, but that social dynamics are often far more powerful in the lives of people who are poor or affluent than we are willing to acknowledge.

As a critical educator, I reject the call for objectivity and neutrality—both of which are impossible for humans. I, instead, seek to be transparent in my call for confronting the failures of our culture and our schools. As Giroux (2010b) argues:

> Paulo [Freire] strongly believed that democracy could not last without the formative culture that made it possible. Educational sites both within schools and the broader culture represented some of the most important venues through which to affirm public values, support a critical citizenry and resist those who would deny the empowering functions of teaching and learning. At a time when institutions of public and higher education have become associated with market competition, conformity, disempowerment and uncompromising modes of punishment, making known the significant contributions and legacy of Paulo['s] work is now more important than ever before. (n.p.).

NOTE

1. Twain's ascribing the quote to Disreali appears to be inaccurate, but Twain's actual quote is accurate.

CHAPTER 1

UNIVERSAL PUBLIC EDUCATION

Two Possible—and Contradictory—Missions

In her "Arts of the Possible," poet Adrienne Rich (2001) identifies the contradictory purposes for universal public education—and what choice we have made in the United States:

> Universal public education has two possible—and contradictory—missions. One is the development of a literate, articulate, and well-informed citizenry so that the democratic process can continue to evolve and the promise of radical equality can be brought closer to realization. The other is the perpetuation of a class system dividing an elite, nominally "gifted" few, tracked from an early age, from a very large underclass essentially to be written off as alienated from language and science, from poetry and politics, from history and hope—toward low-wage temporary jobs. The second is the direction our society has taken. The results are devastating in terms of the betrayal of a generation of youth. The loss to the whole of society is incalculable. (p. 162)

Despite the roots of universal public education in the U.S. (which I turn to below), Rich (2001) recognizes that school is often about silence and stasis, and thus she fears that what is "rendered unspeakable, [is] thus unthinkable" (p. 150). And it is unspeakable and unthinkable that public education has become such an integral part of the U.S. that it has become

Ignoring Poverty in the U.S.: The Corporate Takeover of Public Education, pp. 1–25
Copyright © 2012 by Information Age Publishing

both always on the lips and minds of the public, pundits, and politicians and never genuinely examined at all.

While many people may consider the purpose of public education obvious, as Rich (2001) states, what we expect of our schools is quite muddled and complex, particularly if we listen closely to what people claim as compared with the realities of how we conduct public education. The online world has laid bare the disconnect that often occurs when several people are discussing the same topic but using a term differently:

> It often seems that edu-decision makers and teachers have trouble communicating. Maybe it's because sometimes we really do speak different languages. At the very least, there are a few phrases in the policymaker-reformer-researcher dialect whose meanings change when filtered through everyday teaching reality. (Elden, 2011)

The disconnect about terms within the education field, captured above, is even greater in the wider public discourse. If you follow a discussion thread on a newspaper or online journal piece related to education, you will recognize commentaries flowing from completely different starting points regarding what schools should accomplish, including various views of what "teaching" and "learning" are.

During the first 2 years of Barak Obama's presidency, for example, Secretary of Education Arne Duncan has repeatedly characterized public schools (and its teachers) as an abysmal failure (carelessly using international comparisons and making sweeping generalizations without offering evidence) while simultaneously promoting a utopian faith in what schools can do:

> The promise of universal education was then [1945] a lonely beacon—a light to guide the way to peace and the rebuilding of nations across the globe. Today, the world is no longer recovering from a tragic global war. Yet the international community faces a crisis of a different sort, the global economic crisis. And education is still the beacon lighting the path forward—perhaps more so today than ever before.
>
> Education is still the key to eliminating gender inequities, to reducing poverty, to creating a sustainable planet, and to fostering peace. And in a knowledge economy, education is the new currency by which nations maintain economic competitiveness and global prosperity. (Duncan, 2010c)

The public and political discourse portrays public education as both in crisis and capable of miracles—but rarely is either claim examined or challenged, but rarely do conversations begin with exactly why we have any faith in public education. As well, few making charges of crisis followed by claims of utopian possibilities for education are held accountable for these refrains having been raised throughout every decade for over the past 100 years; consider as one example this from mid-twentieth century:

> Pink-faced, aggressive little John Ward Studebaker, the onetime Des Moines school superintendent who is now U.S. Commissioner of Education, had been looking at the figures. Only four out of ten U.S. children finish high school, only one out of five who finish high school goes to college. (Get adjusted, 1947, n.p.)

The public debate in 1947 revolved around concerns over low graduation rates, but then moved to whether or not high schools should be preparing all students for college. Studebaker's stance from 1947 should give us pause about listening to political leaders comment on the state and purposes of education:

> But most of the 25,000 U.S. high schools were still acting as if all their kids intended to go to college. Studebaker believes that educational reverence for the "whitecollar myth" produces frustrated and maladjusted citizens. Why not frankly admit that most girls would be housekeepers and most men mechanics, farmers and tradespeople—and train them accordingly? (Get adjusted, 1947, n.p.)

During Obama's presidency, Duncan follows a similar pattern to Studebaker's, except now Duncan calls for *increasing* college attendance—although still basing his proposals on the failures of public education. With a historical perspective and a closer inspection of terminology and the ideologies buried in the terminology, however, we should begin to increase our skepticism of the crisis discourse and utopian promises, especially when they come from the mouths of politicians (who conveniently ignore mentioning poverty or the possibility of social inequity).

DEFENDING THE STATUS QUO?: FALSE DICHOTOMIES AND THE EDUCATION REFORM DEBATE

Over the course of 2010, the media-driven education reform debate evolved into an often repeated narrative expressed by the new reformers—Secretary of Education Arne Duncan, Bill Gates, Michelle Rhee, and a growing chorus of celebrities—that has risen to the level of truth with few highlighting that the story just doesn't hold up against evidence. At the center of the new reformers' message are a false dichotomy and a powerful refrain—"the status quo." The false dichotomy fulfills the public's need for a simple good versus evil plot, and the U.S. public seems always game for an "us versus them" approach to anything.

Ironically, the reformer's dichotomy is both misleading and inherently contradictory, if we look carefully at their characterization of the status quo and their insistence that the new reformers are in a battle with *defenders* of the status quo. The nature of the false dichotomy is reflected in President Obama's and Secretary Duncan's responses to the civil rights framework presented by the National Opportunity to Learn (OTL) Campaign, a coalition of organizations committed to civil rights:

> The comments that follow offer critiques of federal efforts that would: distribute resources by competition in the midst of a severe recession; advance experimental proposals dwarfed by the scope of the challenges in low-income communities; and promote ineffective approaches for turning around low-performing schools and education systems. (Civil Rights Framework, 2010, n.p.)

To these critics, as I noted in the Introduction, Obama sent this message on 29 July 2010:

> But I know there's also been some controversy about the initiative [Race to the Top]. Part of it, I believe, reflects a general resistance to change; a comfort with the *status quo* [emphasis added]. But there have also been criticisms, including from some folks in the civil rights community, about particular elements of Race to the Top. (Sweet, 2010, n.p.)

Just 2 days before, Secretary Duncan (2010a) offered a similar refrain:

> We have to challenge the *status quo* [emphasis added]—because the *status quo* [emphasis added] in public education is not nearly good enough—not with a quarter of all students and, almost half, 50% of African-American and Latino young men and women dropping out of high school. (n.p.)

The status quo, then, that the new reformers are presenting with little resistance includes some basic characteristics that are repeated by Duncan, Gates, and Rhee while also being reinforced by the media and celebrities claiming education as their cause—and often this exists within a failure to consider historical context or the nature of the terms being used. The new reformer narrative goes like this: Based on international test score comparisons (Program for International Student Assessment [PISA] was the test *de jure* in 2010), public schools are failing children and U.S. economic competitiveness because those schools are bogged down with "bad" teachers (Bessie, 2010a) being protected by the teachers' unions and because the U.S. has failed to identify high standards and rigorous tests in order to hold those schools and teachers accountable for their failures.

If this status quo were true—and it is not—we should be truly disturbed by the other claim of the new reformers, expressed directly in a blog posting at *The Huffington Post*, titled "New Book Takes Aim at Ed Reformers and Status Quo Defenders," about Rick Hess's book, praised as a criticism of the new reformer movement: "What I find most refreshing about *The Same Thing Over and Over*—in part because I didn't expect it—is that Hess is almost as skeptical of today's self-labeled 'reformers' as he is of status quo defenders" (Snider, 2011).

Status quo defenders? If the picture the new reformers have painted of U.S. public education were accurate (*schools failing children primarily because of incompetent teachers*), who would defend that status quo and for what purpose? Who in this mythical education establishment wants children to fail? What sort of person *would* defend the abysmal status quo identified by the new reformers?

Just as the new reformers are misleading the public about education reform, they are also misrepresenting their critics, demonizing them, in fact, by associating any rebuttals as defending the status quo (Elden, 2011)—or as the president himself stated, being *comfortable* with failing children (Sweet, 2010). So let's step back for a second and reframe this debate, first by clarifying just what the status quo of U.S. public schools constitutes and then by placing that debate in the historical context that reveals the myopic nature of the new reformers.

First, the status quo of public education is not properly characterized with the term "crisis." The central problems we are facing in schools are *historical patterns*—student achievement being strongly correlated with out-of-school factors, such as poverty (Berliner, 2009; Hirsch, 2007; Rothstein, 2010; Traub, 2000); disproportionate drop-out rates among marginalized populations of students; and inequity of teacher assignments to the disadvantage of students living in poverty, students of color, and English Language Learners (ELL) (Peske & Haycock, 2006). The most recent fact of the status quo of schooling is the crippling bureaucracy faced by schools during the past 30 years of accountability—ironically, the exact components of which are at the center of the claims of reform coming from the new reformers (Kohn, 2010a).

And herein lies the discordant nature of the false dichotomy and distortion masked by repeating "status quo" as a tool of demonizing any rebuttals to the claims of the new reformers and distracting us from considering seriously the overwhelming impact of poverty on the lives and learning of children.

The actual status quo of the U.S. includes a tremendous equity gap (Noah, 2010) that benefits those at the top—including all of the faces on the new reform movement—and that is maintained when schools remain overburdened by poverty and bureaucracy. The new reformers are perpetuating inequity through their misrepresentation of failing schools, "bad" teachers, and corrupt teachers' unions in order to perpetuate their own stake in education as a market (Barkan, 2011); in effect, then, the new reformers are the true defenders of this status quo: U.S. public schools are a mirror held up to political and corporate failures that have created a stratified society, with the gaps widening; the achievement gap in our schools is evidence of an equity gap in our society, not primarily a direct commentary on teacher or school quality.

This irony is chilling as well because the sincere critics of social failures in the U.S. and bureaucratic mismanagement of public schools are being demonized and marginalized (Michie, 2011). While the media continues to perpetuate the new reformers' false dichotomies and mischaracterization of defenders of the status quo, the new reformers' solutions for their manufactured status quo fail to stand up to evidence:

> "Race to the Top" and *Waiting for Superman* made 2010 a banner year for the market-based education reforms that dominate our national discourse. By contrast, a look at the 'year in research' presents a rather different picture for the three pillars of this paradigm: merit pay, charter schools, and using value-added estimates in high-stakes decisions.... Overall, while 2010 will certainly be remembered as a watershed year for market-based reforms, this wave of urgency and policy changes unfolded concurrently with a steady flow of solid research suggesting that extreme caution, not haste, is in order. (DiCarlo, 2011)

Again, ironically, 2010 offered us a lesson, but one that isn't very appealing. The public seems willing to accept anything repeated by the elites—millionaires, politicians, and celebrities—but just as quick to disregard evidence from sincere reformers, confirming Rich's (2001) charge about the decision we have made concerning public education.

The purposes of universal public education as a foundational institution of a free people is inextricably tied to our cultural beliefs about affluence and poverty as well as our view of *why* people find themselves in the financial states that they do. Before we can examine fully how the U.S. has ignored and demonized poverty, we must look carefully at how we view and portray education and the purposes of education—especially as education is connected to economic wellbeing.

THE IDEALISTIC (AND ELITIST) ROOTS OF PUBLIC EDUCATION: JEFFERSON AND EMERSON

As I noted above, Secretary of Education Duncan speaks about education in soaring rhetoric that buries assumptions about the purposes for schools, the nature of teaching, and the reality of learning in crisis discourse (framing discussions of education and reform within claimed crises such as the drop-out crisis or the achievement gap crisis) and utopian expectations (stating that education is the sole mechanism for social reform, the single path to individuals rising above the conditions of their lives). Look at these passages from Duncan's speech given to National Council for Accreditation of Teacher Education (NCATE):

> In today's knowledge economy, it is no secret that education is the new game-changer. The days when students could drop out of school and land a good job are over. As all of you know, even high school graduates are finding that the number of good jobs open to them is severely restricted, unless they have some college or post-secondary training.
>
> The global economy magnified many times over the importance of education, so that dramatically-accelerated achievement and attainment are now the key to preparing young people to be successful.
>
> Education is the new engine of economic growth and American prosperity. And more than ever, education must be the great equalizer, the one global force that can consistently overcome differences in background, culture, and privilege.
>
> As the Blue Ribbon panel notes, teachers are the biggest in-school influence on academic achievement and growth. And we know that when it comes to teaching, talent matters tremendously. A recent McKinsey & Company study pointed out a truism that bears repeating: "The quality of an education system cannot exceed the quality of its teachers." Or, as Linda Darling-Hammond puts it: "Every aspect of school reform depends on highly skilled teachers for its success."
>
> In nations that are out-educating us today, the caliber of new teachers is a critical national priority.
>
> By contrast, the United States needs to urgently elevate the teaching profession. And that is why we have launched a national teacher recruitment campaign. (Duncan, 2010d, n.p.)

The diction offered by Duncan is intended to elicit alarm, crisis—"dramatically-accelerated," "critical national priority," "urgently elevate." But that crisis is coupled with claims that education "is the new game-changer" because "education is the new engine of economic growth and American prosperity."

But how much of Duncan's claim is true, and how much is elevated political discourse? And how true are Duncan's words and ideologies to the founding principles upon which universal public education was built? Let's keep Duncan's speech in mind as we consider Thomas Jefferson's and Ralph Waldo Emerson's comments about education from the eighteenth and twentieth centuries, noting specifically the role of poverty and power in all three contexts.

Throughout 2010, Secretary Duncan offered several patterns regarding U.S. public education, including the following (see numerous speeches in References):

- Characterizing public education as a failure, based on graduation rates, test scores, and international comparisons. This claim is regularly expressed in crisis discourse.

- Identifying teachers as the most important element in student achievement (which was qualified on some rare occasions as the most important *in-school* factor). This claim has always been expressed without context or reference to the overwhelming impact of poverty on achievement—80-90% of achievement correlated to out-of-school factors (Berliner, 2009; Hirsch, 2007; Rothstein, 2010; Traub, 2000).

- Stressing the need for improving education as a central element of international competitiveness and creating a world-class workforce. Corporate and competitive needs are highlighted, but the role of universal public education in the health of democracy is absent.

- Characterizing education as *the* avenue to eradicating poverty, restoring U.S. international dominance, and refueling the sputtering U.S. economy. These utopian claims are never weighed against the contrasting crisis discourse, and Duncan never acknowledges ample research showing no direct or singular connection between any country's test scores and economy (Bracey, 2004, 2008).

- Criticizing the failures of No Child Left Behind (NCLB) and the high accountability/testing era while simultaneously calling for national standards, national tests, and teacher evaluations tied to test scores. The discourse in Duncan's speeches is often progressive discourse masking policies that perpetuate increased bureaucratic and mechanistic approaches to education, students, and teachers (Race to the Top, for example).

Popular discourse tends to suffer from presentism—seeing *today* in a state of crisis and *yesterday* nostalgically. But Thomas Jefferson (1900) in 1807 fretted over the lack of support for education in words that seem valid today: "People generally have more feeling for canals and roads than education. However, I hope we can advance them with equal pace" (p. 277). In his roles as public intellectual and political leader, Jefferson rarely strayed too far from arguing for the value of education and a system of universal public education for a thriving democracy. Looking closely at the patterns of Jefferson's beliefs about education—framed against the patterns above from Duncan's 2010 speeches—helps place the current arguments from the new reformers in a historical context that challenges the credibility of their claims—if we truly value the democratic foundations of our public schools system.

Writing to John Tyler in 1810, Thomas Jefferson (1900) made these claims:

> I have indeed two great measures at heart, without which no republic can maintain itself in strength: 1. That of general education, to enable every man to judge for himself what will secure or endanger his freedom. 2. To divide every county into hundreds, of such size that all the children of each will be within reach of a central school in it. (p. 278)

Jefferson connected an education with what critical educators would label today *empowerment,* and he believed that public schools must offer easy access to all children. I believe we should note that Jefferson here and throughout never mentions the role of education in building a workforce or supporting the international competitiveness of a country.

In fact, Jefferson (1900) remains steadfast in the role of education in the empowerment of all people, including those living in poverty:

> The object [of my education bill was] to bring into action that mass of talents which lies buried in poverty in every country for want of the means of development, and thus give activity to a mass of mind which in proportion to our population shall be the double or treble of what it is in most countries. (pp. 275-276)

And,

> The less wealthy people…, by the bill for a general education, would be qualified to understand their rights, to maintain them, and to exercise with intelligence their parts in self-government; and all this would be effected without the violation of a single natural right of any one individual citizen. (p. 50)

Jefferson addresses poverty, without marginalizing people living in poverty or demonizing poverty itself, but he also suggests that education will contribute to the benefit of the entire country—although not our economic power, but "the mass of mind." Intellect and knowledge are embraced for their inherent values, and Jefferson argues a social commitment to public education does not violate anyone's right (which contrasts significantly with the repeated refrain today that taxing for public schools is coercion, government overstepping its bounds).

Consider the following passages from Jefferson's (1900) repeated and impassioned endorsement of universal public education supported by taxation and created specifically to empower people living in poverty to protect themselves from the wealthy and powerful:

> I ... [proposed] three distinct grades of education, reaching all classes. 1. Elementary schools for all children generally, rich and poor. 2. Colleges for a middle degree of instruction, calculated for the common purposes of life and such as should be desirable for all who were in easy circumstances. And 3d. an ultimate grade for teaching the sciences generally and in their highest degree... The expenses of [the elementary] schools should be borne by the inhabitants of the county, every one in proportion to his general tax-rate. This would throw on wealth the education of the poor. (p. 791)

> To all of which is added a selection from the elementary schools of subjects of the most promising genius, whose parents are too poor to give them further education, to be carried at the public expense through the colleges and university. (p. 275)

> By that part of our plan which prescribes the selection of the youths of genius from among the classes of the Door, we hope to avail the State of those talents which nature has sown as liberally among the poor as the rich, but which perish without use, if not sought for and cultivated. But of all the views of this law none is more important none more legitimate, than that of rendering the people the safe, as they are the ultimate, guardians of their own liberty. (p. 276)

> The tax which will be paid for this purpose is not more than the thousandth part of what will be paid to kings, priests and nobles who will rise up among us if we leave the people in ignorance. (p. 278)

> I think ward elections better for many reasons, one of which is sufficient, that it will keep elementary education out of the hands of fanaticizing preachers, who, in county elections, would be universally chosen, and the predominant sect of the county would possess itself of all its schools. (p. 791)

> Science is more important in a republican than in any other government (p.103).

> Preach ... a crusade against ignorance; establish and improve the law for educating the common people. Let our countrymen know that the people alone can protect us against these evils [of monarchial government]. (p. 274)

While Duncan's leadership is ripe for parody because of his predictable patterns that do less than inspire (Farmer, 2011), Jefferson offers refrains that provide the critical foundation upon which we should judge and reform our current pubic schools:

- Universal public education is essential for a democracy and must be accessible to all, regardless of station in life.
- Taxation is necessary to insure the right of public education, and those taxes are not infringing on individual rights, but contributing to the collective knowledge base of the country.
- Education is essential for individual empowerment, insuring each person's ability to protect her/his own liberty.
- Education leads to individual empowerment for the preservation of liberty, but Jefferson also clarifies that power and wealth threaten liberty as much as the possibility of oppressive government.
- Schools should be kept separate from religious influence.
- Knowledge, specifically science, is essential for a democratic republic.

While Jefferson's impact on the genesis of public education and the U.S. university system and libraries is often recognized, Ralph Waldo Emerson tends to remain solely in the American literature classrooms of high school and college—reduced to the merely academic. But Emerson's detailed and powerful consideration of the nature of being an educated American—as distinct from European—is valuable as we consider the purposes of education in a free society. Note the following passages from "The American Scholar" by Emerson (1837/2009):

> In this distribution of functions, the scholar is the delegated intellect. In the right state, he is, *Man Thinking*. In the degenerate state, when the victim of society, he tends to become a mere thinker, or, still worse, the parrot of other men's thinking. (n.p.)

Nature, then, is:

> [t]he next great influence into the spirit of the scholar, is, the mind of the Past,—in whatever form, whether of literature, of art, of institutions, that mind is inscribed. Books are the best type of the influence of the past, and perhaps we shall get at the truth,—learn the amount of this influence more conveniently,—by considering their value alone.... As no air-pump can by any means make a perfect vacuum, so neither can any artist entirely exclude the conventional, the local, the perishable from his book, or write a book of pure thought, that shall be as efficient, in all respects, to a remote posterity, as to contemporaries, or rather to the second age. Each age, it is found, must write its own books; or rather, each generation for the next succeed-

ing. The books of an older period will not fit this…. Hence, instead of Man Thinking, we have the bookworm.

Books are the best of things, well used; abused, among the worst. What is the right use? What is the one end, which all means go to effect? They are for nothing but to inspire. I had better never see a book, than to be warped by its attraction clean out of my own orbit, and made a satellite instead of a system. The one thing in the world, of value, is the active soul. This every man is entitled to; this every man contains within him, although, in almost all men, obstructed, and as yet unborn. The soul active sees absolute truth; and utters truth, or creates. In this action, it is genius; not the privilege of here and there a favorite, but the sound estate of every man. In its essence, it is progressive.

Of course, there is a portion of reading quite indispensable to a wise man. History and exact science he must learn by laborious reading. Colleges, in like manner, have their indispensable office—to teach elements. But they can only highly serve us, when they aim not to drill, but to create; when they gather from far every ray of various genius to their hospitable halls, and, by the concentrated fires, set the hearts of their youth on flame. Thought and knowledge are natures in which apparatus and pretension avail nothing. Gowns, and pecuniary foundations, though of towns of gold, can never countervail the least sentence or syllable of wit. Forget this, and our American colleges will recede in their public importance, whilst they grow richer every year.

Life lies behind us as the quarry from whence we get tiles and copestones for the masonry of to-day. This is the way to learn grammar. Colleges and books only copy the language which the field and the work-yard made. (Emerson, 1837/2009, n.p.)

Emerson's focus moves away from Jefferson's social justice focus but establishes a clear belief in the power of learning to create new knowledge, challenging the value of becoming a slave to tradition. The motifs found in Emerson speak solidly against the conservative nature of many calls for education as a way to instill traditional values and basic knowledge:

- To be educated is to be an original thinker, not, as Emerson warns, a parrot.
- Nature and books provide people suitable environments for learning; for Emerson, nature is the best source above all.
- Books are valuable, but just as Emerson warms about parroting other's thoughts, he also warns against being merely a bookworm.
- Thus, the study of books is an avenue to new learning, new books.
- Students should not be subjected to drill, but offered opportunities to create.
- Learning, then, is best in authentic situations.

The purposes of education and the nature of learning, as expressed by Jefferson and Emerson as essential for individual empowerment and a thriving democracy, are quite distinct from the claims made by the new reformers who have emerged in the first decade of the twenty-first century. Our commitments to consumerism, corporate America, and competition have clearly dwarfed our founding principals based on freedom, equity, and originality of thought.

In the mid-1800s and into the twentieth century, the rise of public education against the dominance of private schools (such as those run by the Catholic church) proved to exacerbate the contradictory purposes identified by Rich (2001) and revealed in the contrast between Jefferson/Emerson and twenty-first century education reformers.

TENSIONS BETWEEN PUBLIC VERSUS PRIVATE SCHOOLING: THE CORPORATE COMPROMISE

"When it comes to selecting a school for their children, the average American parents have little if any choice. The local public school is the only campus in town," writes Smollin (2011), adding, "Politicians and government leaders, on the other hand, have an array of public and private schools to choose from" (n.p.). This opens a piece that explains "41 percent of U.S. representatives and 46 percent of U.S. senators said they send, or have sent, at least one of their children to a private school" (n.p.).

Levy (2011a) soon after offered this about President Obama:

> But now, given the comments Obama made on NBC's *Today Show* while talking about why he and the first lady don't send their children to DC public schools, I'm not so sure. Obama's alleged elitism may not deter his ability to govern, but it does undermine his legitimacy in the face of growing populist sentiment (and not just of the Tea Party), and it further erodes my confidence in his education policies. (n.p.)

The contradictions and even antagonism about the purposes of public education can, in many ways, be traced to the tension between private and public schooling in the U.S.—since that tension represents our cultural assumptions and our commitments to private above public. The tension between public and private schooling can be traced back to the mid-1800s, in fact, where the *threat* of public schools encroached on the monopoly enjoyed by Catholic schools.

Over the past century and a half, public schools have experienced relentless criticism while private schools have received *unwarranted* praise for superiority.

In the mid-1800s, public education was called a "dragon ... devouring the hope of the country as well as religion. [It dispenses] 'Socialism, Red Republicanism, Universalism, Infidelity, Deism, Atheism, and Pantheism—anything, everything, except religion and patriotism,' " explains Jacoby (2004, pp. 257-258). From there, the bashing of public schools continued, judging the quality of our public schools based on drop-out rates (Get adjusted, 1947). We must recognize that the demonizing of public schools and the condemnation of school quality are the way we talk about and view schools in the U.S. as popular discourse and understanding—all steeped in crisis discourse and utopian expectations perpetuated by Secretary Duncan and the new reformers.

While political leaders send the mixed message championed by Duncan—schools are failing *but* education is the key to solving everything—those same leaders practice personal policies, sending their children to private schools, that reinforce the misconception among the public that private schools trump public schools in quality—and, as proponents of private school and school choice tend to add, private schools do better with less money. And embedded in the tension between public and private is a failure to mention poverty and affluence, masking further the impact of poverty on education outcomes and the inequity without our society that is reflected in *all* types of schools, public or private.

What does the public perception of public schools and private schools reveal about our beliefs about schooling and our assumptions about affluence and poverty?

Let's start with facts. In the first decade of the twenty-first century, a solid and growing body of research, likely spurred by the school choice debate, has clarified that private schools do not outperform public schools when characteristics of the students are held constant (Braun, Jenkins, & Grigg, 2006; Lubiensky & Lubiensky, 2006; Wenglinsky, 2007). Further, Baker (2009a, 2009b) has deflated the myth that private schools do more with less. Theses studies help highlight some important aspects of how we view and judge schools as a society, including the following:

- We should avoid making sweeping generalizations about any type of school. Research on private school versus public school quality and spending shows that neither "private" nor "public" is an adequate label for schools since within each, a wide variety of quality and spending exists.
- School type is far less important than the student demographics associated with the school. Even within the new corporate charter school movement that tends to focus on high-poverty populations of students, comparisons among types of schools must consider the characteristics of the students being served; charter systems such as

Knowledge Is Power Program (KIPP) and the Harlem Children's Zone (HCZ) do address high-poverty students like public schools (and unlike many private schools), but that high-poverty population often does not include special needs students at the rate public schools must serve. In short, school quality is highly associated with student populations (more on the charter phenomenon is addressed in Chapter 4).

- The popular view that private schools outperform public schools is strongly tied to public perceptions of affluent people and elite schools. The popular view that elite schools that cater to elite students (usually culled by high-stakes testing such as the SAT, which is most strongly correlated with family wealth and advanced education) are *better* than public schools is factually flawed but a reflection of our cultural faith that elite status comes to those who deserve it (and that *any one of us* is in line for such a reward).

Culturally, we simply cannot bring ourselves to criticize the rich and privileged because we all want to be rich and privileged—and if that wealth and privilege were to come our way, we are convinced it would be deserved. And conversely, we demonize poverty and people living in poverty as a consequence of laziness—something people deserve—because it is the antithesis of the American Dream we cannot challenge. These perverse belief systems are reflected in our views of education.

Giroux (2010b) recognizes that the corporate interests have won over, erasing the roots of progressive and critical education that could have grown from Jefferson, Emerson, John Dewey, and Paulo Freire:

> Public education fares even worse. Dominated by pedagogies that are utterly instrumental, geared toward memorization, conformity and high-stakes test taking, public schools have become intellectual dead zones and punishment centers as far removed from teaching civic values and expanding the imaginations of students as one can imagine. The profound disdain for public education is evident not only in Obama's test-driven, privatized and charter school reform movement, but also in the hostile takeover of public education now taking place among the ultra-rich and hedge fund zombies, who get massive tax breaks from gaining control of charter schools. The public in education has now become the enemy of educational reform. (n.p.)

The erosion of social justice and personal empowerment as central to the purposes of public education and the rise of efficiency driven by the accountability movement are reinforced by our failure even to mention poverty and affluence, except to claim that children living in poverty simply need to work harder, that teachers serving high-poverty schools need to work harder. Failure is not the result of the corrosive influence of poverty, our cultural myths argue; educational failure *and* poverty are evidence of the inherent flaws in the people who fail, the people who are poor.

The great irony we face is that education appears to be needed to change beliefs (just as Duncan suggests about the power of schools), but, as I examine below, our human nature seems wired to resist evidence when that evidence speaks against the "myths that deform us" (Freire, 2005, p. 75)—especially those myths that deform our views of education and poverty.

BELIEF CULTURE: "WE DON'T NEED NO EDUCATION"

"Four in 10 Americans, slightly fewer today than in years past, believe God created humans in their present form about 10,000 years ago" (Newport, 2010, n.p.)—this December 2010 poll also includes the finding that a scant 16% of the U.S. populace accepts evolution without any hand of God involved (Newport, 2010). The U.S. is unique compared to the rest of the Western world, which tends to accept evolution (Owen, 2006), but the comparison is less significant than the inference we can draw about the U.S. and the associated impacts visible in our disdain for not only education, but also the well-educated, the informed: The U.S. is a belief culture. And we have strong, unyielding beliefs about schools and poverty.

And by "belief," I am not attacking genuine religious faith. This discussion is about a belief culture that is quasi-secular, political, and ultimately ideological, even when that belief is connected to religious traditions and stances. As Einstein (1941) offered, both belief and science have value, even as complements to each other: "Science without religion is lame, religion without science is blind" (n.p.)—especially as faith informs our ethics. But in the U.S., we are apt to misuse belief and ignore (or misunderstand) science when we need it most (recall Jefferson's argument about the value of science in a democracy).

While unlike the Western world concerning evolution, the U.S. as a belief culture may reflect ironically what science is discovering about the power of belief over fact as a part of human nature:

> Facts don't necessarily have the power to change our minds. In fact, quite the opposite. In a series of studies in 2005 and 2006, researchers at the University of Michigan found that when misinformed people, particularly political partisans, were exposed to corrected facts in news stories, they rarely changed their minds. In fact, they often became even more strongly set in their beliefs. Facts, they found, were not curing misinformation. Like an

underpowered antibiotic, facts could actually make misinformation even *stronger.* (Keohane, 2010, n.p.)

The U.S. appears on the surface to be a scientific society—we consume the newest and best technology dutifully and with voracity; however, U.S. citizens are largely opposed to scientific ways of knowing and understanding the world: Drawing conclusions about the world based on the weight of evidence (while reserving a fixed conclusion if contradictory evidence reveals itself in the future). Our split personality about science is, in fact, not contradictory; we love to consume ever-changing technology, but that insatiable appetite is about the consumption, not the science.

Consider the pop culture we also consume endlessly. How have we portrayed intellectuals and whom do we love in our entertainment?

From Marlon Brando and James Dean to the Fonz on *Happy Days*, we have adored the uneducated who prove themselves to be better and even smarter than the educated. In fact, if you look carefully at *Friends*, you see an interesting evolution of that narrative. Both Joey and Ross are often portrayed as clueless and bumbling, tapping into our love of those who are not smart. But look closer. The audience as well as the other characters laughs *with* Joey (who is apparently uneducated), and *at* Ross (who has a PhD, who is a scientist, a paleontologist in fact). Look carefully at the episode in which Ross and Phoebe argue about evolution (Crane, Kauffman, Curtis, & Bright, 1995); Ross is shown to be foolish by the cleverer Phoebe (who doesn't embrace evolution, who doesn't value evidence).

This is the America of belief. We cherish stubborn doctrine and clever rhetoric even at the expense of fact (Thomas, 2010s)—and we speak often about tradition. Recently, in my home state of South Carolina—which sits solidly in the Deep South that William Faulkner (1930) captured precisely in the macabre "A Rose for Emily" (yes, in the South we cling to the corpse of tradition, and we are proud of it)—yet another controversy erupted around the celebration of secession: "That some—even now—are honoring secession, with barely a nod to the role of slavery, underscores how divisive a topic the war remains, with Americans continuing to debate its causes, its meaning and its legacy" (Seelye, 2010r, n.p.).

Just as South Carolina has clung to the Confederate flag, the state is proud of being first to secede, of being first to honor state's rights (usually omitting that those state's rights included slavery). "This is not about slavery but tradition!" is the refrain. Try to make a reasoned (evidence-based) argument about secession or the flag issue in the South and you are apt to be the Ross to the multitudes of Phoebes.

South Carolina is not alone, as secession balls were planned throughout the South, where the calls for tradition and state's rights drown out any concerns about slavery. Again, as with those who cling to creationism, many in the South are not swayed by evidence—unless it confirms what they already believe.

The truth is that many in the U.S. are committed to belief over evidence and are simultaneously devoted to consumerism—creating a perfect storm for the political and corporate elites, but also sounding a death knell for the promise of universal public education established by our founders, who happened to be men of reason (although the belief among many Americans is that they were Christian men all; again, don't bother with the evidence).

As Keohane (2010) writes about the findings regarding the power of belief over facts:

> In an ideal world, citizens would be able to maintain constant vigilance, monitoring both the information they receive and the way their brains are processing it. But keeping atop the news takes time and effort. And relentless self-questioning, as centuries of philosophers have shown, can be exhausting. Our brains are designed to create cognitive shortcuts—inference, intuition, and so forth—to avoid precisely that sort of discomfort while coping with the rush of information we receive on a daily basis. Without those shortcuts, few things would ever get done. Unfortunately, with them, we're easily suckered by political falsehoods. (n.p.)

The line from the Pink Floyd song providing the second half of the subhead above, "We don't need no education," is followed by "We don't need no thought control," and this equating of education and thought control is at the heart of the anti-intellectualism supported by the belief culture of the U.S. that has failed the potential of universal public education for a thriving democracy as well as impeding any commitment to social justice.

Recall the arguments about education by Jefferson (1900) from earlier in the chapter—his specific concern for people living in poverty and the role of education in personal empowerment. And here, let's compare Jefferson's comments to Secretary Duncan's (2010e) conclusions about PISA scores from 2009, with our cultural myths and tendency to embrace beliefs despite evidence in mind:

> Here in the United States, we have looked forward eagerly to the 2009 PISA results. But the findings, I'm sorry to report, show that the United States needs to urgently accelerate student learning to remain competitive in the knowledge economy of the 21st century. The United States has a long way to go before it lives up to the American dream and the promise of education as the great equalizer. Every three years, PISA assesses the reading, mathematics, and scientific literacy of 15-year-old students. It provides crucial information about how well our students are prepared to do the sorts of reading, mathematics, and science that will be demanded of them in post-

secondary education or the job market, and as young adults in modern society. Unfortunately, the 2009 PISA results show that American students are poorly prepared to compete in today's knowledge economy. (n.p.)

Duncan gives a brief nod to education as an "equalizer," but he repeatedly connects education to competitiveness, a strong workforce, and reinforcing our "knowledge economy."

These differences, as I noted above, are significant as they feed into our belief culture that values compliance and authority over evidence and skepticism. Jefferson's hope that universal public education would empower people trapped in poverty against the oppression of people with privilege and wealth has been lost in the tidal wave of education for competitiveness and a world-class workforce.

And instead of experts speaking to the public based on evidence, we have a belief culture guided by celebrity based on wealth—Bill Gates (Lyons, 2010) and Oprah—and self-promotion—Michelle Rhee (Thomas, 2010y)—who speak to our cultural assumptions instead of to the evidence from our society and our schools.

As we move into the second decade of the twenty-first century—an era that held great promise for technology so advanced that humanity couldn't imagine its glories—we are faced with *The Big Bang Theory* on Thursday nights. More sitcom fun focused on an objectified young woman next door who is repeatedly exposed as not very bright—but we love her; we laugh with her because she is a certain kind of pretty (consider the lineage to Marilyn Monroe). She enjoys weekly high jinks with four scientists, all of whom we laugh at like Ross, especially the self-proclaimed brightest, Sheldon.

And don't discount that this hilarity is within a show connected with the evolution controversy—the Big Bang—and four university scientists. (But scientific theory is *just a theory* we are reminded by the masses.) We are not Ralph Waldo Emerson's (1841/2009) America, one that is scientific in the purest sense of the word: "Speak what you think today in hard words and tomorrow speak what tomorrow thinks in hard words again, though it contradict every thing you said today" (n.p.).

We are a people clinging to belief, and a belief that is tied to a certain kind of authority that speaks to that belief but can never challenge it. We believe any authority who voices back to us what we already believe. Duncan's (2010e) comments above are messages designed to trigger what people already believe about our schools and international competitiveness. But let's also look at how the media plays a role here that parallels our entertainment industry (more on this aspect is examined in Chapter 3). Consider a recent headline at *The Huffington Post:* "SHOCKING: Nearly 1

In 4 High School Graduates Can't Pass Military Entrance Exam" (Armario & Turner, 2010).

Ironically, this claim isn't shocking since it states what the public already believes (because they have been told the story for decades): pubic schools are failing. But when you read the first paragraph, you can find something that should be shocking:

> Nearly one-fourth of the students who try to join the US Army fail its entrance exam, painting a grim picture of an education system that produces graduates who can't answer basic math, science and reading questions, according to a new study released Tuesday. (Armario & Turner, 2010, n.p.)

The opening doesn't confirm the sensational headline. One-in-four "students who try to join the U.S. Army" is a much different population than all high school graduates (as the headline states). Few readers will notice, and few will challenge the headline, however, because the claim of the headline is something we already believe—just as equating education with readiness for the military appears perfectly appropriate for most Americans (although quite different than Jefferson's charge). At the core of the American belief culture is our acceptance of education as training, education as coercion (Thomas, 2011z), education as normalizing.

And what about those pesky PISA rankings for the U.S.? Again, a simplistic reporting of the ranking fulfills what we believe about schools, so the media perpetuates the distortion despite evidence from China itself that those rankings don't warrant the crisis reaction American media and political leaders have perpetuated. Yong Zhao (2010) notes:

> Interestingly, this has not become big news in China, a country that loves to celebrate its international achievement. I had thought for sure China's major media outlets would be all over the story. But to my surprise, I have not found the story covered in big newspapers or other mainstream media outlets. (n.p.)

While the U.S. uses the PISA rankings to bash schools and call for standardization in order to ensure our global competitiveness, many in China are lamenting the corrosive impact of test-driven education. But that message works against our beliefs, and we are unlikely to hear that message: China seems poised to recognize the failure of standardization, while the U.S. continues to call for more and more standardization. That should be shocking. (As well, when international comparisons of test scores include considerations of poverty, a different message is revealed about the U.S. [Riddile, 2010].)

The belief dynamic has allowed the corporate and political elite in the U.S. to use universal public education to solidify the status quo of their elite positions—reversing Jefferson's ideal. As Alfie Kohn (2010b) has argued (and we have ignored), we use schools to prepare students for a standards- and test-driven system, to perpetuate discipline and self-discipline (Kohn, 2008b), and to squelch human agency and skepticism (Kohn, 2004).

In the second decade of the twenty-first century, we do not have liberals and conservatives vying for the votes and minds of America; we have Corporate Democrats and Corporate Republicans vying through a false dichotomy for the votes and minds of American consumers, too often eager to hear what they already believe. Keohane (2010) explains that the power of belief threatens the promise of democracy:

> This bodes ill for a democracy, because most voters—the people making decisions about how the country runs—aren't blank slates. They already have beliefs, and a set of facts lodged in their minds. The problem is that sometimes the things they think they know are objectively, provably false. And in the presence of the correct information, such people react very, very differently than the merely uninformed. Instead of changing their minds to reflect the correct information, they can entrench themselves even deeper. (n.p.)

And we have a belief culture mesmerized by celebrity authority that perpetuates the marginalization of education and of being educated, being informed (Ramsay, Kull, Lewis, & Subias, 2010). At the center of this false political dichotomy and celebrity leadership, we have universal public education reduced to both scapegoat (Schools are failing to maintain America's place in the global economy!) and the political/corporate tool of creating a compliant workforce and electorate eager to score well on multiple-choice testing.

Throughout the first decade of the twenty-first century, the faith culture in the U.S. fully relinquished expertise to celebrity. Al Gore and Rush Limbaugh have spoken for climate change (the little cousin to the evolution debate), spurred by Davis Guggenheim's *An Inconvenient Truth*. And then Guggenheim's *Waiting for "Superman"* (Martin, 2010) built the platform upon which Secretary Duncan, Gates, and Rhee could lead the charge for education reform supported by Oprah and MSNBC as well as *Real Time* with Bill Maher (Thomas, 2010o) and *The Colbert Report* (Thomas, 2010v).

Watching, listening, and even commenting on the cultural debates over climate change, evolution, and education, I come back to the evolution debate and the cavalier discounting of evolutionary theory by the vocal members of the belief culture: Evolution is just a theory, they state emphatically. "Just a theory" reveals two very important aspects of the failure of the belief culture—how that cultural dynamic leaves us misguided about education and poverty.

First, the statement reveals that most people misunderstand the term "theory." "Theory" is a scientific term (and thus a nuanced term) that is analogous to what lay people would call fact since a theory is the conclusion draw from applying the scientific process to credible and extensive evidence. And that leads to the second important aspect we can draw from the statement.

By conflating "theory" with "hypothesis," the spokespeople for the belief culture are suggesting that "theory" is no better than "belief"—that we shouldn't accept things without evidence. And this is the central problem with a belief culture—espousing erroneous and contradictory ideas while discounting reasonable and evidence-based information simply because that knowledge contradicts tradition.

Leaving a society trapped in the most dangerous aspect of belief, entrenched ideology. Leaving many of us who seek education for empowerment, for human agency trapped in an old song: "We don't need no education/We don't need no thought control...."

Giroux (2011a), writing about Paul Klee's *Angelus Novus*, draws this conclusion about our cultural beliefs, about where our commitments lie:

> Not only has the American public lost its ability, perhaps even its will, to talk about public values such as sharing, caring and preserving, but it can no longer distinguish between a market-driven society and a democratic society. As Sheldon Wolin has insisted, the supportive culture for a viable democracy—"a complex of beliefs, values and practices that nurture equality, cooperation and freedom"—is incompatible with the market-driven values of neoliberalism and their emphasis on a crude consumerism, over-the-top materialism, brutal competition, a culture of lying, a possessive individualistic ethic and an aggressive battle to privatize, deregulate and commodify everything.

FALSE DICHOTOMY:
CALCULATING THE CORPORATE STATES OF AMERICA

In short, if people in the U.S. believed our inequitable economic and political system created poverty, we would be addressing those inequities and not blaming the people trapped in poverty—and we would not be supporting the scape-goating of schools and teachers coming from the new reformers. But, we are not that society; we are the Corporate States of America.

Few people could have imagined the acceleration of corporate influence that has occurred in the first 2 years of Barak Obama's presidency despite the economic downturn associated with those corporations and the election of Obama, who was repeatedly demonized by the Right as a socialist. More shocking, possibly, has been the corporate influence on the public discourse about universal public education, driven by Secretary Duncan and promoted through celebrity tours by billionaire Gates (Thomas, 2010aa) and ex-chancellor Rhee (Thomas, 2010y).

Bessie (2010b) has speculated about the logical progression of the current accountability era built on tests and destined to hold teachers accountable for their students' test scores (despite the evidence that teachers account for only about 10-20% of achievement [Rothstein, 2010])—hologram teachers. And Krashen (2011) believes that the corporate takeover of schools is at the center of the new reformers' misinformation tour. While Bessie's and Krashen's comments may sound like alarmist stances—possibly even the stuff of fiction—I believe we all should have seen this coming for decades.

The science fiction genre has always been one of my favorites, and within that genre, I am particularly fond of dystopian fiction, such as Margaret Atwood's brilliant *The Handmaid's Tale*, *Oryx and Crake*, and *The Year of the Flood*. Like Atwood, Kurt Vonnegut spoke and wrote often about rejecting the sci-fi label for his work—but Vonnegut's genius includes his gift for delivering social commentary and satire wrapped in narratives that *seemed* to be set in the future, *seemed* to be a distorted world that we could never possibly experience.

In 1952, Kurt Vonnegut published *Player Piano*, offering what most believed was a biting satire of corporate American from his own experience working at GE (Reed, 1995). A review of the novel in 1963 describes Vonnegut's vision of our brave new world:

> The important difference lies in the fact that Mr. Vonnegut's oligarchs are not capitalists but engineers. In the future as he envisages it, the machines have completed their triumph, dispossessing not only the manual laborers but the white collar workers as well. Consequently the carefully selected, highly trained individuals who design and control the machines are the only people who have anything to do. Other people, the great majority, can either go into the Reconstruction and Reclamation Corps, which is devoted to boondoggling, or join the army, which has no real function in a machine-dominated world-society. (Hicks, 1963)

Yes, in Vonnegut's dystopia, computers are at the center of a society run by itself like a machine, with everyone labeled with his or her IQ and designated for what career he or she can pursue (although we should note that women's roles were even more constrained than men's, reflecting the mid-twentieth century sexism in the U.S.). Where corporations end and the government begins is difficult in this society that is simply a slightly exaggerated version of the life Vonnegut had witnessed while working at GE before abandoning corporate America to be a full-time writer.

And Vonnegut's fully mechanized and computerized world allows numbers to mask social forces, presenting a world to us not unlike the one in which we live—especially as the growing charge for accountability driven by test scores gains momentum.

For me, however, Vonnegut's *Player Piano* is as much a warning about the role of testing and labeling people in our education system as it is a red flag about the dangers of the oligarchy that we have become. Today, with Gates speaking for not only corporate America but also reforming public education, how far off was Vonnegut's vision?

In the first decade of the twenty-first century, how different is Vonnegut's world to what we have today, as income equity and the pooling of wealth accelerates (Noah, 2010)?

We have witnessed where political loyalty lies during federal government bailouts, as corporate America collapsed at the end of George W. Bush's presidency. With corporate American saved, and most Americans ignored, the next logical step is to transform public education by increasing the corporate model that has been crippling the system since the misinformation out of Ronald Reagan's presidency grabbed headlines with the release of A Nation at Risk (Bracey, 2003; Holton, 2003). If Vonnegut had written this storyline, at least we could have been guaranteed some laughter. But this brave new world of public education is more grim—like George Orwell's *1984*.

Our artists can see and understand when many of the rest of us are simply overwhelmed by our lives. In *Player Piano*, we watch how successful corporate life disorients and consumes workers in order to keep those workers under control. And in the relationship between the main character Paul and his wife Anita, we view the power of corporate life—and the weight of testing and reducing humans to numbers—being magnified by the rise of computers when Paul makes this plea to his wife:

> "No, no. You've got something the tests and machines will never be able to measure: you're artistic. That's one of the tragedies of our times, that no machine has ever been built that can recognize that quality, appreciate it, foster it, sympathize with it." (Vonnegut, 1952, p. 178)

In the novel, Paul's quest and the momentary rise of some rebels appear to be no match for corporate control. Today, I have to say I am no more optimistic than Vonnegut about the prospect of saving public education from corporate greed.

When Secretary Duncan (2010e) offers misleading claims about international test scores and bemoans the state of public schools for failing to provide us with a world-class workforce, and almost no one raises a voice in protest (except those within the field of education, only to be demonized for protesting [Michie, 2011]), I am tempted to think that we are simply getting what we deserve—like Paul at the end of *Player Piano*: "And that left Paul. 'To a better world,' he started to say, but he cut the toast short, thinking of the people of Ilium, already eager to recreate the same old nightmare" (Vonnegut, 1952, p. 340).

Like Kingsolver (1995) in her "Somebody's Baby," Strauss (2011a) makes a bold claim: "Americans don't really think very much of their children." And she does so because the U.S. tolerates one of the highest poverty rates for children among industrialized countries, but she also outlines more proof from the new reformers' refrains—utopian expectations for schools, standardized testing, scape-goating teachers, trivializing childhood, underfunding schools, idealizing charter schools, demonizing teachers' unions.

And this is how I want to frame the rest of my discussion in this book: The U.S. ignores and demonizes poverty by embracing deficit beliefs about teaching, learning, children, and most of all poverty itself. These deficit beliefs are corrosive—and worst of all they are refuted by evidence. One of the worst aspects of our deficit beliefs is captured by the current accountability movement, occurring over the past 30 years, which I now turn to in Chapter 2, "Politicians Who Cry 'Crisis': Education Accountability as Masking."

POLITICIANS WHO CRY "CRISIS"

Education Accountability as Masking

Consider this discussion of U.S. public education:

> For while schools everywhere reflect to some extent the culture of which they are a part and respond to forces within that culture, the American public schools, because of the nature of their pattern of organization, support, and control, were especially vulnerable and responded quickly to the strongest social forces.... The business influence was exerted upon education in several ways: through newspapers, journals, and books; through speeches at educational meetings; and, more directly, through actions of school boards. It was exerted by laymen, by professional journalists, by businessmen or industrialists either individually or in groups, ... and finally by educators themselves. Whatever its source, the influence was exerted in the form of suggestions or demands that the schools be organized and operated in a more businesslike way and that more emphasis by placed upon a practical and immediately useful education. (Callahan, 1962, pp. 1, 5-6)

Currently, does this sound familiar? Maybe even a reference to *Waiting for "Superman,"* Bill Gates, Michelle Rhee, and Arne Duncan? This is in fact from Callahan (1962) from 50 years ago about the state of education.

Ignoring Poverty in the U.S.: The Corporate Takeover of Public Education, pp. 27–55

Callahan (1962) offers a detailed argument that public education was consumed by a corporate and capitalistic faith in *efficiency* during the battle for control of public education during the first half of the twentieth century (also see Kliebard, 1995). Here, and throughout this book, I am making a related point that our education debate and perpetual calls for education reform continue that same dynamic presented by Callahan and deemed a tragedy:

> The tragedy itself was fourfold: that educational questions were subordinated to business considerations; that administrators were produced who were not, in any true sense, educators; that a scientific label was put on some very unscientific and dubious methods and practices; and that an anti-intellectual climate, already prevalent, was strengthened. (p. 246)

These elements of the tragedy—relinquishing education to efficiency—identified by Callahan half a century ago have been replayed and intensified through No Child Left Behind, the Reading First scandal, and the rising attacks on teachers and teachers' unions, all linked directly to calls for accountability, standards, and testing.

Broadly, I reject accountability and standards as an approach to education reform wedded to efficiency because of the inherent failure of honoring efficiency over other goals of public education—democracy, empowerment, justice. And I feel that our pursuit of efficiency has allowed calls for accountability to hide the central weight on education, poverty. Below, with those points remaining my primary concerns, I examine how accountability and standards are mismatched to reforming education as a pursuit of democracy, empowerment, and social justice.

A CRITICAL REJECTION OF THE ACCOUNTABILITY ERA (1983-2001)

As I noted in Chapter 1, Vonnegut's *Player Piano* offers a literary view of the social embracing of a narrow and corporate view of scientific—a powerful social norm that Callahan (1962) demonstrates consumed and drove education throughout the first half of the twentieth century. By 1983, with the release of the politically stained but publicly effective A Nation at Risk, Callahan's warning shifted into a high gear than I suspect he could have never imagined—ushering in the current accountability era that became codified in 2001 with the passing of No Child Left Behind (NCLB).

Much of my discussion below will examine how post-NCLB and reauthorization debates about NCLB are continuing the flawed pursuit of accountability that masks the need to address poverty, but first I want to examine briefly the critical and research-based evidence that we knew accountability paradigms were flawed even and right before the passing of Bush's NCLB legislation based on his pseudo-miracle in Texas. The evidence is powerful that standards are quickly reduced to tests to facilitate accountability, and from that focus on tests, our schools ultimately ask *less* of both teachers and students:

> The need to make test performance the first priority has forced many teachers to push topics and activities that do not appear on the test to the end of the school year, after testing is finished.... Research in the last few decades documents that state testing can significantly affect curriculum and instruction.... Other studies from the NCLB era conclude that the higher the stakes are for educators, the more curriculum and instruction reflect what's on the test—particularly in low-performing schools where the threat of sanctions is strongest. A study of a large urban district from 2001 to 2005 (Valli & Buese, 2007) found that as worries about adequate yearly progress increased, teachers matched the content and format of what they taught to the state test. These researchers concluded that the content of the tests had effectively become the learning goals for students. (David, 2011, n.p.)

Just as Callahan (1962) offered a stern but ignored warning about the cult of efficiency near mid-century, many critical educators exposed the flaws of the standards movement before NCLB was signed into law (Kincheloe & Weil, 2001).

Kincheloe notes that the discussion about education quality, education purposes, standards, and reform have "been disappointing to many scholars, educators, and citizens" (Kincheloe & Weil, 2001, p. 1). Political and public discourse tends to be *transmissional*, lacking a critical element that confronts the assumptions driving the claims and failing to require evidence for those claims except for the status of the person behind the claims: "The unstated assumptions behind technical visions of the characteristics of educated people involve a computer-like conception of the human mind where storage and retrieval of data are its central features" (p. 3), explains Kincheloe. The static and authoritarian discourse about education and education reform, then, failed to rise to discussion and remained trapped in a conflating of "technical" with "rigorous" (itself a problematic term).

"Standards" as a term denoting *challenging* was being misrepresented by the efficiency commitment in American culture driven by consumerism, capitalism, and corporate agendas—the narrowest and most distorted conception of science that honors *measurability* over human complexity or uniqueness: "Technical standards that focus simply on performance on standardized tests remove the all-important meaning-making process from the everyday life of the classroom" (Kincheloe & Weil, 2001, p. 4). To shift from technical standards grounded in efficiency to challenging standards grounded in critical awareness, Kincheloe explains that "the *significance* of information that students learn is important, not just the *acquisition* of such data" (Kincheloe & Weil, p. 6, emphasis in original). The accountability era begun in 1983 and codified in 2001 perpetuated authoritative identification of fixed knowledge and the transmission of that knowledge to passive and receptive students through teachers as service worker: "Such pseudo-learning constitutes an uncritical absorption of other people's agendas without an understanding that an agenda is present in the process" (Kincheloe & Weil, p. 6). Combined with the influence of efficiency norms is the masking allure of objectivity.

Agency is hauntingly absent from claims made about education and by education reformers over the past thirty years. Students, teachers, and the public are addressed and characterized as lacking agency, as if agency is not central to democracy or even being fully human (Kincheloe & Weil, 2001). *The most offensive irony in the authoritative masking of agency is the concurrent call for holding those students and teachers accountable without honoring their agency to make decisions.* As well, this irony functions within a call for objectivity that denounces *political* voice by educators or in the classrooms *through* the political—and often partisan—and public dynamics that call for and implement technical standards, high-stakes testing, and punitive accountability mandates.

The critical call for "standards of complexity" (Kincheloe & Weil, 2001, p. 97) was offered and ignored, like the warning from Callahan (1962), just as the U.S. chose to move forward with a bipartisan commitment to the most overtly technical standards, testing, and accountability process ever mandated by the federal government, NCLB. And the decade since NCLB has revealed we are likely to keep pushing in the wrong direction.

THE NEGLECTED "TOP LEVEL KIDS" AND HOLLOW CALLS FOR ACCOUNTABILITY

The twenty-first century Western world, driven by American corporate and consumer ideology, is a perpetual media culture that depends on sound bites and *the next thing*, leaving the public reduced to media consumers never allowed time to reflect on the information. Volume and speed have consumed and obliterated nuance, ethics, and accuracy. For example, numerous media outlets reported the *fact* that Secretary Arne Duncan made speech after speech about education and education reform, but none paused long enough to verify *what* Duncan said or to examine his claims against the evidence, against the assumptions of those claims.

The education debate during the Obama administration has been characterized by celebrity spokespersons supported uncritically by the media; as Adam Bessie (2011) exposes, "Unfortunately, the mainstream media has unquestioningly bought into this limited conception of educational reform." Rare is the unmasking of oversimplified and misinformed messages from Duncan, Bill Gates, and Michelle Rhee. But, the new media—Internet-based journalism and blogging with interactive commentary through discussion boards—exposes the perfect storm that has matched the new reformers' misleading narrative about defenders of the status quo (Thomas, 2011b) and the public's concern for the neglected "top level kids" as expressed in this commentary at a blog posting on *The Huffington Post*:

> As a teacher in a very mixed socio-economic school district, I find that MOST resources get put into helping the lower scoring/economically disadvantaged children, while very little is used to help promote and push forward the high achievers. This may come across as very crass, but the high achievers are going to be our nation's leaders and business executives; the ones who create the new innovations and push our country to new heights. Why are we so opposed to making our top level kids better?
>
> Now, should we neglect those who are not the "top level kids?" ... At the end of the day, all kids have the opportunity to be successful in the American public schools if they work hard and desire to be successful. Do all kids start off with the same resources or ability levels? No. But "real life" outside of school is not going to be kinder to them because of it. If they have twice as many obstacles, they need to work twice as hard to overcome them. The market place shows no mercy to the disadvantaged. We do these students a disservice if we coddle them. (Grether, 2010, n.p.)

The reason the new reformers' distorted charges that "bad" teachers (Bessie, 2010a)—and not the debilitating influence of poverty, supported by the weight of evidence—are at the root of failing schools is effective lies in the cultural assumptions that guide the beliefs of the public (Keohane, 2010). The new reformers are using celebrity to speak to the cultural faith in rugged individualism as an inherent quality of the chosen who either "work twice as hard" to succeed or fail as they deserve, the belief argues.

The reader comment above demonstrates that the public embracing an ideology driven by rugged individualism, pulling ones self up by the boot straps, and rising tides lifting all boats shifts all culpability to the individual; even when we concede that the "market place shows no mercy," we seem unconcerned about the *ethical* results of Social Darwinism built into our consumer culture. In fact, we believe that Social Darwinism helps lift the elite to the top, as they deserve—again, despite the evidence to the contrary. These connected claims, then, feed the call for and support of standards and accountability.

As one brief example, consider the move under George W. Bush to end college admission policies that considered race *as that contrasts with* the use of legacy in college admissions, a longstanding practice that benefited Bush himself and apparently offers a huge advantage to those already privileged (Lewin, 2011). Public opinion tended to rail against race-based college admissions as unfair (or at least the mainstream media portrayed public opinion that way), but you are hard pressed to find much concern about the very real advantage of legacy admission policies. This is the America that demonizes those living in poverty while idealizing those living in wealth.

We are encouraged to rush to protect and defend those at the top—billionaires and "top level kids"—but somehow people living in poverty or struck by unemployment need to suck it up, work twice as hard, and see adversity as an opportunity. The myth of the neglected "top level kids" has the same momentum of cultural faith as the calls for "no excuses" schools—populated primarily by children living in poverty, of color, and speaking home languages other than English (see Chapter 4 for a full discussion of "no excuses" charter schools)—and accountability for schools and teachers.

When I was growing up—and I was a "top level kid" according to the education system—I was offered innumerable gifts by my parents, who were wonderful but far from perfect (which is often a key element in being wonderful). From my father I learned more than I can catalog here, but one of the greatest lessons is ironic because I came to embrace a philosophy *opposite* of one my father's frequent responses to my argumentative nature: "Do as I say, not as I do."

As an educator who taught in a rural high school for 18 years but now teaches elite students at a selective university—all "top level kids"—I have learned and have tried to honor the value of being a model for those beliefs and actions that we expect of our students; in fact, I expect more of myself than of my students—although, like my parents, I am not perfect. Throughout the current reform debate as I worked as an educator and scholar—writing about and examining often the rise of the new reformers in education (Duncan, Gates, and Rhee)—I have been reminded of my father's "Do as I say, not as I do," and more recently, I was struck by another formative influence on my life, George Carlin (2004), specifically this rant from *When Will Jesus Bring the Pork Chops?*:

> I get weary of this zero tolerance bullshit. It's annoying. To begin with, it's a fascist concept; it's what Hitler and Stalin practiced. It allows for no exceptions or compassion of any kind. All is black and white—no gradations. But even more important, it doesn't solve anything. The use of such a slogan simply allows whichever company, school or municipality is using it to claim they're doing something about a problem when, in fact, nothing is being

done at all and the problem is being ignored. It's a cosmetic non-solution designed to impress simpletons. Whenever you hear the phrase zero tolerance, remember, someone is bullshitting you. (p. 84)

Parallel to Carlin's distrust, I find the relentless calls for "accountability"—from student accountability at the beginning of the standards era in the early 1980s to the more recent mantra about "bad teachers" and teacher accountability—to be as hollow as "Do as I say, not as I do" because those calling for accountability are billionaires, celebrities, politicians, and political appointees—all of whom through their affluence and status tend to live *outside* anything resembling accountability.

With the new reformers speaking celebrity to the mythologies driving public opinion and masking evidence about the reality of U.S. public education and the reform that system does need, educators have an obligation to speak expert to celebrity by consistently addressing the following facts:

1. Poverty is the overwhelming correlation with student achievement in the U.S. and throughout the world. Several studies show out-of-school factors account for 80-90% of achievement: The Joseph Rowntree Foundation has shown 86% of achievement is connected to conditions outside of the schools (Hirsch, 2007), Berliner (2009) has outlined six out-of-school factors overwhelming academic achievement, Rothstein (2010) places the hysteria about teacher quality in its proper context of social inequity, Traub (2000) has detailed the historical failures of schools to overcome social influences on achievement since the 1960s, and even the faux crisis expressed about 2009 PISA scores has been exposed as greater evidence of the corrosive nature of poverty rather than the quality of U.S. schools (Riddile, 2010).

2. Teacher and school quality is, obviously, important (again, see Rothstein, 2010), but there is no evidence that teacher quality is one of the main problems facing schools. But teacher assignment is impacting students negatively—since studies show that students living in poverty, students of color, and ELL students are assigned to teachers with less experience and who are often un- or under-qualified/certified (Peske & Haycock, 2006). Despite claims that public education is neglecting the top students, the evidence is to the contrary—students who excel tend to be disproportionately more affluent than the students struggling and those students succeeding increasingly find themselves in the most challenging courses (often designed to weed out so-called weaker students) with the best teachers. Public education should not be expected to cure poverty, but public education should be held culpable for stratify-

ing students further by the conditions of their lives outside of school since schools-within-schools are a reality of many schools across the U.S. (view the HBO documentary *Little Rock Central: 50 Years Later* for a vivid insight into this phenomenon).

3. The current new reformer calls are increasing the status quo, not changing it (Kohn 2010a)—accountability, standards, and testing have been tried for three decades in 50 separate experiments that have all hurt more than helped. Despite the persistent misuse of SAT data to demonize, label, and rank the quality of schools across the U.S., SAT data offer one vivid and valuable message that is almost always ignored: SAT scores are most directly correlated with parental income and parental level of education (Thomas, 2010l), and these students are among the most affluent and learning in advanced classes taught by the best teachers.

4. Critical educators and researchers are against the traditional status quo of public schooling, which is characterized by accountability, standards, testing, and stratification (the elements of "reform" proposed by the new reformers); we have been calling for educational reform for a century, highlighted by the work of John Dewey, Paulo Freire, and an often ignored contemporary community of educators and scholars: Stephen Krashen, Susan Ohanian, Henry Giroux, bell hooks, Joe Kincheloe, Walt Gardner, Stephanie Jones, Adam Bessie, and many others. Critical educators are seeking evidence-based and humane schools that support democratic principles above corporate and consumer interests—and that is the message that the corporate and political elite want to squelch. Education professor Gregory Michie (2011) captures the inverted reality of whose voice matters in the education debate: "Then again, I'm an education professor, so what do I know about schools? Maybe only this: If you really want to understand what's going on in them and the direction we need to be headed, don't ask Bill Gates or the Business Roundtable. Ask a teacher" (n.p.).

5. The U.S., like the countries the new reformers claim have successful education systems, must make social reforms that support educational reform (Thomas, 2010h). Schools alone cannot change society; the evidence is overwhelming and clear on this. When Secretary Duncan (2010c) speaks to utopian expectations for education—"Education is still the key to eliminating gender inequities, to reducing poverty, to creating a sustainable planet, and to fostering peace" (n.p.)—we must acknowledge that schools *alone* have never and will never correct the inequities in society. Duncan's idealism is as corrosive as the 100% proficiency mandates of NCLB

because they both assure the ultimate perception of failure. In short, celebrity reformers have the formula backward when they claim education can cure poverty. Instead, we should heed Martin Luther King Jr. (1967) from his "Final Words of Advice": "We are likely to find that the problems of housing and education, instead of preceding the elimination of poverty, will themselves be affected if poverty is first abolished" (n.p.).

6. Accountability for accountability's sake misrepresents teaching and learning as an isolated and direct relationship between one teacher and one student. Teaching and learning are social and multifaceted human acts that are beyond simplistic views of "accountability" or causation. While new reformers often use international comparisons to demonize U.S. schools (Thomas, 2010x), they tend to ignore that countries such as Finland reject simplistic teacher evaluations linked to student test scores. Further, data, again, caution against using student tests as evidence of causation about teacher quality (Baker et al., 2010).

Each of the six points above is being masked and distorted by corporate and political elites who expect a compliant media and a public too overloaded with information to question claims that match their assumptions. The distorted education reform debate offers educators a chance to rise about false dualities of conservative/liberal and traditionalist/progressive, to speak expert to celebrity as *radicals*, as Howard Zinn (1994) implores in his memoir *You Can't Be Neutral on a Moving Train*:

> From that moment on, I was no longer a liberal, a believer in the self-correcting character of American democracy. I was a radical, believing that something fundamental was wrong in this country—not just the existence of poverty amidst great wealth, not just the horrible treatment of black people, but something rotten at the root. The situation required not just a new president or new laws, but an uprooting of the old order, the introduction of a new kind of society—cooperative, peaceful, egalitarian. (p. 173)

The misleading concern for the so-called neglected "top-level kids" is one strategy used within the calls for standards and accountability that detracts us from addressing poverty. Another powerful rhetorical strategy is framing education always in a state of crisis.

"CRISIS" DISCOURSE AS POLITICAL STRATEGY

"The Boy Who Cried Wolf" is a well-known Aesop fable that offers a moral about the dangers of lies. While this tale is a simple but accurate message, the world of fable is rarely a fair reflection of the world of reality. In our real world, the villagers appear less perceptive than those encountered by the shepherd boy of fable since politicians for a century have found political capital in crying educational "crisis" while pointing always at our schools and our teachers. Unlike the villagers who exposed the shepherd boy's lies, we dutifully turn in any direction politicians point and ask not for a shred of proof.

"It is rather the same thing that is happening to the English language. It becomes ugly and inaccurate because our thoughts are foolish, but the slovenliness of our language makes it easier for us to have foolish thoughts," George Orwell (1946, n.p.) warns in his "Politics and the English Language." Few examples are better for proving Orwell right (and Aesop wrong) than political language addressing, ironically, the education of children throughout the U.S. But, as Orwell adds, "If one gets rid of these habits one can think more clearly, and to think clearly is a necessary first step towards political regeneration" (n.p.).

The language of choice for politicians is "crisis," and the wolf of choice for politicians is "education." When Barack Obama entered the White House, many hoped for his message of change, but the education policy and discourse coming from Obama and Secretary of Education Arne Duncan are disturbing evidence of the status quo: corporatist and positivistic approaches to school reform designed to keep everyone looking at schools in order to hide the massive inequities in the lives of children and their families over our shoulders as we remain transfixed on schools and teachers.

For example, David Sirota (2010), writing in *The Seattle Times*, has exposed the power of politicians to distract through cries of crisis about education:

> Of course, 30 years into the neoliberal experiment, the Great Recession is exposing the flaws of the Washington Consensus. But rather than admit any mistakes, neoliberals now defend themselves with yet more bait-and-switch sophistry—this time in the form of the Great Education Myth. (n.p.)

The political slight of language works this way: Cry wolf (or assume the frantic mantle of Chicken Little, "Our schools are failing! Our schools are failing!"), and the villagers will never look at the inherent flaws in our society, flaws that keep the corporate elite in power, that keep the political elite in power, that relentlessly carve an ever-widening gap between the haves and have-nots (Noah, 2010).

Secretary Duncan is proving to be a master of crisis discourse, cloaking his corporate commitments in the language and settings of authentic civil rights. Duncan (2010b), speaking on behalf of the Obama administration, stood in Little Rock, Arkansas, where he reminded his audience of Dr. Martin Luther King, Jr., and Central High. And there he made his direct case, crying wolf about the need to focus on teacher quality:

> The big game-changer for us, however, in terms of both formula and competitive programs, revolves around the issue of teacher quality. Nothing is more important and nothing has a greater impact on the quality of education than the quality and skill of the person standing in the front of the class—and there is so much that needs to change in the way that America recruits, trains, supports and manages our teachers. (n.p.)

Nothing?

Duncan's wolf comes just months after this sobering truth about childhood in the United States:

> The rate of children living in poverty this year will climb to nearly 22%, the highest rate in two decades, according to an analysis by the non-profit Foundation for Child Development. Nearly 17% of children were living in poverty in 2006, before the recession began. (Szabo, 2010, n.p.)

In his Arkansas speech, Duncan mentions teachers over four dozen times and poverty none. And while he waves his arms and draws our eyes toward the claimed failure of teachers in our failed schools, invoking a crisis in teacher quality (to join the drop-out crisis and the achievement gap crisis), the truth about what matters in student achievement remains ignored, silenced.

And while a powerful body of research proves Duncan's claims about teacher quality false—the dominant influence on student achievement is poverty, not teacher quality (Berliner, 2009; Hirsch, 2007; Traub, 2000)—exposing the political lie doesn't require that we villagers go that far. The annual hand wringing over SAT scores is all we need.

Near the end, of course, of a discussion of 2010 SAT scores in *Education Week*, a recurring truth is shared:

> Students' scores continued to reflect their family income and parents' education. Those in the lowest-income brackets, and whose parents had the least education, scored 125 points or more below their peers at the top of the family-income or parental education grid. (Gewertz, 2010, n.p.)

Students who take the SAT are a unique population of students, more affluent and more likely to take advanced coursework than the entire population of U.S. students. Yet among the elite students in our schools, who also disproportionately have access to the most experienced and fully certified teachers (Peske & Haycock, 2006), SAT scores are most strongly correlated with parental income and parental educational attainment.

And that truth can be verified for every year the SAT has been administered, decades of data refuting decades of politicians crying wolf about failing teachers and schools in crisis to keep the villagers from looking at the social forces keeping those villagers in place while the corporate and political elite enjoy the fruits of their persistent deception. The use of crisis discourse helps perpetuate the increasingly effective calls for accountability, yet another mask for ignoring poverty during the standards era.

"THE TRUTH IS ALWAYS HARD TO SWALLOW"— AND OTHER IRONIES

Secretary of Education Duncan's Arkansas speech failed to mention poverty even once, but he referred to teachers over four dozen times. And these facts of language were telling in a time when many educators are challenging the call to increase teacher accountability, including a disturbing shift to value-added modeling (VAM). The *Los Angeles Times* publishing teachers' names along with evaluations of those teachers based on VAM has fueled the debate. But the careful and detailed challenges to the many flaws with holding teachers accountable for student achievement (Baker et al., 2010) are not shaking the Obama/Duncan persistence at placing the focus of school reform on teachers while ignoring the substantial evidence that the primary influences on student achievement are the conditions of childrens' homes and communities.

Duncan's rhetorical strategy became predictable since he made compelling statements, which he later contradicted in the policies he supported—and he wrapped his speeches in the language of civil rights to feed the perception that the Obama/Duncan educational plan embraces the continuing call for our society to address our social failures.

For example, the language below seems to place Duncan (2010c) among those recognizing that school failures happen within social failures:

> Instead of holding only schools accountable we want to hold districts and states more accountable. No school is an island, operating in isolation. Instead of prescribing specific and often impractical interventions for the vast majority of schools from Washington—we want to offer a clear definition of success and let most schools figure out how to get there. We must better support creativity and innovation at the local level, which where the best ideas will always come from. (n.p.)

But if we look carefully, and hear the rest of this speech, we see that the policies are entirely focused on teacher quality, teacher accountability, and teacher culpability. Yet, the central claim about the primary influence of teachers is factually untrue. Teacher quality does matter, but teaching effectiveness is dwarfed by the lives of the children any teacher teaches.

Duncan (2010c) further proves the willingness of the administration to treat schools as if they exist in social vacuums by making international comparisons: "Today, there are many different approaches to strengthening the teaching profession—both here in America and in countries that are outperforming us like Finland and Singapore." But Duncan fails to acknowledge or address the disparity in childhood poverty between Finland and the U.S. (Adamson, 2005, 2007). And then the crux of Duncan's focus on teachers is found here: "The truth is always hard to swallow but it can only make us better, stronger and smarter. That's what accountability is all about—facing the truth and taking responsibility and then taking action" (n.p.). For the Obama/Duncan administration, then, accountability is about "the truth and taking responsibility and then taking action." But that may be more compelling in rhetoric than in reality, especially when we expose the truth against the claims and when we hold those calling for accountability accountable themselves.

In reality, when using test scores to hold people accountable is turned on those at the top who make such claims, the message somehow changes. As Chancellor of DC schools, Michelle Rhee represents in reality what Duncan has been promoting through his speeches—accountability for teachers through rigid evaluation systems that lead to firing those teachers deemed weak. But shortly after firing teachers, Rhee appeared unwilling to have the same accountability dynamic applied to her tenure over DC schools, as posted on the Schools Matter blog:

> According to Rhee and the Oligarchs who built her, one-shot tests appear to be perfectly valid when it comes to firing teachers and making decisions on teacher pay and job security. However, when it comes to Rhee's own accountability to do what she identified in 2007 as her top priority as schools chief (to close the achievement gap), such tests are only isolated data points that should be looked at over time. You see, the gaps are not closing as Rhee's raging arrogance had led her to predict. (Horn, 2010a, n.p.)

So here is one truth that is truly hard to swallow: Accountability built on tests is appropriate for teachers, but not for a chancellor who creates that same dynamic for those teachers.

But the holes in Duncan's plans do not stop there. Another mistake is that the Obama/Duncan administration is failing to acknowledge the social sources of educational struggles while promoting Race to the Top (RttT). This competition for funding has recently revealed itself as a plan deaf to the true problems facing schools, as posted on a recent Rural Education blog at *Education Week*:

[Howley Caitlin's] research fleshes out the numbers behind an obvious but important point: While states with large rural populations such as North Carolina and Georgia won Race to the Top money, missing in action are almost all the states with highest numbers of small, rural schools—and many in the high rural-poverty belts the Rural School and Community Trust has identified in the Rural 900, a list of the highest-poverty rural school districts in the nation. (Schulken, 2010, n.p.)

In short, yet another truth hard to swallow, poverty and out-of-school factors do not matter in school reform because teachers are the primary component of student success, according to Duncan, and market forces (competition in RttT) will provide the objective field upon which school reform will make itself clear.

While Duncan continues to offer claims about truth that ironically avoid the truth, our main concern should be with not swallowing claims of "truth," but a willingness to open our eyes and first see the truth—and then to have the moral courage to do something about children living in poverty in the wealthiest country in the history of human civilization. The standards and accountability era has shifted our eyes toward "top-level kids" and characterized public schools in crisis in order to keep us distracted. Another strategy within the standards movement is the singular and simplistic focus on test data and the misuse of international comparisons—which ironically serve to highlight the power of poverty once we strip away the careless use of data and rankings. Let's look at the flawed pursuit of test scores next.

BITTER LESSONS FROM CHASING BETTER TESTS

In a *New York Times* Op-Ed, E. D. Hirsch Jr. (2009) argued, "We do not need to abandon either the principle of accountability or the fill-in-the-bubble format. Rather we need to move from teaching to the test to tests that are worth teaching to" (n.p.). This refrain parallels the contradictory messages coming from the Obama administration that claims supporting a change to the culture of testing in NCLB, but then argues for better testing. Secretary of Education Duncan (2009), in a speech about NCLB reauthorization acknowledged concerns about testing, but immediately took the same position as Hirsch: "Until states develop better assessments—which we will support and fund through Race to the Top—we must rely on standardized tests to monitor progress—but this is an important area for reform and an important conversation to have" (n.p.).

A better test is all we need?

Nothing could be further from the truth. We have been searching for the perfect test for a century now in education, and that has led us to the reliability and validity traps. In other words, technically Hirsch is right, but authentically, a test will never be anything more than a pale reflection of what any student knows. Let's consider first something we claim is much less important than education (although that claim may be tenuous)—football. It would be quicker and cheaper to design a multiple-choice test that is well designed (high reliability and validity) and replace all football games, including playoffs, with those tests in order to determine high school, college, and professional championships. Imagine Friday nights across the U.S. with teams lined up in desks bubbling frantically to reach the state championship!

But we would never stand for this.

Somehow, however, this is exactly what we call for again and again as a solution for improving the education of our children in a free society—higher standards, more testing, and greater accountability. The flaws of testing and accountability are failing our students and our society:

- A culture of testing perpetuates the misconception that teaching and learning somehow exist within an educational vacuum—as if the lives of children are suspended when they walk through the doors of school. Accountability principles that hold people accountable for conditions beyond their control will always fail, but that is what we do in education.

- Test data are never a pure representation of learning. A test score is impacted by effort of the student, quality of the test, conditions of the testing day and time, and a number of other factors that have nothing to do with learning. Multiple-choice tests, as well, are always impacted by guessing. But a central error in our faith in and use of testing is that testing can be valuable for offering broad patterns related to large groups of students, but it is terribly inefficient and ineffective for any individual student. The main mistake we make over and over is placing high stakes on single tests for individual students and now teachers.

- Teaching to a test reduces learning to a static body of knowledge and is the lowest possible characterization of teaching and learning. A basic argument of John Dewey (1938/1997) that we have failed to see in this country is that education can never fully anticipate what any student needs to know, but schools can prepare children to be expert learners, something that a multiple-choice test as a goal or a measurement can never achieve. Testing, then, shifts the conversation to the acquisition of static knowledge, but adult human agency in a free society manifests itself in the organic nature of being that is about the process of interacting with knowledge.

- The best test possible can only be an approximation of learning. Any test must reduce what is being measured and depend on statistical approximations to create the perception that we are measuring something much larger than we are. As Popham (2001, 2003) has argued, a test provides us data from which to make inferences, but at best those inferences are approximate—unless you make the test so direct and simplistic as to create a situation where we are collecting data that means almost nothing.

- Once we make any test sacred, that test replaces the larger and more authentic goals of school. Instead of reading, students take test-prep to be tested on reading; instead of writing, students take test-prep to be tested on writing … and the list goes on. Testing and teaching to a test are always asking less of our students. As well, the history of the standards and accountability era has taught us that standards are always reduced to *what is tested*.

Correlations, validity, and reliability are powerful in the world of statistics, and they sound impressive when we call for making our schools more challenging. But in the end, teaching and learning are human endeavors that are messy, chaotic, and nearly impossible to reduce to simple measurements. Calls for better tests are merely digging a deep hole even deeper. The solution to better schools is not better tests but challenging students to read, write, and think for hours each day throughout the school year, never lifting their heads or pencils to get ready for a test (although they certainly should for rest, play, or pursuit of something of interest).

But we must place a more challenging school day—one not concerned with tests—within a social commitment to the lives of children outside of school as well. Hungry children care little about tests or reading. If we want better and even eager readers in this country, we don't need better reading tests: We need students who are actually reading. If we want highly literate and critically thinking young people to enter and rejuvenate our free land, spending much of their schooling trying to get a higher test score is not the solution, regardless of the test they are chasing. And if we persist in calling for better tests while ignoring the burden of poverty on children's lives, those children will continue to learn the bitter lesson about what we truly value as a people. A connected obsession with tests includes comparing test data from the U.S. internationally—a practice that proves to be more masking and even less credible than calls for better tests in the U.S.

FINNISH ENVY

While I recognize that Freudian psychology has mixed credibility within the field of psychology, I believe if we put the new reformers in education—Secretary Duncan, Gates, Rhee, and their ilk—on the psychiatrist's couch we'd be likely to diagnose them all with Finnish Envy, and a considerable degree of delusion as well.

First, we should be clear that the current psychoses among the new reformers in education are nothing new. Consider the Golden Age of U.S. education, as praised by Rhee herself (Thomas, 2010v), the 1950s. According to Rudolf Flesch, author of *Why Johnny Can't Read—And What You Can Do About It* (Why Johnny Can't Read, 1955):

> Only in the U.S., reported Flesch, is there any remedial-reading problem. In Britain, kindergarten children read *Three Little Pigs*; in Germany, second-grade pupils can read aloud (without necessarily understanding all the words) almost anything in print. By contrast, average U.S. third-graders have a reading mastery of only 1,800 words. Why is the U.S. so far behind? Says Flesch: "We have decided to forget that we write with letters, and [instead] learn to read English as if it were Chinese." (n.p.)

And Admiral Hyman Rickover's *Swiss Schools and Ours: Why Theirs are Better* (1962) and *American Education, a National Failure; The problem of our schools and what we can learn from England* (1963) offered even more bashing of U.S. schools, including making (not a surprise) international comparisons and calling for national standards:

> To some critics, the situation cries out for a "national curriculum" to equalize schools. Loud among them is Admiral Hyman G. Rickover, who calls local control "the greatest obstacle to school reform." Says Rickover in a tendentiously titled new book, *Swiss Schools and Ours: Why Theirs Are Better*: "I know of no country that has brought off successfully a really thorough reform of the school system without making use of some national standard that sets scholastic objectives." (Education, 1962, n.p.)

Half a century later, the country is being bombarded *still* with charges that U.S. schools are failing. The messages have changed little, but they come in misleading documentaries like *Waiting for "Superman"* and through the left-wing media perpetuating false information about international results on tests (see the *Huffington Post* article and its discussion of other media outlets—all of which are perpetuating the same misleading claim that international education comparisons show the U.S. is failing [Berdan & Weiner, 2010]).

Earlier in the first decade of the twenty-first century, under the George W. Bush administration when Margaret Spellings held the position of Secretary of Education, we saw what was coming: Political misinformation to protect political agendas when Spellings exposed herself as either incompetent or dishonest by claiming that NAEP test scores proved NCLB a success (Hoff, 2007). Pallas (2009c), Bracey (2007), and Ravitch (2009a) have discredited Spellings's claims about NCLB producing NAEP gains, but those facts found little traction in the press. More recently, the stakes and the misinformation have morphed even further into the absurd because we have little distinction now among the many interests using our public schools as political, corporate, and ideological footballs—Secretary Duncan, Rhee, Gates, corporate charters (KIPP), Teach for America, and celebrities such as Oprah Winfrey, John Legend, and Andre Agassi (Thomas, 2010v).

One refrain they all seem to share is a fascination with Finland, specifically the much praised Finnish schools. But when we hear U.S. schools criticized and Finland identified as the gold standard for reform, we rarely hear that U.S. children suffer under the weigh of poverty (20+%) that is significantly higher than the childhood poverty rate in Finland (3-4%). The new reformers like to show selected rankings (test scores comparing apples to oranges) while hiding others (childhood poverty).

And those same new reformers who have identified bad teachers and protective teachers' unions as the central problems with U.S. schools also fail to share that virtually all teachers in Finland belong to unions, have their graduate education paid by the government, and work collaboratively within a system that does not use high-stakes testing (Snider, 2010). The blog Schools Matter struck the nail on the head by characterizing the use of Finland by the new reformers as cartoonish (Horn, 2010b), except this isn't funny at all.

While the contradictions and distortions currently being promoted by the new reformers and reinforced by every aspect of the media are proving to be a disservice to U.S. schools, its students, and the entire country, those of us who care about those schools and children should take a moment to call the reformers' bluff: Let's be like Finland, except we can't just focus on schools alone.

The truth about test data and international comparisons is that poverty and social realities remain the primary factors reflected in both the data and the comparisons. That education reformers persist in *distorting* and *misusing* data and comparisons suggests either incompetence or fixed ideological agendas that are willing to sacrifice evidence for goals other than education reform. The use of test data and international comparisons, then, prove to be another way the standards and accountability movement masks and even ignores the role of poverty in society and schools. Now let's turn to the inherent failure of unified standards themselves.

WHY COMMON STANDARDS WON'T WORK

With the blessing and encouragement of President Obama and Secretary Duncan, we are establishing "common-core standards" to address the historical claim that our public schools are failures. In the 1890s, a similar lament was voiced by the group known as the Committee of Ten:

> When college professors endeavor to teach chemistry, physics, botany, zoology, meteorology, or geology to persons of 18 or 20 years of age, they discover that in most instances new habits of observing, reflecting, and recording have to be painfully acquired by the students—habits which they should have acquired in early childhood. (Report, 1994, n.p.)

Their solution? Almost exactly what the current common-standards pursuit offers us. In fact, the bureaucratic approach to schools—establish content, prescribe content, and measure student acquisition of that content—has been visited and revisited decade after decade for more than a century now, and always with little or no regard to out-of-school factors. It has always failed, and always will.

This time around, we should use the creation of and debate about national standards to reject a failed solution for the ignored problems facing our schools—and our society. Today's attempt at national standards, the recently released work of the Common Core State Standards Initiative (The standards, 2010) in English language arts and mathematics that is being adopted separately by states, fails first because the standards are based on two flawed assumptions: that we somehow, in the twenty-first century, don't already know what to teach (we do and have for decades); and that somehow a standard body of learning matches what humans need and what a democracy that values human freedom wants (it doesn't match either).

Next, the standards movement further de-professionalizes teaching at the K-12 level. Chemistry professors in college, for example, do not need a set of standards to teach chemistry; part of the appropriate expectations for their job is to be scholars of their field and adept at teaching that body of knowledge. (In fact, a central problem we could address instead of arguing about a set of standards is that, at the K-12 level, we trivialize the need for teachers to be knowledgeable, and at the college level, we trivialize a professor's need to be skilled at teaching. Educators at any level need both.)

Further, to standardize and prescribe expectations is, in fact, to lower them. Common standards also devolve into asking less, not more, of students, since they are invariably tied to the narrowest possible types of assessment. Some clichés have become clichés because they are true. The truism "Give a man a fish and he eats for the day; teach a man to fish and he eats forever" captures perfectly the flaw with a standards approach to education: Prescribed standards of learning are giving children fish, not teaching them to fish because all of the work to engage with knowledge is left to some authorities outside the classroom to identify and to the teacher in the classroom to dispense.

Standards-driven education removes intellectual engagement and agency from teachers and students, rendering classrooms lifeless and functional, devoid of the pleasure and personal value of learning, discovering, and coming to be. Common standards also begin by assuming that acquiring content is all that matters in learning. To create a standard body of knowledge is to codify that the students themselves do not matter—at least in any humane way. The standards movement envisions children as empty vessels to be filled by the prescribed knowledge chosen for them—certainly a counterproductive view of humans in a free society.

A call for higher standards speaks to our human quest for improvement, but that call conflates "standard" with "expectation," and the two terms are not synonymous in the way we need for improving education. Yes, we should have challenging expectations for teachers and students, but those expectations can never be and will never be any more standard than one human to the next. To standardize and prescribe expectations is, in fact, to lower them.

Offering some type of national standards as a solution for the failure of public education implies that a lack of standards exists and that the supposed lack is somehow the cause of our educational problems. And that central flaw is at the heart of what is most wrong about the new common-core standards, because the creation of those standards is drawing our attention away from the actual causes of educational problems.

A call for national standards ensures that we continue doing what is most wrong with our bureaucratic schools (establish-prescribe-measure) and that we persist in looking away from the largest cause of low student achievement: childhood poverty. A call for national standards is a political veneer, a tragic waste of time and energy that would be better spent addressing real needs in the lives of children—safe homes, adequate and plentiful food, essential health care, and neighborhood schools that are not reflections of the neighborhoods where children live through no choice of their own.

Education is in no way short of a knowledge base. And even if it were, tinkering (yet again) at a standard core of knowledge while ignoring the dehumanizing practices in our schools, and the oppressive impact of poverty on the lives of children, is simply more fiddling while the futures of our children smolder over our shoulders and we look the other way. As Mathis (2010) explains, the entire argument for national standards fails both from internal inconsistency by its advocates and the weight of evidence:

> The Obama administration has stated its commitment to research-based and evidence-based ("what works") policy making. Thus, it is troubling that the common core standards initiative lacks a convincing research base. In May 2010, the administration did publish a "research summary" concerning its proposals to achieve "college- and career-ready students," and a few pages were devoted to common core standards (the remainder of the research summary focuses on accountability and capacity). The summary presents standards as a valid and meaningful reform tool, but the support for this statement is primarily in the form of a critique of the existing system. As Gerald Bracey noted, there is no evidence that the simple act of raising standards or making them uniform across states will, in fact, cause increased student learning. Similarly, Grover Whitehurst did not find, following his 50-state analysis, a relationship between standards and performance. At the very least, there appears to be faint evidence or promise for this reform in proportion to the massive, national undertaking it has become. (n.p.)

In the long view of history, declaring public education a failure and calling for high expectations has been a refrain for over 100 years; most recently, the current accountability era lasting three decades has offered us 50 separate experiments in standards, testing, and accountability leading to the same exact claims of failure and a need for higher—and now unified—standards. This is ample proof that the pursuit of standards is folly and a tragic mask hiding the weight of poverty on children's lives and learning.

2020 VISION FOR NO CHILD LEFT IN POVERTY

However, what if we rethought our pursuit of national standards? But not education standards.

What if we pursue a 2020 vision for No Child Left in Poverty, modeled on the NCLB legislation under George W. Bush, federal policies being revised by the Obama administration?

Since many leaders and the public seem unwavering in support of establishing standards, gathering evidence of compliance with those standards, and holding someone in authority accountable for that achievement as the primary mechanism for reform, I believe that same process must be applied to the single greatest influence on student achievement, poverty.

Numerous studies along with decades of data from the College Board on the SAT (College Board, 2005, 2010) support one major fact of student achievement: Student outcomes on assessments of learning are more strongly tied to the educational attainment of the parents and the income of the parents than any school or teacher factors (Berliner, 2009; Hanushek, 2010; Hirsch, 2007; Traub, 2000). In June 2010, the news on childhood poverty in the U.S. was alarming with rates climbing above 20% (Szabo, 2010).

And throughout the first decade of the twenty-first century, the U.S. stands as one of the richest and most powerful countries in the world that also has one of the highest rates of childhood poverty among other affluent and powerful countries (Adamson, 2007). To solve problems, we must address the sources of those problems, and if standards/measurement/accountability represent the dynamic this country embraces for solving those problems, then my 2020 vision for No Child Left in Poverty is where we must make our next commitment.

First, we must set high and rigorous standards for poverty. Just as NCLB calls for 100% proficiency in academic achievement by 2014, the 2020 vision must set as its benchmark that there be no childhood poverty by 2020. Once we have standards of childhood poverty established, and that process must begin now and move swiftly, we must clarify the poverty data that will serve as the evidence for compliance with the standards. Crucial to our place in the international market place, of course, is complying with international comparisons of childhood poverty among the most powerful countries in the world. The call for higher standards for childhood poverty must be aligned with our standing among world powers as we seek to maintain our place in the worldwide market place.

The most important element of any standards and accountability is acknowledging that using standards and accountability suggests that those with the power to make changes are somehow unmotivated. Accountability provides the motivation needed to make change happen. Finally, then, once we establish standards for eliminating childhood poverty and gather the necessary data, we must hold every Representative and Senator accountable for the childhood poverty in their districts. If childhood poverty is not eliminated by 2020, those Representatives and Senators in failing districts must be replaced with more highly qualified and motivated people.

One aspect of this standards movement that will be unique is that I am calling on the U.S. House and Senate, led by President Obama, to put this legislation to a vote among every teacher in the U.S. Since NCLB and all federal and state legislation related to education are established and imposed onto schools and teachers by the ruling bodies in our states and nation, and since my 2020 vision plan would hold the politicians accountable, an act of good faith would be to give the vote for the plan to those teachers who are being held accountable for the education of America's children, regardless of the affluence of those children.

The 2020 vision for No Child Left in Poverty can address our historic failure to have high standards for the conditions of children's lives and schools, or at least, we can turn over both the House and Senate within a decade. While many will call *this* call for standards and accountability far-fetched, I feel it has far more credibility than NCLB and similar calls for education accountability. Nevertheless, what we need is not just social reform or just education reform—we need education reform that is couched in a larger social acknowledgement and addressing of poverty in the lives of children and then families.

POLITICAL REFORM MUST PRECEDE EDUCATIONAL REFORM— WORDS MATTER

In his *Leading Minds*, Howard Gardner (1996) examines highly effective leaders and the disturbing dynamics behind their success. The great irony of powerful leadership is that these leaders speak simplistic messages aimed to connect with the simplistic assumptions of the wider public— accountability and testing ring true within a simplistic message, but poverty is too complex since it challenges deeply held ideologies among the public. If our leaders were somehow always benevolent and wise, this pattern could in a paradoxical way benefit society, but our leaders tend to be as misguided as the populace to whom they speak—and lead.

For example, in the U.S., we are often guided by our misconceptions and our mythologies, regardless of whether or not either is accurate. Political leaders and the average citizen depend on, for example, a conflating of demonizing terms such as socialism and Marxism with the *acts* of totalitarianism. In other words, when we speak against socialists, we are in fact challenging the oppressive fact of totalitarian government, but we take little time or care with words, as Orwell (1946) warns, and thus simply charge any effort to use government as an act of socialism, thus totalitarianism. As Gardner (1996) shows, we allow no room for nuance, and leaders who remain black-and-white (consider George W. Bush's "for us or against us" language after 9/11) are politically successful—although political success is not necessarily what is best for our society.

It is somewhat fully American to be skeptical and even cynical of the government. Calls for no government (or at least better government) in the U.S. stretch back to Henry David Thoreau's "Civil Disobedience."

And this disdain for government is fully reinforced by our mythologies, specifically our trust in rugged individualism, and extends to our contradictory attitudes toward public schools. So the language used by politicians, echoed in the media, and embraced by the wider public is steeped in misinformation, oversimplification, and a cyclic carelessness that insure we remain essentially fixed in a fruitless pit of our own digging.

And this is where education, public education, comes into play.

Many who champion the power of education—from Thomas Jefferson to John Dewey to George Counts to Paulo Freire—have embraced and claimed that education is the *causational* tool for social reform. This is a compelling myth, as compelling as rugged individualism. But like rugged individualism, education as social reform *as it is being promoted by the new reformers* (not as espoused by critical and progressive scholars) proves to be one of the "myths that deform" (Freire, 2005, p. 75). Public schools, in fact, have proven themselves to be both a reflection of our society and burdened by the very worst of our society—thus unable to be the social reform mechanism that many hope they would be.

Yet, in 2010, under the Obama administration (a leader consistently demonized by the Right as a socialist, a big government advocate set to take away American liberties), we are facing educational policies driven by corporatist assumptions—competition, accountability, and measurement—and not ideologies driven by socialism or Marxism, or even the power of collaboration inherent in democracy. At the center of the federal discourse and policies, promoted by Secretary Duncan, is the not-so-subtle view that schools and teachers are the central flaws with our public schools. And school and teacher reform (including closing "bad" schools and firing "bad" teachers) can be achieved through rigorous standards, teacher accountability tied to student achievement, and what Duncan and others are calling "transparency" and even the "truth."

From Race to the Top (RttT) to value-added methods of teacher effectiveness to the claim that teachers are the most important element in student achievement to calls for schools to reform the ills of U.S. society, one ignored truth runs through them all: Not a single one of these messages or policies is supported by the weight of evidence. As Orwell (1946) cautions, "the slovenliness of our language makes it easier for us to have foolish thoughts" (n.p.).

For nearly three decades, the U.S. has implemented bureaucratic education reform through an accountability model to address historic failures reflected in the schools but created by the social inequities we never name, never acknowledge, and never address. The harsh reality is that society and schools have a symbiotic relationship that allows inequality to remain because those who win the game always believe the rules are fair—and fear changing the rules since new rules could mean new winners.

Thus, educational reform must come within political reform, and both must be the result of new ways in which we speak about our society and our schools, including the following:

- Poverty is a powerful force in any person's life, but even more so in the lives of children. Childhood poverty is the dominant influence on any child's academic achievement; therefore, society needs to address childhood poverty and also insure that our public schools stop perpetuating inequity in the schools through tracking, teacher assignments, authoritarian discipline practices, and narrow standards-based high-stakes testing.

- Accountability must be reframed as a term and as a political message. To hold any free human accountable for behavior chosen and conducted by that human is a fact of freedom since freedom should not insure license. As a harsh example, I am free to smoke cigarettes, but not free to impose that smoke on others who choose not to smoke; yet, my choice to smoke carries with it *my accountability for the health consequences of my actions.* However, the political use of accountability in the school reform movement fails to comply with the basic tenants of ethical accountability. Teacher accountability (including the recent move toward value-added methods) ignores that teachers have little or no choice in the standards imposed on their work, the tests used to hold them accountable, and (most significantly) the lives their students live outside of their classrooms. Teacher accountability as it is now being practiced is a political distraction and little more than holding teachers accountable as nonsmokers for the consequences of second-hand smoke.

- The accountability flaw is directly linked to the mixed messages and policies related to teaching as a profession. The political and public charge that teachers must be held accountable *as all professions are* seems always to call for only part of the conditions for professionals—accountability. Teachers must be afforded professional autonomy first before professional accountability can be both ethical and potentially productive. Instead of holding teachers accountable for bureaucratic standards and tests not of their making and test scores produced by the students more strongly correlated with those students' lives than anything the teacher can provide, teachers must be afforded autonomy to practice their profession while being held accountable for that which they can control—the opportunities to learn in the classes each day. Their content, their lessons, their assessments.

In Arthur Miller's (1954) *The Crucible*, the audience is forced to consider the power of the accusers. John Proctor challenges us with "Is the accuser always holy now?" And in the graphic novel *Watchmen* (Moore & Gibbons, 1986, 1987), the work is carried by the refrain "Who watches the watchmen?"

And therein lies the power of words.

Political charges against the failure of schools and teachers mask the failure of the accusers. Political calls for accountability of those schools and teachers distract us from holding the politicians themselves accountable. Partisan politics of the worst kind is an act of distraction and sleight of hand known to pickpockets and thieves. As Gardner (1996) reveals to us, politicians are effective by being simplistic, by speaking to the assumptions that mindlessly drive us. The most damning irony of all is that we remain in a cycle of politics that uses education as a scapegoat to distract us from the rules of the game that keep the winners winning and the losers preoccupied.

Political sleight of hand and rhetorical masking are intended to distract us from looking closely at the inequity inherent in our consumer/corporate culture—a culture that has created the winners who want to suggest they deserve their privilege (and hide that they also believe the losers deserve to lose). Instead of standards, then, I believe we need to confront our society, and then reform education to empower us all in the pursuit of equity.

"DON'T ASK, DON'T TELL": THERE'S A REASON CAPTAIN AMERICA WEARS A MASK

With the release of *The Tillman Story*, Pat Tillman's brother, Richard, appeared on Bill Maher's *Real Time* (Maher, 2010) and offered yet another narrative of Pat's life and death, one the Tillman family is willing to tell, but one the American public and ruling elite are unwilling to ask about or retell. Richard was frank and struggling on Maher's HBO show, which included a clip from Pat's memorial where Richard made a blunt and impassioned effort to tell the truth about his brother in the face of the political need to maintain American Mythology (which parallels the masking of the education reform debate)—even when those myths are deceptive, even when those myths are at the expense of people.

Pat Tillman was a stellar athlete who succeeded in college and rose to unique status in the NFL, where he did a very *un-American* thing, stepped away from a multi-million dollar contract, to do a very *American* thing, enlist in the military after 9/11 in order to serve his country. The news and political stories of Tillman's decision played down the apparent rejection of materialism in Tillman's volunteering to serve in the military, but the official stories began to craft a narrative starring Pat Tillman as Captain America. Apparently, we could mask a not-so-subtle challenge to our materialistic existence and consumer culture as long as that masked hero would justify our wars.

Then Tillman died in the line of duty.

Then the U.S. government was exposed for building a story around Tillman's death that was untrue: Pat was killed by "friendly fire" (a disarming term for an incomprehensible and gruesome fact of wars) and not at the hands of the enemy as officials initially claimed—to Pat's brother who was also serving and nearby, to Pat's family, and to the entire country (White, 2005).

Then Richard Tillman, still boiling with anger, said on Maher's show that Pat should have retaliated in order to save himself against the "friendly fire." (Maher, 2010).

Beyond the continuing chasm between the real life and death of Pat Tillman and the narratives created around him, the release of the documentary presents the American public with a story that isn't very flattering. *The Tillman Story* depends on the ambiguous meaning of "story," as a synonym for "narrative" and "lie," to offer another layer to the growing truths and distortions connected with why Pat Tillman joined the military, how he died, and the complex human being who he was. Now, if we place the Tillman *stories* against the debate in the military over "don't ask, don't tell," we notice that in this culture we endorse masking reality as a good and even honorable thing. We confront the Great American Myth that never allows us to ask, much less tell.

This military policy based on deception is ironically our central cultural narrative, one the ruling elites perpetuate as political success depends upon speaking to our cultural myths instead of to reality. We are a country committed to don't ask, don't tell. Pat Tillman's life story and the corrupted narrative invented by politicians and the military to hide the truth and propagandize at the expense of a man and his life are tragic and personal myths that we are still *ignoring*—willful ignorance. If the ruling elite will fabricate preferred stories at the expense of a single person, we can expect the same about the institutions central to our democracy, such as our public education system and teachers.

This complex narrative around Tillman is a disturbing confirmation of the "myths that deform" (Freire, 2005) inherent in the "banking" concepts of education (Freire, 1993). In this new era of hope and change, the Obama administration, we must be diligent to ask and tell, especially when it comes to our public schools. The false dichotomy of Republican and Democrat, conservative and liberal, is a distraction from the reality of the political elites expressing corporatist narratives to ensure the balance of power favoring the status quo. Leaders are often compelled to maintain cultural myths because black and white messages are politically effective.

President Obama and Secretary Duncan are now leading a renewed assault on public education, and directly teachers, under the banner of civil rights—just as Pat Tillman's life and death were buried beneath claims of *patriotism* raised like Captain America's shield so no one could see behind it. The reality that Obama and Duncan cannot ask or tell about is poverty—and its impact on the lives and learning of children. Acknowledging poverty is an affront to the American Dream; confronting poverty is political dynamite. Blaming teachers and schools instead without offering the evidence works because this is a message we are willing to acknowledge and hear (Giroux, 2010a).

For example, a group from the ruling elite of schools, self-described as "educators, superintendents, chief executives and chancellors responsible for educating nearly two and a half million students in America," placed themselves squarely in the context of President Obama's and Secretary Duncan's charge against teachers and the status quo; their manifesto states: "As President Obama has emphasized, the single most important factor determining whether students succeed in school is not the color of their skin or their ZIP code or even their parents' income—it is the quality of their teacher" (How to fix our schools, 2010, n.p.).

The names of the leaders—Klein, Rhee, Vallas—are impressive, and their sweeping claims are compelling—except that the substance of their message is false (Krashen, 2010). Narratives are powerful, and telling those narratives requires diligence, a willingness to say something often enough to make the created story sound more credible than reality, until the truth is masked beneath a web of narratives that makes truth harder to accept than the lies that seem to conform to all the myths that mislead us (rugged individualism, pulling oneself up by the bootstrap, a rising tide lifts all boats).

"Let's stop ignoring basic economic principles of supply and demand" speaks to our faith in the market, and "until we fix our schools, we will never fix the nation's broader economic problems" triggers our blind willingness to compete and our enduring faith in schools as tools of social reform (How to fix our schools, 2010). They are compelling because we have been saying them for a century.

Just as the fabricated story of Pat Tillman and his sacrifice justified war.

"I don't believe that even the best teachers can completely overcome the huge deficits in socialization, motivation and intellectual development that poor students bring to class through no fault of their own" (Gardner, 2010c) sounds weak, fatalistic, in the face of our myths, the words of soft people eager to shift the blame. It is something we dare not tell. Just as the smoldering facts of Pat Tillman's death remain too hard to ask about and too hard to tell. But only the latter are supported by evidence. But only the latter contradict the Great American Myths about which we dare not ask, we dare not tell.

Captain America wears a mask for a reason: The myth is easier to look at, easier to tell about than the truth hidden underneath—whether we are asking about and looking hard at the death of a complex man, Pat Tillman, or the complex influences of poverty on the lives and learning of children across our country.

The historical and current calls for standards and accountability are dishonest masks on a false hero, and we must move beyond that, not just unmasking but exposing the flaws in that so-called hero. In Chapter Three, I turn to the power of the media, a power that is being manipulated by political and corporate leaders and squandered by the media itself, to mislead and ultimately perpetuate the false narratives driving the current misguided calls for corporate education reform.

CHAPTER 3

LEGEND OF THE FALL

The Education Debate in the Media

Two persistent and powerful cultural narratives perpetuated among mainstream Americans are that the media and the public education system are corrupted by a liberal bias. These narratives tend to be reinforced by the corporate and political elite, but are uncritically accepted by the general public—and reinforced, ironically, by that media being labeled "liberal."

As I have been discussing so far, particularly in Chapter Two while examining the technocratic and corporate-based accountability era of the past thirty years in education, U.S. public education is not liberal (and certainly not critical in the tradition of Freire); in fact, it is highly traditional and driven primarily by corporate interests in a compliant work force. As Kohn (2008a) has explained:

> Despite the fact that all schools can be located on a continuum stretching between the poles of totally progressive and totally traditional—or, actually, on a series of continuums reflecting the various components of those models—it's usually possible to visit a school and come away with a pretty clear sense of whether it can be classified as predominantly progressive. It's also possible to reach a conclusion about how many schools—or even individual classrooms—in America merit that label: damned few. The higher the grade level, the rarer such teaching tends to be, and it's not even all that prevalent at the lower grades. (n.p.)

Ignoring Poverty in the U.S.: The Corporate Takeover of Public Education, pp. 57–87
Copyright © 2012 by Information Age Publishing
All rights of reproduction in any form reserved.

Here, in this chapter, I confront a similar mischaracterization as it relates to the education debate of the media, which is primarily a corporate media, not a liberal media.

As a result, the corporate-driven reform agenda facing public education as we move into the second decade of the twenty-first century is being reported on *uncritically*, and thus, the media is complicit in ignoring poverty in the U.S., when it isn't marginalizing people living in poverty by reinforcing deficit views of poverty and those trapped in it (which I will address more fully in Chapter 7).

Increasingly, the media is more and more difficult to characterize as entertainment and journalism blur. And as the new media evolves (such as the blogosphere has, emerging as an open media, both recreating and influencing media and journalism), public consumption of what counts as credible becomes more complex and volatile. In this chapter, I will focus on that blur, but with a consideration primarily of how media presents a pattern of messages through a variety of avenues (from *Huffington Post* to *The Daily Show* to *Real Time with Bill Maher* to CNN and *Newsweek*). Education and education reform are consistently misrepresented while poverty and people burdened by poverty are marginalized, stereotyped, and ultimately ignored.

WAITING FOR THE LIBERAL MEDIA

One of the strongest patterns of a cultural tendency to ignore poverty in the U.S. is the intersection of the so-called liberal media and liberal education system—especially in the most extreme examples of liberal/progressive and blurred media such as Bill Maher's HBO series, *Real Time*.

Maher presents his viewers with a mix of satire and serious considerations of topics and ideas often ignored in our wider public discourse. During his October 15, 2010 episode—with panelists John Legend, Markos Moulitsas, Dana Loesch, and Dan Neil—Maher shifted the discussion to education after identifying the documentary *Waiting for "Superman"* as a great film (Maher, 2010b).

After praising the documentary, which has received unmatched media support including a week-long focus on education by NBC and an episode of *Oprah* dedicated to the film, Maher offered facts he had learned from the film. While Maher at first appeared to have accepted the film uncritically, he did turn on the basic argument of the documentary—that the teaching profession is bloated with bad teachers who need to be weeded out in order to save our schools and those children trapped in bad schools—and raised the possibility that educational struggles include far more than a weak teaching core, including the powerful impact of poverty. While I found Maher's initial praise of *Waiting for "Superman"* and his willingness to embrace the messages of the film as facts disappointing, his opening challenge to blaming teachers presented a perfect opportunity for the panel discussion to serve the audience and the education debate well. Instead, viewers witnessed several snapshots of everything that is wrong with the current national discussion about education portrayed uncritically through the media.

First, Maher's acknowledging the film as a great film and factual is a snapshot of our cultural habit of embracing as true those messages that match what we already believe (regardless of the evidence). As Thomas Jefferson (1900) warned: "The moment a person forms a theory, his imagination sees, in every object, only the traits which favor that theory" (p. 865). *Waiting for "Superman"* is less fact and more cultural narrative designed to reinforce societal assumptions that avoid confronting any aspects of our mythologies that could render those myths untrue—such as the powerful impact of poverty and inequity on educational outcomes.

Consider another snapshot: John Legend, musician, took the moral baton during the discussion after Maher's opening comments about the film. Legend wrote the music for the documentary and has established himself as a spokesperson for education reform, which he qualifies by his friendship with economist Dr. Roland Fryer. This snapshot is complex and powerful. Just as we should pause before embracing *Waiting for "Superman"* as sincere or authoritative, we should be able to question why Legend—or even Fryer—deserves his status as educational reformer.

Legend has rhetorical capital as a successful African American male who has risen above challenging life conditions, including having attended a "drop-out factory," as Maher stated. And Legend is bright, passionate, and talented. In his *Huffington Post* piece, Legend (2010) catalogs facts, similar to the facts Maher lists from the documentary, reinforcing the decades-long mantra that our public schools are failures based on international comparisons of test scores (including the ubiquitous Finland reference); and then he makes his central argument:

> So what do we do? Give up? Move to Finland (#1 across the board)? Canada (#2 in reading and science)? Shrug our shoulders and blame the kids and their parents? No, we can't afford to do that. Ensuring that ALL American children can access a quality education is the civil rights issue of our time. We cannot stand idly by and allow this institutionalized inequality to continue. (n.p.)

Do John Legend's status and background qualify him for being a spokesperson for educational quality and reform? I think not, especially when his claims are corrupted by misleading data and sweeping narratives that speak to myths, not facts.

Legend is the personification of rugged individualism, and he speaks against the recognition of social failures—which he characterizes as blaming children and parents while carefully not raising the possibility that social inequity may be to blame—and to our enduring faith that schools can change society. And Legend leads to a third snapshot: An exchange between Legend and Loesch, a Tea Party leader and spokesperson.

When Maher pushed against blaming teachers and asked about the influence of poverty on any school's, any teacher's, and some parent's ability to help children, Legend and Loesch presented what every American wants to hear—they rose above their backgrounds, including single-parent homes (like Obama, and even Bill Clinton), poverty, and high schools as drop-out factories. Loesch's mother worked multiple jobs and had time to insure her education, she countered to Maher's argument that people living in poverty may be unable to attend to their children's education because of the weight of their lives.

And here is where all of the snapshots from this episode of *Real Time* converge: Cultural narratives speaking to rugged individualism, to everyone pulling herself or himself up by the bootstrap, are reinforced daily by those people who have excelled—including the media, which affords disproportionate access to having a voice to the wealthy and the famous (those outliers who through their media saturation seem to prove the rugged individualism exceptionality to be a norm). We are a culture who raises exceptionality to the expectations of the normal. This becomes the message of our narrative: *Legend overcame, and so should all African American males. Loesch overcame, and so we cannot let a single-parent home off the hook.*

Let's not turn to the facts in the face of cultural myths, however, because the data clearly show that Legend and Loesch are *exceptions*, not the norms. But normalizing the exceptional allows us to raise our heads and stick out our chests while blaming those who fail for their failure. Those people living in poverty are simply not holding up their part in the American Dream, we suggest and even state. Teachers and our public schools are failing our children, we add.

As Legend (2010) proclaimed in his *Huffington Post* piece: "We know how to fix our schools. We just need to DO it. *Waiting for 'Superman'* highlights some schools that are working against all odds" (n.p.). Like Legend and Loesch, that *some* schools have been designated as miracles (and little effort is made by the media to confirm the claims of miracle) is evidence that *all* schools can do the same; if schools are failing, they are to blame because "we know how to fix our schools."

One exceptional school, one exceptional person—these legends are *outliers*, not norms, and legends should not guide us, especially when we are addressing our children, especially when we are addressing children who face lives of poverty not of their choosing. To persist in normalizing exceptionality is one of the patterns unmasking that the media is willing to ignore poverty as a result of the norm of inequity in our society—as well as a willingness to ignore that our schools often reflect that inequity.

WAITING FOR "SUPERMAN": A TALE OF TWO FILMS

The media fascination with *Waiting for "Superman"* is an excellent commentary on how we are failing, again, our public schools, not a proclamation that our public schools are failing us. In fact, we should all set aside either praising or bashing *Waiting for "Superman,"* and instead, we should step back and look at the assumptions and distortions exposed by the debate surrounding the documentary. As well, we should ask that during this flurry of inspection of schools that everyone takes the time to look at another documentary that offers a much better basis upon which to have a debate, *Hard Times at Douglass High*.

First, while many educators have presented a passionate and evidence-based refuting of *Waiting for "Superman"* (Bessie, 2010a; Gardner, 2010d; Ginsberg, 2010; Haimson, 2010; Ravitch, 2010b, 2010c; The real facts, 2010), the media, from Oprah to NBC, have lined up to praise uncritically not only the film but also the inherent implications of the film—that high accountability is needed and works, that charter schools are superior to our public schools, that teacher quality is paramount to school reform, that teachers' unions are central to the failure of schools. Some supporting the film argue that the documentary is *not* making some of the claims listed above, but I contend that what a text *intends* doesn't matter in the face of what a text *does place into the discourse*.

Next, we must acknowledge that *Waiting for "Superman"* is coming into the cultural awareness of Americans at the exact same time that President Obama and Secretary Duncan are repeatedly stating to the country that we must weed out bad teachers. Obama's and Duncan's speeches offer this refrain about teacher quality while never once acknowledging the power of poverty over children's lives and learning. In short, the film reinforces a misleading cultural narrative being perpetuated by the two most powerful voices in national public education (see Chapter 1). The intent and forces behind *Waiting for "Superman,"* along with the media's embracing of the film and the narratives coming from the film and about the film, need to be exposed and examined carefully. But intent is a difficult animal to corral.

Here, I want to offer an alternative, then, to the somewhat naïve and clearly uncritical embracing of *Waiting for "Superman"*: View and consider the HBO documentary *Hard Times at Douglass High*. While *"Superman"* allows us to ignore or marginalize the impact of poverty, *Hard Times* confronts us with the realities of children trapped in real lives burdened by poverty—lives they do not leave at the door when they enter schools.

In *Hard Times*, the daily realities of many students, the administration, and the teachers paint a graphic picture of the complexity, and often *futility*, of sincere and deep human effort (since the school choice crowd believes schools need competition, implying, of course, that teachers simply aren't working hard enough): What else could this school do? What else could these teachers do? What can these children do in the face of the lives they have been dealt through no choice of their own?

Frankly, I don't care what the purpose or intent of *Waiting for "Superman"* is. I have no patience for the film, or the failed responses to the film that perpetuate distortions and mis-directions about education, teachers, children, and lives spent in poverty. We have ample evidence that the primary causes of student achievement lie in the homes and communities of children, not in their schools (Berliner, 2009). As long as we continue to argue about more rigorous accountability, higher standards, and better tests (Kovacs, 2008), as long as we continue to weave tales of "miracle" where none exist, as long as we allow anyone in power (politicians, corporate CEOs, education superintendents and chancellors, union leaders, *anyone*) to speak in monologues instead of dialogues (the authoritarian versus the authoritative), while continuing to ignore the facts of poverty in the lives and learning of children, we persist in failing our schools and those children.

IRONIC LESSONS IN EDUCATION REFORM FROM BILL GATES

While the American public, media, and politicians placed their faith in *Waiting for "Superman"* and ignored *Hard Times at Douglass High*, Barkan (2011) recognized the powerful driving force of billionaires moving to the forefront of education reform:

> Hundreds of private philanthropies together spend almost $4 billion annually to support or transform K-12 education, most of it directed to schools that serve low-income children (only religious organizations receive more money). But three funders—the Bill and Melinda Gates Foundation, the Eli and Edythe Broad (rhymes with road) Foundation, and the Walton Family Foundation—working in sync, command the field. Whatever nuances differentiate the motivations of the Big Three, their market-based goals for overhauling public education coincide: choice, competition, deregulation, accountability, and data-based decision-making. And they fund the same vehicles to achieve their goals: charter schools, high-stakes standardized testing for students, merit pay for teachers whose students improve their

test scores, firing teachers and closing schools when scores don't rise adequately, and longitudinal data collection on the performance of every student and teacher. (n.p.)

The media, specifically, has focused on Bill Gates as one of the Supermen-de-jure—despite Gates having no experience or education in the field of education beyond his choosing education reform as a hobby; in fact, like many of the new reformers, Gates is a product of private schooling:

> But there is one thing that characterizes a surprisingly large number of the people who are transforming public schools: they attended private schools.... Bill Gates (Lakeside School, Seattle) has donated billions of dollars to public schools with the proviso that they carry out his vision of reform, including tying teacher tenure decisions to students' test scores. In November, Mr. Gates and Mr. Duncan (University of Chicago Laboratory School) called on public school leaders to increase class size as a way of cutting costs in these hard times. The two men suggested that schools could compensate by striving to have an excellent teacher in every classroom. The private school Mr. Gates attended has an average class size of 16, according to its Web site. The home page says the best thing about Lakeside School is it "promotes relationships between teachers and students through small class sizes." Mr. Duncan's private school has an average class size of 19. (Winerip, 2011)

While the media masks poverty in the U.S., it also fails to acknowledge that expertise—or the perception of expertise—is more often linked to affluence and privilege than to experience, scholarship, or education, as is the case with Gates. Strauss (2011b) has identified that Gates' access to leading educational reform is tied directly to his wealth, and Rothstein (R. Rothstein, 2011) has outlined Gates' repeated misunderstanding and misrepresenting of educational research and data. Yet, Gates continues to receive virtually a free pass—with access to a bully pulpit unavailable to the very teachers he has tended to marginalize and even demonize.

One powerful example of the Gates phenomenon is an interview at *Newsweek* by journalist Daniel Lyons (2010), who posed a series of questions to Gates and Randi Weingarten, president of the American Federation of Teachers—highlighting not what we need to address in our public schools but proving further that the media, celebrity/billionaire experts, and bureaucrats are themselves incompetent and should not be leading a discussion about education. Also central to the failure of the media is the use of Weingarten as an implied balance in the interview—yet, as I will avoid addressing directly her comments, her role as union president fails the discourse nearly as much as Gates himself.

The *Newsweek* interview is driven by corporate assumptions about education and reform, including the questions themselves, the sweeping and unsupported claims made by Gates, and the rebuttal position Weingarten assumes throughout. Neither Lyons, Gates, nor Weingarten ever challenge competition, standards, testing, or international comparisons in any sophisticated or evidence-based ways. Instead, the interview perpetuates Gates as a real reformer, a credible expert on education.

As I will detail below, this interview confirms Alfie Kohn's (2010a) unmasking the new reformer movement dominating public discourse about education and education reform:

> For a shrewd policy maker, then, the ideal formula would seem to be to let people enjoy the invigorating experience of demanding reform without having to give up whatever they're used to. And that's precisely what both liberals and conservatives manage to do: Advertise as a daring departure from the status quo what is actually just a slightly new twist on it. (n.p.)

Lyons, Gates, and Weingarten—like Secretary Duncan and former DC chancellor Rhee—personify Kohn's "ideal formula": Continue and even expand the status quo by calling the reforms an attack on the status quo. The *Newsweek* piece, perpetuated in the Education section of *The Huffington Post*, is flawed from the start, however, with each question framing the potential answers within misinformation and distortion. As well, we cannot discount that the entire discussion is also restricted to elites themselves—authorities who have benefited well from the current system, leaving us to wonder why they would want to change anything.

If we can't change the questions posed by Lyons, we can at least imagine what the answers should have been *if a powerful element of the discourse about education were not intent on ignoring poverty and social inequity.*

First Question: "Our schools are lagging behind the rest of the world. Why is that? How did we fall so far behind?" (Lyons, 2010, n.p.).

Gates is predictable in his answer, starting with "A lot of other countries have put effort into their school systems. So part of it is the competition is better" and then moving from international comparisons and market forces to making unsubstantiated and misleading statements about overspending on education in the U.S. with poor returns.

The Answer We Need: International comparisons are being distorted—and are a stale mantra of public school detractors reaching back into the 1950s. Consider the relentless bashing of public schools in the mid-twentieth century by Admiral Rickover (comparing the U.S. to the Swiss and British) and the charges that public school students couldn't read from Rudolph Flesch (Thomas, 2010v; Why Johnny Can't Read, 1955).

Test scores in each nation have *never* been shown to be directly or positively correlated with that country's economy; and, international test comparisons gloss over populations being compared (Bracey, 2008)—first, the U.S. has over 20% childhood poverty compared to Finland's 3-4%, thus the populations are different, not the quality of the schools since about 80-90% of achievement is tied to out-of-school factors.

When we consider poverty in an analysis of PISA scores from 2009, the source of much hand wringing (Duncan, 2010e), the comparisons expose the social inequities tolerated by the U.S. (Riddile, 2010)—not the failure of the schools. And if we find ourselves enamored with Finland because of their high test scores, we must be prepared to accept the full picture of that envy since Finland rejects most of the exact reforms the new reformers are proposing. As well, Finland offers government support for teachers' advanced degrees, a teacher force that is virtually 100% unionized (Sahlberg, 2010).

So the short answer is that the U.S. is lagging the world in addressing childhood and overall poverty, and that reality is reflected in our schools—not caused by them. But Gates never makes this assertion and the media never begins with this premise.

Second Question: "Bill, you mentioned that the top quarter of our teachers are very good. But that's probably the case in Finland, too. It can't be the case that every teacher in Finland is some amazing teacher." And, "You say 'counsel people out of the profession.' Is that something you can't do now?" (Lyons, 2010, n.p.).

Here, Gates makes sweeping claims about Finland's teachers being under a "personnel system" and teachers in the U.S. receiving "no evaluation" and "no feedback." Gates is allowed to perpetuate what Horn (2010b) has characterized as a "cartoon version" of education in Finland.

The Answer We Need: Teacher quality is only a small percent of achievement (Berliner, 2009; Hirsch, 2007; Rothstein, 2010; Traub, 2000), and there is little evidence that teacher quality is the most or even one of the main problems with student achievement in public schools. But the provable problem with teacher quality is teacher assignment. Peske and Haycock (2006) show that students in poverty, students of color, and ELL students are in classrooms with the least experienced teachers who are often un- or under-qualified/certified.

Teacher quality does matter in terms of what happens once students are within the walls of schools, but we seem blind to the long-standing tradition of assigning the most experienced and best qualified teachers to the elite students, who are already experiencing advantages in their full lives outside of school.

Third Question: "Randi, you've talked about moving from the industrial age into a knowledge economy. But aren't unions just relics of the industrial era? Does the concept of a union itself make sense in a knowledge economy?" (Lyons, 2010, n.p.).

Although the question is aimed at Weingarten, Gates jumps in after she offers a brief two-sentence reply—"Of course it does. You look at the different countries that are vastly more successful than we are, and they're all unionized"—a fact ignored often by neoliberal reformers who enjoy making selective international comparisons to bash U.S. schools. Gates immediately discounts widespread unionization in other countries by claiming that U.S. unions have "work rules" that are not present in those countries—again making a claim without evidence and skirting the fact that strong unionization exists in the exact countries championed by Gates and other reformers.

The Answer We Need: Finland's teachers are essentially 100% unionized. In the U.S., states with the strongest teachers' unions correlate positively with the highest test scores (although a shift in how test scores are examined can achieve contradictory conclusions). That union bashers ignore this data is telling, but pro-union use of the data is equally revealing. Unionization and its impact on school quality are, in fact, much more complex than either side tends to acknowledge.

Simply put,

> "Sweeping statements one way or the other on this should be viewed with suspicion," Rotherham said, in a review of claims about the connection between unions and school quality... Weingarten's claim that states that have lots of teachers in teacher unions tend to be the states that have done the best in terms of academic success is perhaps technically correct—at least by some measures. But the empirical scientific research on this subject is—in the words of Burroughs—"limited, ambiguous and incomplete." Further, there is even less evidence to support the implication that strong unionization is the *cause* for one state performing better than another. (Randi Weingarten says students, 2010)

Union bashing, like union advocacy, tends to fail because of oversimplification and conflating correlation simplistically with causation.

Fourth Question: "Should we have a national curriculum in the United States?" (Lyons, 2010, n.p.).

Gates implies that the national standards movement is both something being resisted by the states and something driven by the states, but he glosses over one key fact—for 30 years the U.S. has had 50 separate standards experiments that have resulted in a national consensus that our schools are failing despite NCLB's accountability mandates placed on top of the standards experiments. Like Duncan, Gates appears to believe that we just need *better* standards: "I think this is going to be a good thing. It's going to drive some efficiency. This curriculum's not just a standard where they arbitrarily pick things. It's actually a better curriculum" (Lyons, 2010, n.p.).

The Answer We Need: The short answer is "No." The pursuit of standards, testing, and accountability has failed since A Nation at Risk in 1983 spurred the current era. More of the same, except centralized nationally, is highly unlikely to do anything except waste precious time and money on the misguided goal of "standard" at the expense of addressing child-hood poverty and in-school equity for student/teacher assignments (Thomas, 2010c, 2011l). The call for national standards is the exact wolf in sheep's clothing that Kohn (2010a) has warned us about—masking the status quo in reform discourse.

Fifth Question: "What about this notion of giving tenure to teachers? That seems ridiculous." And, "Bill, when you talk I can hear the frustra-tion in your voice. Does this stuff drive you crazy?" And, "To me, Bill's graph seems to demonstrate the effect of organized labor on any industry. You could say the same thing happened in Detroit" (Lyons, 2010, n.p.).

Lyons's "ridiculous," "frustration" (to Gates), "stuff," and "crazy" immediately marginalize any genuine consideration of unions and lays at Gates' feet the entire authority on the issue. Gates responds with an abrupt "No," and lists, without support, a flurry of reasons unions fails, suggesting that they allow teachers to be shielded from credible evalua-tions following three consecutive "we spend more" claims. Eventually, the discussion turns to the graphs often wielded by Gates.

The Answer We Need: Tenure is about due process and academic free-dom. Let's start the discussion of tenure with accurate information. The tenure mantra is similar to the union mantra from the new reformers. Since they consistently misrepresent their claims—and fail to show evi-dence to substantiate their claims—we can rest assured that their motives are as specious as their arguments. Is tenure a concept worth debating? Of course, if we genuinely feel due process and academic freedom are irrelevant to the profession of teaching.

Is there any credible evidence that the tenure debate is essential for addressing the most pressing issues facing our schools? I see no evidence for this, so for now I believe the tenure debate is a false debate intended to distract us from the real issues facing our schools—the failure of politi-cal and corporate leaders to fulfill the promise of a free and equitable U.S. and to address the weight of poverty on children.

Also, Bill Gates' graph is oversimplified and distorting for a reason—to promote his agenda. Bracey (2006) warns about the inherent distortions found in most data-based graphs and charts. But more directly, Fung (2011) has exposed the distortions in Gates' charts and Gates' complete lack of understanding data and statistics (also represented by his repeated misrepresentation of international tests score data): "It's great that the Gates Foundation supports investment in education. Apparently they need some statistical expertise so that they don't waste more money on unproductive projects based on innumerate analyses" (n.p.).

Lyons's (2010) questions set the stage for yet another major media outlet to perpetuate the corporate and bureaucratic agendas of America's elite—at the expense of both the debate about education and our schools themselves. U.S. citizens are falling victim to what scientists are discovering about human nature—we allow our beliefs to drive our commitments even in the face of facts contradicting those beliefs (Keohane, 2010).

And there is where we stand, suckered—suckered by billionaires, suckered by celebrities, suckered by the media (who appear to be simply passing on misinformation because of their own gullibility). And ironically, education is the exact remedy needed to stop this vicious cycle. I suspect that is why the leading elites in this country are offering the status quo in reform discourse, hoping to keep us uninformed and themselves in charge—as long as we refuse to pull back the curtain and examine the inequity in society and the corrosive impact of poverty on children.

But Gates continues to hold court on education and have access to the most prominent media outlets. In his *Washington Post* Op-Ed Bill Gates (2011), builds to this solution for education reform:

> What should policymakers do? One approach is to get more students in front of top teachers by identifying the top 25 percent of teachers and asking them to take on four or five more students. Part of the savings could then be used to give the top teachers a raise. (In a 2008 survey funded by the Gates Foundation, 83 percent of teachers said they would be happy to teach more students for more pay.) The rest of the savings could go toward improving teacher support and evaluation systems, to help more teachers become great. (n.p.)

Gates also includes his own foundation's survey to give his claims the appearance of evidence-based reform, but this claim, and the continuing free pass Gates and other education hobbyists and celebrities receive from the media and the public, reveals several ironic lessons in education reform:

- *Wealth and celebrity do not equal expertise.* The U.S. is a celebrity culture, and we revere wealth because we aspire to wealth. Why do we listen to Dr. Phil and Dr. Oz? Because Oprah endorsed them—not because they offered the public credible expertise in their fields. The current education reform debate is being driven by wealth, celebrity, and life-long bureaucrats—not by the expertise and experience of millions of teachers, scholars, and researchers who have credible evidence about the problems that face our public education system and the likely solutions that would move us closer to the promise of that system in our democracy.

- *Teaching and learning are not the simple transmission of a set body of knowledge from an authoritarian teacher to a passive classroom of students.* The smoldering charges that our schools are overburdened by "bad" teachers, and thus we need to improve our teaching core, has distracted us from considering *first* exactly what the teaching/learning process should look like in universal public education system built to support a free people and a democracy. The new reformers have framed teaching as *both* the most important element in educational outcomes—although evidence refutes that simplistic claim (Ravitch, 2010c)—and a simple act of transmitting knowledge to a large group of students to raise test scores linked to national standards. If we need the best and the brightest and if teachers alone can overcome the weight of poverty, then reducing teaching to a service industry contradicts internally an argument that is also easily disproved since both initial claims are false. Teaching and learning are messy, idiosyncratic, and nearly impossible to measure or trace to single points of causation—and Gates lacks the experience or expertise to make any conclusions about teacher quality.

- *The political and corporate elite as well as the general U.S. public simply do not respect teachers and do not value education.* The U.S., as the wealthiest and most powerful country in the history of humanity, has made and can make anything happen we want. We move forward with wars when we decide we should, we bail out failing banks when we feel we should, we make a whole host of celebrities wealthy when we want (and we never hold them accountable for their egregious lack of respect for anything), and we could eradicate childhood poverty and support fully a vibrant and world-class education system—if we wanted to. But we don't.

- *Evidence doesn't matter, but it should.* As the first point above suggests, the public seems content with celebrity and wealth, but skeptical of evidence (Thomas, 2011g). I have had dozens of experiences offering public commentary on education, citing extensively why I hold the positions I do, but one of the most common replies I receive is, "Anybody can make research say whatever they want." While I empathize with the sentiment, this belief is flawed because it oversimplifies the research debate in the same way that the new reformers oversimplify the education reform debate. The truth about research is that *one* study is interesting, but that one study proves little. Once research has been peer-reviewed, while no guarantee, that study gains credibility. Then, as research builds to a *body* of peer-reviewed research with clear patterns, we reach safe ground for public claims and policy. Neither cherry-picking studies to advance an agenda nor being cavalier and cynical about research is conducive to advancing humanity through our greatest gifts as human—our scientific pursuit of knowledge.

- *Poverty is the unspoken and ignored weight on education outcomes, and while U.S. public education needs significant reforms, education reform will never succeed without the support of social reforms addressing childhood poverty and income equity.* This final ironic lesson from a billionaire holding forth repeatedly on education reveals its problem by the obvious complexity of the statement itself. The sentence is too much for our sound-bite culture that politicians feel compelled to appease. While we revel in making international comparisons to demonize our schools (Riddile, 2010), we fail to acknowledge international evidence of how to address school reform. Let me suggest two international approaches we should be considering, both from the Joseph Rowntree Foundation (UK)—a compilation of evidence on the impact of poverty on educational success (Hirsch, 2007) and a detailed consideration of wide-scale social and education reform (Goodman & Gregg, 2010). But the new reformers will conveniently never mention these international reports because they begin with the problem of poverty instead of blaming the schools

As we enter the second decade of the twenty-first century, U.S. political leaders and the public appear disgusted with the public education system, but this sentiment has been with us since the Committee of Ten declared education inadequate in the 1890s. We must, then, come to terms with two facts: (1) We must drop utopian claims about education because education is not the *sole key* to overcoming social failures, but a single element in the larger working of our society, and (2) claims of crisis in education are misleading since the problems we are considering (student outcomes and drop-out rates, for example) are patterns that have existed for over a century.

Many are arguing that the new reformers must be valued since they are creating a debate about education and rattling the cage of an entrenched status quo that is failing. I find this argument weak since we have no evidence that inexpert celebrity claims are resulting in a close consideration of what is truly wrong with our schools and what should be pursued to create the world-class schools we claim we want (see the discussion below about other celebrity reformers). In fact, this current round of school bashing and calls for accountability and reform are an intensifying of the exact same failed solutions we have tried for three decades—all the while ignoring the genuine problems driven by poverty and the weight of evidence for what reforms would work.

And this leads to a question I have: If Bill Gates had no money, who would listen to him about education reform? No one—the same as who should listen to him now.

SUPERMAN OR KRYPTONITE?: GEOFFREY CANADA

The celebrity education reformer tour includes more than Bill Gates, and another star, based on the misleading *Waiting for "Superman,"* is Geoffrey Canada who continued his misinformation tour on *The Colbert Report* (Colbert, 2011) where celebrity reformer Michelle Rhee had earlier revealed her lack of historical perspective and expertise concerning education (see a discussion of Rhee below).

Canada made his second appearance with Colbert, but this time he came in as the face on the Harlem Children's Zone (HCZ)—mislabeled as a "miracle" (Pallas, 2009a, 2009b) and representing the selective corporate interest in school reform. When Canada's HCZ is useful for the new reformers to discredit public education, scapegoat teachers, or dismantle teachers unions, Canada is Superman, but when Canada's commitment to addressing the out-of-school factors that overwhelm student achievement challenges the misinformation coming from those new reformers, Canada and his HCZ is suddenly kryptonite (Whitehurst & Croft, 2010).

What's the truth?

First, we should be growing more and more suspicious of the celebrity tours dominating our media with misinformation that reinforces America's strongest misconceptions about our society, poverty, and schools. From Rhee speaking to Colbert and on CNN to John Legend on *Real Time* and to Gates being interviewed with Randi Weingarten in *Newsweek*, the public has been convinced that "bad" teachers are being protected by corrupt teachers' unions, thus dragging our schools, our children, and our society into decay. All while rarely, if ever, mentioning poverty.

And Canada keeps that drum beating by opening on Colbert with a sweeping claim: America, it seems, is for the first time in 30, 40, or 50 years taking education seriously. I wonder what the Committee of Ten would say about that after they made their claim about school failure in the 1890s (Report of the Committee of Ten on Secondary School Studies, 1894). Like Rhee, Gates, and Duncan, Canada makes claims and recommendations about education that are offered in a historical and research vacuum—appealing to the ahistorical perspective that warps public opinion.

The truth is that assertions made by Canada and all the reformers are the exact same narrative that has been driving political discourse about schools for a century—simplistic international comparisons, crisis discourse about graduation rates, discrediting teachers and teaching as a profession, and a complete failure to mention or address social inequities and childhood poverty. And here once again during the celebrity tour, Canada makes a plea *for a group of children who couldn't fit into the economy* (Canada's characterization), lamenting the high prison rate in the U.S. But, he never mentions poverty directly—as Duncan is prone to do in his numerous speeches about education reform.

Worse still, by implication, Canada places the focus on the children themselves for not fitting in—never a question raised about the U.S. economy or social inequity. While it appears to be fair game to demonize schools, teachers, and above all else teachers' unions (one joke toward the end of the interview resulted in Canada saying "both" to Colbert's mock question about whether we should blame teachers' unions or teachers' unions), it is beyond reproach even for Canada, a man who came from poverty himself, to say "poverty" or to challenge the status quo of American politics and corporate consumerism.

Instead, Canada promised a 100% graduation rate at the HCZ (not evidence of what has been accomplished, but rhetoric about what could be), railed against the achievement gap (conveniently omitting that the achievement gap reflects the social equity gap [Noah, 2010]), repeatedly endorsed the credibility of testing, and built to the most powerful distortion of all coming from the new reformers: "We've got to hold the adults responsible.... We've allowed our schools to fail these kids with no consequences," stated Canada.

These charges sound compelling and trigger America's faith in myths about rugged individualism, pulling ones self up by the bootstraps (for which Canada stands as a shining example of making the exceptional the norm against which we are all judged), and rising tides lifting all boats. But the new reformers are calling for accountability from perches upon which they themselves face no accountability—wealth (billionaires in some cases), political appointments, and celebrity. Calling for *other* people to be held accountable while ignoring context and standing outside the accountability machine yourself is a hollow and cowardly call—even when people have the best of intentions, as does Canada.

As we find ourselves in the second decade of the twenty-first century— with our universal public education system under an onslaught of misinformation and corporate manipulation—we are better off turning away from the celebrity reformers and instead heeding the education resolutions from Mike Rose (2011), notably regarding the media:

> To have the media, middle-brow and high-brow, quit giving such a free pass to the claims and initiatives of the Department of Education and school reformers. There is an occasional skeptical voice, but for any serious analysis, you have to go to sources like The Nation or Pacifica radio. Journalists

and commentators who make their living by being skeptical—David Brooks, Nicholas Kristof, Arianna Huffington—leave their skepticism at the door when it comes to the topic of education. (n.p.)

RHEE'S EDUCATION CELEBRITY TOUR: LEGEND OF THE FALL

The U.S. is floundering at the bottom of international comparisons of education, and what makes this worse is that in the grand ol' 1950s, the U.S. was at the top—at least that is one story offered by Michelle Rhee on an episode of the *Colbert Report* (Colbert, 2010). Like the discussion of *Waiting for "Superman"* by John Legend on Bill Maher's *Real Time*, the celebrity tour of Rhee, who eventually lost her job as chancellor of schools in DC, raises some real problems about not only what our self-appointed educational leaders are saying about education, but also how our so-called left-wing media helps (directly and indirectly) to perpetuate misinformation about our education system—misinformation that is being promoted to mask the real issues about poverty in our culture that the political and corporate elite do not want to face.

Rhee, in her interview with Colbert, made several sweeping claims about schools, and as is the nature of contemporary media (recognizing, of course, that Colbert is satire), she is allowed to make those claims without any evidence and without anyone raising a hand to ask, "Really?" Let's unpack now just the one claim about the U.S. being number one in education and graduation in the 1950s.

First, Rhee is following a clever playbook of the new education reform movement: Make partial claims that few people will question because the claims *sound* true. While I find the claim itself misleading, even if the claim is true, Rhee is referring to the U.S. public education system *before* integration and the civil rights movement impacted a public education system that had closed doors to many American citizens. In short, the education system of the 1950s was an incomplete one that shunned many people marginalized by race and poverty.

Rhee trusts that most people embrace a misguided nostalgia for the past, a nostalgia lacking evidence for such faith in a better time, but once we actually return to that Golden Era, the message then is somewhat confusing in the light of Rhee's claims. Let me recommend some reading: Admiral Hyman Rickover's *Swiss Schools and Ours: Why Theirs are Better* (1962) and *American Education, a National Failure; The problem of our schools and what we can learn from England* (1963)—both built on the argument that throughout the 1950s U.S. public schools were clear failures when compared internationally (sound familiar?), and educational reform was needed to address the crisis.

Or recall the *Time* article about Rudolf Flesch (Why Johnny can't read, 1955) or his own book—*Why Johnny Can't Read—And What You Can Do About It* (1955).

The full truth, of course, is that corporate and political elites have been making the same exact charges heard from Rhee, Secretary Duncan, Gates, and Canada, unwarranted and without much resistance, for at least half a century. Rhee's misinformation is nothing new, but it is finding renewed traction because these messages are being reinforced through the cult of celebrity, and that cult of celebrity is being driven through the so-called left-wing media just as easily as anywhere else—*Oprah*, Maher's *Real Time*, *The Colbert Report*.

The message must be challenged, however, and it must come from the field itself—educators and scholars alike. When the usual claims and patterns are raised, we must do as much maligned educator and activist Bill Ayers (2001) has implored us to do, "Talk back, speak up, be heard" (p. xv).

Now, what are the claims, and how must we offer rebuttals?:

- All cries of educational crisis are misleading. A crisis requires drastic responses quickly; our education system is a reflection of historical patterns that require patience and nuance in facing and addressing those patterns. We do not have education crises; we have lingering and systemic social failures. But for reformers such as Rhee, a crisis allows her confrontational and acerbic style to find justification; whereas, in a measured setting, she is exposed as without merit.

- Education leadership that has no experience or expertise doesn't deserve to be at the head of the reform table. Celebrities—Oprah, Gates, John Legend, Andre Agassi—are not experts in education just because they have fame and money. Leadership and money are not the credentials needed to drive educational reform. But Rhee presents a twist on the lack of experience and expertise driving education reform; Rhee has a few years as a teacher, but she entered education through Teach for America, feeding into the growing sentiment that educators do not need education degrees or certification.

- Data doesn't prove much of anything when the data is cherry-picked, and incomplete. As Rhee in her Colbert interview demonstrated, the new education reform celebrities have learned the power of incomplete statistics; offer just enough data to trigger popular assumptions—as long as those popular assumptions fuel the corporate agenda. When a simplistic and obvious claim about education is made, we must always assume it is false. The truth about education is nuanced and complex—and numbers can lie, especially when driven by an agenda.

- Let's be more like Finland? Well, let's do that, but not the way Secretary Duncan, Gates, and Rhee have claimed. Let's admit the genuine influence of socialism in Finland, along with their commitment to healthcare and sex education. Let's consider that the government pays for all teachers' graduate courses, leading to every teacher having a Master's degree before teaching. Let's consider that nearly all teachers in Finland are unionized. And let's note that Finland does not use standards-driven testing to label students, teachers, and schools (Horn, 2010b). And let's consider that childhood poverty is about 3-4% (while the U.S. child poverty rate is over 20%) (Adamson, 2005, 2007).

- International comparisons of test scores? What about international comparisons of childhood poverty? When we stoop to rankings, we are always risking yet more oversimplification and distortion (Bracey, 2004), but when our political and corporate elite cherry-pick rankings (test scores) while avoiding the big picture (childhood poverty rankings), we are once again falling victim to factual but misleading statistics. State schools in all countries are a reflection of social realities of that country—not data that can be used to compare the educational quality among countries.

Historically, the political Left has been a direct and indirect supporter of public education. That tradition does not mean the Left gets a free pass. President Obama and Secretary Duncan have abandoned democratic principals and the promise of public education for a free people; they have abdicated those principals for the lure of corporate ideology. The so-called left-wing media is following right along. I happen to like Bill Maher and Stephen Colbert, but, again, that doesn't mean they are above being called on the carpet for their negligence (and the negligence of the media across the board). And it is negligence to allow and even embrace the distortions driving the new educational reform movement being fueled by a celebrity elite who have no business representing the education agenda of a free society that claims to value academic freedom, human empowerment, and the hope of democracy not yet fulfilled.

After announcing that U.S. education is a complete failure, unlike the Golden Era of the 1950s, on *The Colbert Report*, Rhee brought her celebrity crisis tour to CNN where she charged, once again, that public education is a failure based on recent PISA scores, ranked internationally. But is U.S. education in crisis as Rhee claims? If it is, then we either need to change the definition of the word or admit that a crisis can last more than a century because every single claim made by Rhee has been tossed at education since the mid-1800s.

On January 15, 2009, a jet crash-landed in the Hudson River. That's a crisis. The pilot, crew, passengers, and rescue personnel had to take quick and even drastic actions because the situation was life-or-death and bound by time. Education is not a crashed jet. There is always time to make corrections to decisions made by children and their families (such as dropping out); there is always time to receive the education someone needs. Crying "crisis" fails any hope of educational reform because it distorts reality and places unrealistic expectations on a human endeavor that is complex and cumulative over a long period of time.

Interestingly, in her charges of "crisis," Rhee espouses the sort of double talk we hear form Secretary Duncan. *Education is in crisis; it is failing our children and country!* But, according to Rhee, it is central to saving our economy and keeping us competitive internationally, a false claim (Bracey, 2008) that is a popular refrain for Duncan (2010c). Amazing! This institution, U.S. public education, that has been identified for over a century as a complete failure, is simultaneously also "the key" to erasing every evil known to humans, including keeping us number one in the world!

But Rhee goes beyond simple double-speak (crisis/failure v. our only hope). She also perpetuates misinformation (and likely knows better) about teacher quality, the teaching profession, tenure, and teachers' unions. In her CNN interview, she continued the false refrain that tenure is a job for life (tenure, in fact, is about academic freedom and due process, not a guarantee of a job regardless of expertise or quality), calling for merit pay and the ability fire those pesky "bad" teachers who, by implication, are characterized as the central problem with education (masking the fact that poverty, not teacher or school quality, accounts for about 80-90% of student achievement).

Rhee, and Duncan, we must consider are *political appointees*. Is it somewhat contradictory and problematic for political appointees to call for (idealized) corporate standards for hiring, firing, and paying the teacher workforce in the U.S.? Is it even more disturbing that Rhee is making these charges while doing her celebrity tour in order to secure *another* political appointment?: "Oh, and in addition to starting that organization [Students First], she has also spent a great deal of time advising Republican governors—Chris Christie, Rick Scott, and now John Kasich—on how best to crush public employees' unions. She is doing it for the children" (Pareene, 2011).

For me, the new reformers—Rhee, Duncan, Gates, Canada, and others—are without credibility because their messages are factually inaccurate, historically blind, and ethically challenged (reflecting a "do as I say, not as I do" mentality of the hypocritical authoritarian). The agenda of the new reformers is clearly about using education as a political capital to move themselves further along—this is not about reforming schools, but about advancing careers (and brands) within a corporate model.

But there is something beyond the hypocrisy of calling for corporate models for hiring, firing, and paying teachers from political appointees making double, triple, or more above what the average teacher makes. There remains the culpability of the media. CNN, *HuffingtonPost*, *The Colbert Report*, *Oprah*, *Real Time* with Bill Maher—these media outlets are not Fox News. They are often charged with being the "liberal media," but they invite and endorse the exact misguided commentary I have identified above—and while free speech means Rhee, Duncan, Gates, and Canada have every right to make their claims (although I am not sure free speech should *encourage* dishonesty), free speech and freedom of the press, I believe, allow and even encourage someone somewhere to raise a hand and say, "That's misleading." (Or, "Wait a minute; that's not even true.")

And that "someone" must include the media in a democracy. If it is true that public education is failing us (and that is true, but not the way the new reformers claim), then it is also true the media is failing us.

On CNN, Rhee marched out the platitude that this generation will be the first generation less well educated than their parents. Well, let's start there: "That's misleading."

It is conjecture, at best, and impossible to navigate (or even prove) at worst—making it ideal political discourse designed to manipulate. We need education reform, but if anyone looks back over the past 150 years, what we need for certain is educational discourse reform, starting with holding the new education reformers accountable (since they seem eager to push accountability) for their lack of expertise, for their lack of historical context, and for their misinformation.

That would be a lesson more valuable to the children of this country than any test prep we could muster to raise our PISA scores.

Yet, in 2011, *Time* included Rhee on its list of the 100 most influential people, along with Geoffrey Canada, and never mentions the many failures and controversies surrounding her tenure in DC:

> None of that is even hinted at in the brief Time write-up by—oh, look, it was written by David Guggenheim, who directed "Waiting for 'Superman,'" the pro-reform propaganda film that convinced a bunch of supposed liberals that lazy teachers are the only reason why underprivileged children in impoverished, segregated school districts don't perform very well on bubble tests. (Pareene, 2011, n.p.)

The continual bungling of reporting on the new reformers shows that while claims of educational failure may be misguided, claims that our media is failing seem well founded

OUR DEBATE CULTURE: SOMEONE WINS, BUT NEVER THE TRUTH

One semester, a colleague asked a few other professors and me to participate in a student debate as part of his first year seminar. Our role in the debate was to evaluate the debate, and of course, choose a winning side. During the debate, I came to recognize something about the debate itself, the college freshmen involved, and ultimately our American culture as well as our media that leaves me certain that our commitment to winning and rugged individualism insures that we will continue, despite our potential for growth, to sacrifice Truth for the sake of winning.

Academia has long valued the formal debate and by extension assigning students argumentative essays—both of which often include the caveat that students should set aside what they truly believe and practice arguing a position (apparently regardless of their investment in that position). In fact, many teachers have argued themselves for decades that students would benefit *more* by choosing a position with which they disagree. In formal debates and argumentative essays, a premium is placed on the act of argument itself. While I watched and thought about evaluating my colleague's class in their debate, I noticed that one team was clearly winning because that team had one student who was sharp and relentless (she could easily be described as having assertive qualities found in Michelle Rhee, for example).

I genuinely had no idea which team posed the better points, offered credible evidence, or presented the most valid argument (I thought both teams were failing on all three, actually), but I know which team was clearly winning the argument. The students debating looked a lot like watching Glenn Beck, or listening to Rush Limbaugh, or even Bill O'Reilly. Argument as a skill is about passion and the ability to think quickly, but lost in the *act* or competition is concern for what we would assume is a higher goal: The Truth (or as close as we can come to The Truth).

I concede that Beck, Limbaugh, O'Reilly, and the whole array of pundits one might conjure as influential in popular culture are *not* classic debaters, particularly since they regularly hold court with monologues. But I also must add that I see very little difference in these pundits and a classic debater (or a writer skilled in rhetoric) because the skill of argument is so powerful that Truth is apt to get subsumed in either case. Take for example how American culture has twisted one of its sports icons, Vince Lombardi.

Lombardi's status in American lore is firmly built on his image as a winner, and our faith in winning is (ironically) tied to our belief in the rugged individual—even when the winners themselves are part of team sports. Lombardi *alone* was able to will his teams to victory, we believe. When people invoke Lombardi, we often hear his pearls of wisdom (similar to the mythology around John Wooden), but one of the sayings most often attributed to Lombardi, "Winning isn't Everything... it's the only thing," appears to be a misquoting. While whether or not Lombardi said these words is an intriguing nugget for historians to unravel, I believe it is more important that culturally Americans *want* this to be true because it captures exactly what is most wrong with our society.

Winning is everything, and Truth be damned. (And by extension: Wealth is everything—consider Gates again—and ethics be damned.) I often sit after any election season, feeling disappointed and resigned to being a pointless voter. But I am compelled now to argue that democracy has not failed us; we have failed democracy. And education along with the media is culpable here.

Our debate culture is directly and indirectly fostered in schools when we teach debate and assign argumentative essays. As well, the real world through the media teaches our children and all of us each day that winning is valued, that the act of winning is valued. And that we care little for what is eviscerated in the wake of winning.

American culture is committed to the rugged individual (idealized in our portrayals of Gates, Canada, and Rhee), the personification of winning in the face of all odds. And our education system works to reinforce that mythology instead of providing children with the opportunities to seek Truth in the name of cooperation, in the name of community. By glorifying rugged individualism, by championing winning at all costs, we have demonized collaboration and cooperation, we have demonized (again ironically) the precious few Universal Truths that have managed to survive within this jaded species called humanity.

The best debater, the person most effective at argument, I have ever witnessed is Kurt Vonnegut. In his works, he offers thousands upon thousands of arguments about the value of human kindness, but he never allows himself once to sacrifice Truth for his arguments or even his art. Because he knew that art is Truth, Truth is art. For me, the same could be said about the democracy we have failed: Democracy is Truth, Truth is democracy.

Instead, we in the U.S. are a mere collection of individuals bound and determined to fight it out until only one stands, and in that process everyone loses—especially the Truth. Our political system is simply an opposing pair of teams playing for the championship, except they dress like the debate team and tend to proceed as if they are competing for the trophies so prized among students who have been lured into the world of politics as combat. And most of the rest of us stand on the sidelines, fans, having chosen sides and hoping that our team wins so that the other team loses— so that we are right and they are wrong.

I think we can do better in our schools, and I believe we must demand that our media seek the Truth instead of perpetuating our debasing debate culture—one that idealizes but ignores hard truths such as the plight of poverty in our wealthy nation.

JOURNALISTS, MEDIA FAIL EDUCATION REFORM DEBATE

Malcolm Gladwell has garnered a significant amount of fame and respect as a writer of nonfiction, as a journalist and public intellectual. Gladwell's 2009 advice in *Time*, then, to aspiring journalists stands as both provocative and illustrative of the problem at the heart of media coverage of education and the education reform debate:

> The issue is not writing. It's what you write about. One of my favorite columnists is Jonathan Weil, who writes for Bloomberg. He broke the Enron story, and he broke it because he's one of the very few mainstream journalists in America who really knows how to read a balance sheet. That means Jonathan Weil will always have a job, and will always be read, and will always have something interesting to say. He's unique. Most accountants don't write articles, and most journalists don't know anything about accounting. Aspiring journalists should stop going to journalism programs and go to some other kind of grad school. If I was studying today, I would go get a master's in statistics, and maybe do a bunch of accounting courses and then write from that perspective. I think that's the way to survive. The role of the generalist is diminishing. Journalism has to get smarter. (Altman, 2009, n.p.)

The media has changed dramatically, both in types of access to information and in the breadth of that access, in the past couple decades—including the rise of blogs, allowing virtually anyone to "publish" as a journalist. The irony in this media evolution is that while even Gladwell seems to confront the professional preparation of journalists narrowly and while the new media has opened the door to journalism to any writer regardless of direct training or experience in journalism, the education profession is experiencing a convoluted media-driven assault on its professionalism.

To add insult to injury, the so-called "liberal" media reports, perpetuates, and makes credible daily a neoliberal, corporatist attack on the equally labeled "liberal" public school system. The media sits at the center of the current education reform debate, playing a powerful role that deserves no better than an "F" for the failure of the vast majority of that media to do as Gladwell implores: To rephrase, most educators don't write articles, and most journalists don't know anything about education, except how to report uncritically baseless and tired criticisms and assumptions.

The high-profile examples are easy to cite: *Waiting for "Superman,"* Gates interviewed in *Newsweek* (and virtually everywhere else), Rhee and Canada on *The Colbert Report* (and virtually everywhere else), and episodes and segments of *Oprah* and *Real Time* with Bill Maher, as I have addressed above. While high-profile media coverage and distortions of the education debate are powerful, the incessant drip of flawed media coverage occurring at all levels is equally corrosive. For example, in December 2009, *The Greenville News* (Greenville, SC) published an Op-Ed by Dr. Jameson Taylor, "Educating Entrepreneurs Will Create Prosperity," claiming that public schools are failing based on NAEP scores. Then, Taylor proclaims:

> A new report by the South Carolina Policy Council shows that school choice programs in the counties of Clarendon, Hampton, Lee, Marlboro and Williamsburg could create 123 small businesses and 379 additional jobs. In fact, a statewide school choice initiative could create thousands of new jobs. These jobs are not teaching or administrative positions created by more state spending, but jobs created by the students themselves. (n.p.)

For the average reader, an Op-Ed by Dr. Taylor, identified as director of research at the South Carolina Policy Council, and a report from SCPC authored by economist Sven Larson present an authoritative message that matches two cultural narratives that are robust but lacking in evidence—simplistic claims of public education failure and the power of the free market. I was immediately skeptical about the Op-Ed and the report since I was then working on a book on parental school choice (Thomas, 2010a); the claims about schools and the conclusions of the study failed to match what I was examining in my research.

Several months later, the National Education Policy Center (NEPC) released a review of Larson's study and concluded: "As a result of its uncritical acceptance of an earlier flawed study and in its introduction of additional untenable assumptions, the report offers findings that are unlikely to be valid and is of little use in informing policymakers and the public about the effects of vouchers" (Roy, 2010, n.p.). The NEPC also awarded Larson's study the "Magic Potion" Award in their 2010 Bunkum Awards.

When I submitted a rebuttal Op-Ed to *The Greenville News*, what happened? The editor said that I had already been afforded my say on school choice in previous pieces and that the Jameson piece provided balance to the debate—not a single bit of interest in the accuracy or credibility of the balance, though. In the past decade, we have, in fact, ample evidence that think-tanks have assumed many of the surface features of credible research—experts with credentials, slick publications, citations—without following through on the essential element of high-quality evidence, peer review (Welner, Hinchey, Molnar, & Weltzman, 2010). Molnar (2001) has noted "news reports of education research frequently do not appear to take account of whether such research is peer reviewed" (n.p.).

Further, Yettick (2009) released a study of how educational research is portrayed in the mainstream media, focusing on educational reporting in three major publications—*New York Times*, *Washington Post*, and *Education Week*. Yettick discovered that university and government-funded research received the most media coverage, but that proportionately, think-tank reports were overrepresented by the media. University research occurred 14 to 16 times more often than think-tank reports, but the media covered university research only twice as often: "As a result, any given think tank report was substantially more likely to be cited than any given study produced by a university," Yettick (2009, n.p.) concludes.

Yettick (2009) proposes three recommendations for combating this phenomenon among education journalists reporting on research. First, in order to improve the quality of evidence stakeholders receive through the media, reporters should begin to seek out peer-reviewed research through all entities conducting research. While not without flaws, peer-review remains the gold standard of evaluating research, as reflected in the medical and pharmaceutical fields. Before any research can be deemed credible, we must know the who's and how's of the research process. Peer-review provides oversight for bias and corruption in the research process, but it also adds nuance to the discourse.

Next, reporters dealing with educational research should implement peer-review strategies on think-tank reports themselves; if no peer-review is available, or if the reporter is unable to find an expert to help evaluate the report, Yettick (2009) explains, "the article might include the sentence, 'Other experts in the field have not yet had an opportunity to assess this study, which has not gone through peer review, a process that serves as an important quality control for research in education'" (n.p.).

Finally, all media reports of educational research should provide an active link to the research itself, facilitating stakeholders drawing their own informed conclusions about the quality of the research. Yettick (2009) also provides in the study useful appendices that should guide us all as we contemplate the value of any research or report we come across. One appendix details dozens of think-tanks and the ideology of each. The media covered think-tank reports during the time of the study ranging, out of 99 think-tanks, from 11% liberal to 52% centrist and to 34% conservative.

When the media reports in the same way on a think-tank study that is not peer-reviewed as the media reports on a peer-reviewed university study, the implication is that the evidence is equal—when it is highly likely that the evidence is not of equal validity. Advocacy reports, whether from the left, center, or right, are just that, advocacy.

For example, in his popular "Class Struggles" column in *The Washington Post*, Jay Matthews (2011), who has earned a reputation as a journalist with credibility about education, weighed in again about vouchers, "Vouchers Work, But So What?" The piece focuses on an updated report from the Foundation for Educational Choice (Forster, 2011), as Matthews characterizes:

> Greg Forster, a talented and often engagingly contrarian senior fellow at the Foundation for Educational Choice, has expanded a previous study to show that nearly all the research on vouchers, including some using the gold standard of random assignment, has good news for those who believe in giving parents funds that can be used to put their children in private schools. Students given that chance do better in private schools than similar students do in public schools, the research shows. Public schools who are threatened by the loss of students to private schools because of voucher programs improve more than schools that do not have to worry about that competition, the research also shows. (Matthews, 2011, n.p.)

Matthews' position as a journalist focusing on education and the surface credibility of the think-tank report combine to mask, once again, what lies behind the report—the earlier incarnation of "Win-Win" was promoted with the same positive claims about choice, but later unmasked in a review:

> This new report purports to gather all available empirical evidence on the question of the competitive effects of vouchers, finding a strong consensus that vouchers help public schools. But the report, based on a review of 17 studies, selectively reads the evidence in some of those studies, the majority of which were produced by voucher advocacy organizations. Moreover, the report can't decide whether or not to acknowledge the impact of factors other than vouchers on public schools. It attempts to show that public school gains were caused by the presence of vouchers alone, but then argues that the lack of overall gains for districts with vouchers should be ignored because too many other factors are at play. In truth, existing research provides little reliable information about the competitive effects of vouchers, and this report does little to help answer the question. (Lubienski, 2009, n.p.)

At the very least, the updated "Win-Win" should be placed in the context of the earlier flaws in the 2009 version; but we should also expect to withhold endorsing this version until the work is reviewed.

Yettick (2009) opens her analysis with this argument about the importance of media coverage of educational research: "Because the research featured in these outlets influences policymakers, practitioners and parents, it is important to know who produces the educational research mentioned in the news media" (n.p.). Combined with Gladwell's advice, Yettick's recommendations are a start, but I am certain that education reform will continue to fail if the media continues to fail the public discourse about our society, our schools, and our need for that reform.

ACCOUNTABILITY? START AT THE TOP

For nearly two decades, I taught high school English in rural upstate South Carolina. During about the last half of that part of my career, I also served as the soccer coach—a role that added valuable nuance and perspective to my role as a teacher and mentor to young people. Soccer is a spring sport in South Carolina since high schools tend to use the football fields for soccer. Each spring, one of my greatest headaches as a soccer coach was navigating spring break, which invariably fell near the end of the regular season and disrupted our practice schedule as we headed to the playoffs. Parents and players alike tended to push against my belief that we needed to practice at least some of the week (I wanted all of the week, by the way).

One year, after a particularly difficult wrestling match over when and if we'd practice during spring break, I was driving my wife to the Nissan dealership on the Tuesday of spring break and my cell phone rang. The voice on the other end was the captain of the soccer team, to whom I said something like, "Hey, Jason, what's up?"

Within a few seconds, I realized that my entire soccer team was waiting for me at the field for the practice I had fought for and then completely forgotten to attend. The next morning at the scheduled practice time, I was there early and I set out to run 10 laps around the soccer field—double the required five laps for players who missed practices. As my players arrived, one by one, they joined me on the laps.

I never said a word about my laps, although I apologized for missing the practice the day before, but my players knew what I was doing—and most, I think, realized that I had chosen to run more laps than I required for them. This story is not self-aggrandizement. I have failed far too often in my life as a teacher, coach, parent, and husband—and this space doesn't afford me the space needed to catalog those failures.

This story is to state that, despite my many failures, I believed in and practiced one Golden Rule of teaching, coaching, and mentoring young people: Hold yourself to higher standards than you ask of those over whom you are granted authority.

Each time I read the repeated claims coming from the new reformers—Duncan, Gates, Rhee, and Canada—I think about my days in the classroom and on the field. These new reformers reached their positions of authority in education reform, first, without any real expertise (similar, I must admit, to how I became a varsity soccer coach without ever having played the game). Next, one of the central refrains of their message has been teacher accountability.

I have raised concerns about the tragic flaw of hubris (Thomas, 2011m), which led me to muse about a classic text:

"Ozymandias"

by Percy Bysshe Shelley

I met a traveler from an antique land
Who said: Two vast and trunkless legs of stone
Stand in the desert. Near them, on the sand,
Half sunk, a shattered visage lies, whose frown,
And wrinkled lip, and sneer of cold command,
Tell that its sculptor well those passions read
Which yet survive, stamped on these lifeless things,
The hand that mocked them, and the heart that fed;
And on the pedestal these words appear:
"My name is Ozymandias, king of kings:
Look on my works, ye Mighty, and despair!"
Nothing beside remains. Round the decay
Of that colossal wreck, boundless and bare
The lone and level sands stretch far away.

Like Ozymadias, the new education reformers are oblivious to their own failures, as is the media (Pareene, 2011), yet they continue to tout their accomplishments—that are little more than "the decay of that colossal wreck." So how have the new reformers fared when placed against their claims?

What about Duncan's Chicago miracle? Evidence suggests that we have no miracle, but mirage (Horn, 2009), and Andrew J. Coulson (2009) makes this cogent suggestion for Duncan: "Secretary Duncan has said that state and district officials should not make inflated claims about student achievement based on misleading state test scores, and has used the NAEP to fact check their claims. He's right about that" (n.p.).

And, Gates' small schools experiment? While Gates himself declared the experiment a failure, Marshak (2010) explains that Gates' small school experiment actually exposes Gates' own inability to understand the education dynamics he claims to reform. But ample evidence reveals both that Gates is inexpert and remains unsuccessful as an education reformer (McKenzie, 2007), including his failure to understand statistics and the charts he repeatedly uses to make his claims (Fung, 2011).

Rhee's DC success? Possibly the best example of too-good-to-be-true (Gillum & Bello, 2011). While the truth about Rhee has been mounting for some time—both her incompetence and her lack of success (Clawson, 2011)—those of us in education have known this all along. Some are starting to see that Rhee is no miracle worker, but she does fulfill a script, as Lyons (2011) notes in a piece titled "Michelle Rhee: Education Reform Huckster"—"Presumably because Rhee's tale fits so conveniently with Jeffersonian idealism that sees potential genius everywhere, it was treated as gospel throughout the national media" (n.p.).

Canada's Harlem miracle? Only in the press, although the press seems convinced that Canada is an expert in education—and he is not—and the source of education miracles—again, he is not.

But this is not anything new; we can also backtrack. Bush and Paige's Texas miracle? Another mirage, as Ravitch (2011b) explains and as careful consideration of the data reveals (Klein, Hamilton, McCaffrey, & Stecher, 2000).

Accountability appears to be something those driving the reform are using to mask the lack of expertise or accomplishment among the reformers themselves. And the media is playing right along, unwilling and possibly unable to hold the reformers themselves accountable—unwilling and possibly unable as well to discern that the education reform debate is being misrepresented as badly as education is itself.

There is no support for the status quo, and there is a credible but often silenced recognition that the new education reformers lack the exact experiences and expertise needed to drive true education reform. As Anthony Cody (2011b) has explained, "The 'reformers' have used the power of the media and government, and billions of dollars in philanthropic money to push anyone who questions their strategies off the stage up to this point" (n.p.). Despite having little to no expertise and only claims of success where no success exists, the new reformers have built false statues for their own benefit.

If accountability is truly what must drive education reform (and I doubt this is true), then we must start at the top, or we are left only with the crumbling bravado of self-appointed experts at the expense of children, education, and the promise of a free society. And we must demand that the media unmask the reformers and speak about and to the poverty that shackles nearly one in four children in the U.S., resulting in education outcomes that appear to condemn the very universal public education system designed to address inequity.

Against the failures of the new reformers and the silence as well as masking perpetuated by the media, Kovacs (2008) makes this plea to educators:

> Schooling as if democracy matters is a political project, plain and simple, and our refusal to engage is akin to fiddling while Rome burns. In hopes of thwarting the Anti-School Movement in order to create spaces so educators can school as if democracy mattered, I encourage the reader [of the author's essay] to become more involved with politics; to listen to teachers, students, and parents; to contact local and state representatives; to speak at board meetings and before civic organizations. Your informed voice must be shared outside the halls of the academy, to do otherwise guarantees more of the same. (n.p.)

In Chapter 4, I turn to a media darling—charter schools. The shift at both ends of the political spectrum during the Obama administration has been a universal embracing of charter schools, despite the education format being co-opted by corporate entities. The charter movement is proving complex since many advocating charter schools are directly claiming to be concerned about poverty—no longer ignoring poverty, but this willingness to speak about and against poverty doesn't bring the promise we may have hoped to find under the first African American president of the U.S.

CHAPTER 4

THE GREAT CHARTER COMPROMISE

Masking Corporate Commitments in Educational Reform

The shifting but persistent advocacy for school choice has found its newest manifestation in the growing corporate charter school movement, which is the current culmination of stalled promises for choice that are abandoned for the next promise yet to be discredited:

> This is a notable possibility in view of the claim that voucher programs have not been shown to harm academic achievement. In fact, the "do no harm" promise is far removed from earlier claims about the potential for vouchers to improve student performance. Over a decade into this reform, some advocates are moving away from optimistic claims about school choice achievement outcomes, and many are instead highlighting parent satisfaction as evidence of success. (Lubienski & Weitzel, 2008, p. 484)

Along with the shift to charter schools as a source of competition and market forces—tossing aside vouchers and tuition tax credits—school choice advocates have begun to claim that choice is primarily designed to help those trapped in poverty and denied the choice middle- and upper-class families enjoy (without challenging or question either the value of parental choice or the accuracy of the claim).

Ignoring Poverty in the U.S.: The Corporate Takeover of Public Education, pp. 89–122
Copyright © 2012 by Information Age Publishing

Corporate charter schools such as the Harlem Children's Zone (HCZ) and Knowledge Is Power Program (KIPP) serve primarily—and sometimes exclusively—high-poverty populations of students who are African American. A disturbing irony of the school choice movement absorbing the charter school movement is that its claimed and real focus on high-poverty children of color is in fact perpetuating our ignoring poverty by stereotyping African American and high-poverty children, segregating them in charter schools that embrace "no excuses" and "pedagogy of poverty" ideologies.

"Closing the achievement gap" and "no excuses" are powerful refrains of the current corporate reform movement in public education because the phrases simultaneously acknowledge poverty *and* help perpetuate the masking and ignoring of poverty. Focusing on "achievement" and "no excuses" allows the norm of rugged individualism to highlight individual failure and responsibility while disregarding social influences and boundaries impacting those individuals facing poverty and thus the achievement gap.

HIGHLIGHTING AND IGNORING POVERTY: TWENTY-FIRST CENTURY CHARTER SCHOOLS

Poverty impacts public and political discussions of education both when it is acknowledged and in its absence. Powerful refrains about public education and education reform for over a century have focused exclusively on schools and teachers, leaving poverty completely out of the discussion. Both the political Left and Right benefit from focusing on individual responsibility and market forces in order to avoid any culpability for the economic elite in terms of income and opportunity inequity in our society.

Some of the most persistent and corrosive motifs of political discourse about schools suggest that schools are the sole avenue to social reform and to individual productivity, that success and failure in our schools and in society are primarily driven by the ambitions and abilities of each individual (winners deserve to win and losers deserve to lose), and that references to poverty or other social hurdles are mere excuses for those who want to avoid accountability. As I will examine further below, political and public discourse often identify and champion "miracle" schools that prove schools can succeed if only everyone is making the necessary effort.

While the rugged individualism and market forces arguments persist, directly from the Right and covertly from the Left, a disturbing and new approach to the education reform debate is the rise of the charter school movement, specifically charter schools that are run with a corporate model, such as KIPP, and charters that are driven by personalities or philanthropists, such as the HCZ. These new manifestations of charter schools have benefited from natural disasters—Katrina in New Orleans—and from uncritical media and political endorsements, Canada's HCZ being endorsed by *The New York Times* and President Obama.

The new charter movement is also distinct because these charter schools tend to serve monolithic populations of poor African American children while underserving special needs children and English language learners (ELL). Since these new charter schools are stepping into the most challenging segments of the public school system, few of the schools receive any criticism from the children and families they serve, the media, the public, or politicians. Charter schools simultaneously maintain tax-funded schooling and create quasi-market based entities since parents choose to enroll their children in the schools.

The new reformers—Gates, Rhee, Duncan, and Canada—have ridden the wave created by *Waiting for "Superman"* and its message that "bad" teachers are at the heart of failing public education (and that evil teachers' unions are allowing their "bad" teachers to remain in the field). And that aspect of the new reform movement seeks to ignore entirely the role of poverty in the lives and education of children by labeling any reference to poverty as an excuse—focusing almost exclusively on simplistic international test score comparisons that, in fact, discredit their own claims when poverty is considered in those rankings. But the new education reform movement has begun to have it both ways (acknowledging and marginalizing poverty), by embracing and championing charter schools that address exclusively high-poverty children and communities.

Most of the charter schools the new reformers support, however, are careful to identify poverty as an obstacle that cannot be used as an excuse, resulting in the rise of "no excuses" policies in these schools that require parents and students to sign detailed agreements about their commitment to the extended school days, regimented class structures, scripted student behaviors, and rigid requirements for students to remain in the schools. This "new paternalism" is presented as the necessary mechanism for enculturating children living in poverty (almost all of whom are children of color) into middle-class norms of behavior. Few people other than scholars of poverty, culture, and race raise concerns about the "no excuses" policies of the new charter movement; in fact, "no excuses" ideology is nearly universally applauded.

Klonsky (2011) identifies the new charter movement as a contemporary manifestation of Social Darwinism, designed to pit those living in poverty against each other. The high-poverty charter schools that are often populated by students chosen by lottery from a pool of families wanting to enter the schools perpetuate competition among families who feel trapped both in lives of poverty and in public schools that have been labeled failures by the accountability system and by the media. The popular discourse reinforces the specter of failure while the "no excuses" charter schools themselves institutionalize rugged individualism and the very real threat of being thrown out of the charter schools since other families are always waiting to enroll.

By cultural default, the new charter school movement is embedded in a market and corporate paradigm that shifts all of the expectations and outcomes to the commitment and abilities of the individuals. Community, cooperation, social justice, and cultural forces are simply ignored, washed from the debate through the "no excuses" refrain. As Klonsky (2011) explains, many elements of the new reform movement merge under the seemingly practical call for charter schools and "no excuses" ideology:

> Schwartz, a Teach For America (TFA) alum—no shock there—directs the so-called *Level Playing Field Institute*. He actually performs a service by articulating the anti-democratic social theory behind many current corporate reform policies. However, his plea to U.S. corporations to increase their support for school re-segregation and creaming via charter schools is redundant. The corporate world, including power philanthropists like Gates, Broad, Walton and Bradley, is way ahead of him in this regard. It was the Bradley Foundation, in fact, that underwrote the publication of *The Bell Curve*, by Charles Murray which was based on the Social-Darwinist theory that black and Latino students lacked the academic potential held by white and Asian students and therefore should be tracked away from college preparatory programs. (n.p.)

While acknowledging poverty, the new charter movement enables TFA, corporate America, billionaire/millionaire entrepreneurs, and classist scholars to perpetuate stereotypical claims about people trapped in poverty, shifting the blame to those in poverty and masking the power of those elites who, in fact, do control what conditions exist in U.S. society.

Along with the uncritical faith in "no excuses" ideology driving corporate charter schools is the concurrent trust that we can and thus should close the achievement/poverty gap. A central component of NCLB forces states and schools to report test data by subgroups, a policy designed to expose decades of schools and states hiding the low achievement of subgroups—notably children of color, children from poverty, special needs students, and ELL students. Once the data were exposed and delineated, the gaps in achievement became the focus of education reform and millions upon millions of tax dollars. This focus on the achievement gap, however, stalled at the correlation between student characteristics and student outcomes, in part because culturally we ascribe to the "no excuses" ideology that drives the new charter movement.

Yet, careful consideration of all test data—including state accountability testing, national normed testing, and the SAT—reveal that test scores overwhelmingly reflect the status of any child's life far more than the quality of the school or of that student's teachers. As Mathis (2011) laments, "Scientifically disproven years ago, the 'Beat the Odds' myth is still the excuse of convenience for justifying claims that schools can single-handedly overcome poverty" (n.p.). As long as the ruling elite maintains the "no excuses" mantra and as long as that same ruling elite claims to be addressing the achievement gap, schools and teacher, along with the students and their families, will remain the target of what needs reforming.

Mathis (2011) makes a compelling case that seeking to close the achievement gap is corrosive:

> There is great harm in this myth, that schools can do it all. It provides the excuse for politicians, vested interests and advocates to wrongly declare schools "failures." It gives a false justification for firing the principals and teachers who work with our neediest. It tells us a complex society does not need to invest in its skills or its children. It serves as a moral cloak for actions that are technically unjustified—as well as just plain wrong. (n.p.)

Baker (2011), along with many others, adds that measuring, identifying, and then addressing that achievement/poverty gap is nearly impossible. The political and corporate commitment to charter schools, "no excuses" ideology, and closing the achievement gap remains popular, but they are all flawed—destined to exacerbate, not eradicate, the conditions of poverty they appear suited to address (Thomas, 2011v).

The shift politically toward charter schools is spread across partisan and ideological lines that continue to separate support for school choice. Once a proponent of school choice and the accountability movement, Ravitch (2010c) summarizes the great charter compromise, focusing on the narrative created by documentaries such as *Waiting for "Superman"*:

> The message of these films has become alarmingly familiar: American public education is a failed enterprise. The problem is not money. Public schools already spend too much. Test scores are low because there are so many bad teachers, whose jobs are protected by powerful unions. Students drop out because the schools fail them, but they could accomplish practically anything if they were saved from bad teachers. They would get higher test scores if schools could fire more bad teachers and pay more to good ones. The only hope for the future of our society, especially for poor black and Hispanic children, is escape from public schools, especially to charter schools, which are mostly funded by the government but controlled by private organizations, many of them operating to make a profit. (n.p.)

Like Ravitch, I am skeptical, and now I will turn to looking carefully at the charter school movement that allows corporate and political interests to address poverty by ignoring poverty through compelling cultural refrains of "no excuses" and "closing the achievement gap."

THE CORPORATE TAKEOVER OF AMERICAN SCHOOLS: HIGH-POVERTY NEIGHBORHOODS

The top positions in public education across the U.S.—for example, Secretary Duncan, recent chancellors Joel Klein (New York) and Michelle Rhee (Washington, DC), and former Chancellor Cathleen P. Black (New York)—reflect a trust in CEO-style leadership for education management and reform. Along with these new leaders in education, billionaire/millionaire entrepreneurs have also assumed roles as education saviors: Bill and Melinda Gates, and Geoffrey Canada. This corporate element is strongly reflected in the new rise of charter schools as the focus of how to reform public education; as well, the corporate model allows the ruling elite to continue to promote the value of the market system without identifying the market's role in the economic inequity throughout the U.S.

Gates, Canada, Duncan, Klein and Rhee have capitalized on their positions in education to rise to the status of celebrities, as well-praised in the misleading documentary feature *Waiting for "Superman"* (Thomas, 2010m), on Oprah, and even on Bill Maher's *Real Time* (Thomas, 2010o). What do all these professional managers and entrepreneurs have in common? Little or no experience or expertise in education. (Instead, they have degrees in government and law, along with nontraditional entries into education and strong ties to alternative certification, such as Teach for America). Further, they all represent and promote a cultural faith in the power of leadership above the importance of experience or expertise. The rise of corporate charter schools and corporate leadership in school reform reinforce the contradictory addressing and ignoring poverty that sits within the larger school reform discourse, a debate that seeks to fulfill corporate interests at the expense of those living in poverty.

When Klein quit his post as chancellor in New York—soon after Rhee left DC—the fact that he was leaving for a senior position at News Corp and that his replacement would be a magazine executive (whose tenure would be cut short just as Rhee's was) sent a strong message: The implication was that the American public distrusts not only schools, but also teachers and education experts; this distrust reinforces the allure of charter schools, which aggressively distinguish themselves from "failing" government schools while simultaneously accepting tax funding.

More telling, however, is the appointment of Duncan as Secretary of Education under President Obama. This appointment of a CEO-style leader of schools in Chicago comes under a Democratic administration and, ironically, a president once demonized as too friendly with the radical left within the education community. Like Obama, Secretary Duncan has led refrains against bad teachers (Thomas, 2010q, 2010i), while ignoring the growing impact of poverty on the lives of children and on schools. One very visible effect of this trend for recruiting CEO-style leaders and billionaire entrepreneurs is the new commitment to corporate-sponsored charter schools—such as KIPP and the HCZ among the most high profile.

The messages coming from the new reformers of public education in the U.S., then, are that government has failed and that only the private sector can save us. But is that message accurate?

The corporate push to take over public education is, in fact, masking the failures of corporate America. And, in turn, this masks that America has failed public education, rather than public education has failed America. The standards, testing and accountability movement is built on a claim that education can change society. The corporate support for the accountability movement and the "no excuses" charter school movement seeks to reinforce that claim because, otherwise, corporate America and the politicians supporting corporate America would have to admit that something is wrong with economic and political structures in the U.S. But the evidence isn't on the side of corporate America.

The Joseph Rowntree Foundation has shown that only 14% of pupil achievement can be attributed to the quality of the school; 86% of that achievement is driven by factors outside of education (Hirsch, 2007). David Berliner (2009) has also established six out-of-school factors that overwhelm the effectiveness of education against poverty and expanding social inequities. Yet, the causational relationship between poverty and educational outcomes are never addressed in the new charter movement and the rising commitment to corporate-style school leadership. Instead, the corporate message is that poverty will not be used as an excuse.

In the U.S., achievement gaps and failure in state schools reflect larger inequalities in society (Noah, 2010; Thomas, 2011v), as well as dysfunction in corporate, consumer culture. The schools did not cause those gaps or failures—although it is true that, far too often, they perpetuate the social stratification. And the evidence shows that schools alone will never be able to overcome powerful social forces (Mathis, 2011).

The real failure, which is the message being ignored along with poverty, is that one of the wealthiest countries in the world refuses to face the inequities of its economic system, a system that permits more than 20% of its children to live in poverty (Szabo, 2010) and to languish in schools that

America has clearly decided to abandon, along with its democratic principles. Thus, Americans are being sold charter schools and corporate
school leadership in part in order to address the achievement gap paralleling the equity gap in our society, but we are in fact ignoring poverty
and the root causes of poverty—the exact corporate culture we are being
told to allow to run our schools.

The public, I believe, is easily led and misled because of our faith, our
tendency to be a belief culture, as I discussed earlier. Charter schools support is further evidence of this reality because we are seeking not just
charter schools, but *miracle* schools.

RECONSIDERING EDUCATION "MIRACLES": WHY WE BELIEVE CHARTER TRUMPS PUBLIC

"We may have found a remedy for the achievement gap," proclaimed
David Brooks (2009, n.p.) in an Op-Ed for *The New York Times*. Brooks
titled the piece "The Harlem Miracle," about the Promise Academy of the
Harlem Children's Zone (HCZ). Brooks concluded that Dobbie and
Fryer's (2009) claim that the charter school had closed the achievement
gap between blacks and whites proved the reformers right and the educational establishment wrong. Throughout 2009, and uncritically, HCZ was
championed by NPR, *Edutopia, 60 Minutes, Time,* and the *Washington
Post*—where Shulman (2009) added, "Now the Obama administration
seeks to replicate [President and CEO Geoffrey] Canada's model in 20 cities in a program called Promise Neighborhoods and has set aside $10
million in the 2010 budget for planning" (n.p.).

The HCZ experiment includes a charter school that offers both social
and educational support for students and parents, designed to lift the
families out of poverty by addressing the entire zone of each child's life.
Paul Tough has chronicled the ambitious program in *Whatever It Takes,*
although the book explores the HCZ with far more complexity than any
of the outlets noted above. The rush to replicate the HCZ offers important lessons that have more to do with how we distort research than how
we can reform schools. Repeating patterns exposed by Molnar (2001) and
Yettick (2009) concerning the failure of mainstream media to report on
educational research, the media and political reactions to the "Harlem
Miracle" prove again that many have misrepresented what data from the
Promise Academy reveal—mainly that there was no miracle. (This parallels the claims of the "Texas Miracle" under then-governor Bush—a claim
also later discredited by scholarship that the mainstream media ignored.)

But, educational reform must be about improving the lives of children,
not declaring ideological winners, not "reproduc[ing] the dominant ideol-

ogy" (Freire, 1998, p. 110). The new reformers, in their quest to support corporate interests, must deflect the corrosive power of poverty (and claim "no excuses") in order to shield corporate America, but also must appear to be concerned about the underprivileged (and claim "closing the achievement gap") for public gain. For the new reformers to win, the debate must be simplistic.

Aaron Pallas (2009b), responding directly to Brooks (2009), noted that Dobbie and Fryer (2009) base their claims of closing the achievement gap on one test result of ten at two grade levels. Further, Pallas explains that advocates gloss over that those students did not close the gap on the Iowa Test of Basic Skills the same year. In short, making claims that HCZ research provides "a remedy for the achievement gap" overstates for the wider public what the data support. Proclaiming "miracle" exposes our flawed silver-bullet mentality, not a remedy for closing the achievement gap.

For HCZ to show us how to reform public schools, we must know how HCZ schools compare and differ from public schools in order to identify what causes any success. And we must resist allowing the media and politicians to drive through distortion what we say, believe, and implement concerning our schools. Beneath faith in "miracle" charter schools, "no excuses" ideology, and utopian goals of closing the achievement gap is a complex truth that admits the power of poverty to overwhelm the possibilities of public education.

One difference is that HCZ schools include virtually no ELL or special education students (Miron, Urschel, Mathis, & Tornquist, 2010; Frankenberg, Siegel-Hawley, & Wang, 2011), populations public schools must serve. Another difference is that although Brooks (2009) discounted the value of low student-teacher ratios, the HCZ schools have, according to the *60 Minutes* report, one adult for every six children (Schorn, 2006), again unlike public schools addressing high poverty populations.

Further, HCZ schools address the social conditions of children living in poverty along with reforming schools. But advocates discount the impact of the social support (Whitehurst & Croft, 2010) and champion the most disturbing and least challenged aspect of the Harlem experiment—"no excuses schools," Brooks (2009) explains, adding, "The schools create a disciplined, orderly and demanding counterculture to inculcate middle-class values" (n.p.).

The claim of "no excuses schools" masks the rise of "new paternalism" schools that implement oppressive practices in pursuit of raising scores, increasing graduation rates, and improving college attendance—all mechanistic assumptions about education in a free society—while seeking to discredit progressive educational ideologies (Whitman, 2008; Landsberg, 2009). Diane Ravitch (2009b) has questioned HCZ's commitment "to impose middle-class values on poor and minority children." Ravitch argues, "But I don't think that our schools need to be boot camps to teach courtesy, civility, respect for others, self-discipline, and other virtues necessary for democratic life" (n.p.).

"New paternalism" schools implement the worst aspects of racism and classism, notably that the problems we face are inherently in the children themselves. If we persist in conforming all children to the system, we are ignoring the possible (and likely) flaws in society, standardized testing, and bureaucratic schooling. When the media and politicians speak with authority in ways that confirm our stereotypes and prejudices, those corrupted views are confirmed—absolving those with the best of intentions of any wrong-doing. "No excuses" charter school support allows the ruling elite to ignore and marginalize those living in poverty while claiming to help them.

We, then, are left with some disturbing lessons hidden by distorting what HCZ "no excuses" charter schools reveal.

First, we must distinguish media and political advocacy from evidence, especially when we are faced with claims of "miracles." Brooks (2009) claims the Promise Academy alone closed the achievement gap, but Dobbie and Fryer's (2009) study admits, "*We cannot, however, disentangle whether communities coupled with high-quality schools drive our results, or whether the high-quality schools alone are enough to do the trick* [emphasis in original]" (p. 4). Next, we must seek the full picture, even when faced with the complexity of data and statistical claims of relevance. Brooks's conclusions drawn from Dobbie and Fryer's paper are questionable and conflict with Paul Tough's book on HCZ.

As well, we must make accurate comparisons with public schools when considering educational experiments. HCZ schools have conditions and populations *unlike* high-poverty public schools. What has worked for individual HCZ students (and the definition of "worked" remains controversial at best) may not work in public school reform—and more importantly, the methods that create the data used to determine improvement may all be more harmful than any perceived positive outcomes. And many of the successful elements in the HCZ experiment have been supported by research for decades, but rarely implemented in public schools.

Finally, if the HCZ experiment is important to the children being served now and for the lessons we can learn, and it is, then we must acknowledge its successes and its problems honestly. But to manipulate evidence to declare ideological winners and losers fails the children and society we seek to serve. Ultimately, we must set aside the pursuit of "miracles" and face the realities of poverty in an ever-increasingly inequitable society, an inequity that is reflected in but not caused primarily by our schools.

KNOWLEDGE IS POWER PROGRAM: THE IRONY OF THE NAME

While the HCZ has the allure of Geoffrey Canada as a self-made minority millionaire turned entrepreneur, and one that chose to help poor children at that, KIPP charter schools appear to be popular throughout the U.S. solely for their "no excuses" ideology and their ability to maintain their status as highly successful schools when public schools fail. KIPP self-describes its program by triggering key motifs:

> KIPP, the Knowledge Is Power Program, is a national network of free, open-enrollment, college-preparatory public schools with a track record of preparing students in underserved communities for success in college and in life... KIPP builds a partnership among parents, students, and teachers that puts learning first. By providing outstanding educators, more time in school learning, and a strong culture of achievement, KIPP is helping all students climb the mountain to and through college. Every day, KIPP students across the nation are proving that demographics do not define destiny. Over 80 percent of our students are from low-income families and eligible for the federal free or reduced-price meals program, and 95 percent are African American or Latino. Nationally, more than 90 percent of KIPP middle school students have gone on to college-preparatory high schools, and over 85 percent of KIPP alumni have gone on to college. (Knowledge is Power Program, 2011, n.p.)

"Free," "open-enrollment," "college-preparatory," "public schools," "strong culture of achievement," "demographics do not define destiny"— these refrains trigger, as I have discussed above, our faith in the rugged individual and our willingness to acknowledge poverty as long as we do not allow the root causes of poverty to be examined, as long as we keep the focus of accountability on the children and parents in poverty.

Central to KIPP is its Five Pillars, which are driven by the "no excuses" ideology and powerful rhetoric:

> *High Expectations.* KIPP schools have clearly defined and measurable high expectations for academic achievement and conduct that make no excuses based on the students' backgrounds. Students, parents, teachers, and staff create and reinforce a culture of achievement and support through a range of formal and informal rewards and consequences for academic performance and behavior.
>
> *Choice & Commitment.* Students, their parents, and the faculty of each KIPP school choose to participate in the program. No one is assigned or forced to attend a KIPP school. Everyone must make and uphold a commitment to the school and to each other to put in the time and effort required to achieve success.

More Time. KIPP schools know that there are no shortcuts when it comes to success in academics and life. With an extended school day, week, and year, students have more time in the classroom to acquire the academic knowledge and skills that will prepare them for competitive high schools and colleges, as well as more opportunities to engage in diverse extracurricular experiences.

Power to Lead. The principals of KIPP schools are effective academic and organizational leaders who understand that great schools require great school leaders. They have control over their school budget and personnel. They are free to swiftly move dollars or make staffing changes, allowing them maximum effectiveness in helping students learn.

Focus on Results. KIPP schools relentlessly focus on high student performance on standardized tests and other objective measures. Just as there are no shortcuts, there are no excuses. Students are expected to achieve a level of academic performance that will enable them to succeed at the nation's best high schools and colleges. (Knowledge is Power Program, 2011, n.p., http://www.kipp.org/about-kipp/five-pillars)

These foundational principles are followed on KIPP's web page by a Commitment to Excellence pledge that must be signed by all involved, students, parents, and teachers (Knowledge is Power Program, 2011). The pillars and commitment pledge embrace measurement, self-reliance, accountability, choice, and a whole host of cultural norms that trigger most of the middle-class belief systems that define Americans. And KIPP has a catchy, if eerie, slogan: "Work hard. Be nice."

Like the praise for the HCZ, advocates of KIPP tend to focus on the rhetoric, ideology, and press releases of the organization itself, rarely taking care to see if the claims are true or if the KIPP model offers any realistic evidence of how to reform public schools. Ironically, knowledge about KIPP is powerful, but not the way the KIPP advocates might hope.

As a tax-funded public charter school system, KIPP, unlike traditional public schools, must advocate for enrollment of its students; in other words, good publicity and public support ensure that KIPP schools, and their investors, thrive. As I will examine below, advocacy causes real concerns for the education reform debate, but here, let's look at the truth about KIPP beneath the advocacy.

Much about the allure of KIPP and the power of its message in the education reform debate—as well as how we view and address poverty—is in a debate about the charter schools in Valerie Strauss's blog, The Answer Sheet at *The Washington Post*. While the new reformers' messages gained traction throughout 2009 and 2010, especially with the success and uncritical acclaim offered to *Waiting for "Superman,"* the charter movement broadly and KIPP narrowly received a great deal of attention and thus support.

Before the *"Superman"* bump, KIPP and other charter schools existed on the edges of the public consciousness and the world of educational research. As a result, we have a great deal of advocacy and media about KIPP, but far too little scholarship and research. Just as Pallas (2009b) exposed the false claim of "miracle" about the HCZ, we should be skeptical of claims of any high-flying school—since we have a long history of deflated claims of "miracle" from Bush's "Texas miracle" to Duncan's "Chicago miracle." In Strauss's blog, Kahlenberg (2011a) addressed KIPP schools because Strauss and fellow WaPo colleague Jay Matthews disagreed about KIPP, with Matthews an advocate and Strauss a skeptic.

Kahlenberg (2011a) examined a central criticism of KIPP schools, attrition rates. When most people compare types of schools—charter with public or private with public—they fail to consider the significant difference between schools that can and do select, charter and private, and schools that must enroll and serve any and all students. Kahlenberg identifies one of those distinctions:

> The big difference between KIPP and regular public schools, however, is that whereas struggling students come and go at regular schools, at KIPP, students leave but very few new children enter. Having few new entering students is an enormous advantage not only because low-scoring transfer students are kept out but also because in the later grades, KIPP students are surrounded only by successful peers who are the most committed to the program. (n.p.)

When examining KIPP schools and their success as well as relative success compared to public schools, we must keep in mind that many of the differences between KIPP and public schools may have more to do with creating the outcome differences than the pillars or signed commitments; as Kahlenberg concludes:

> It may well be, in fact, that high attrition rates are a key explanation for KIPP's success in raising test scores. When KIPP tried to take over a regular public school—where the students are not self-selected, but are assigned to the school; and where students not only leave, but large number of students enter—KIPP abandoned the field after just two years. KIPP long ago realized that what we charge regular public schools with doing is far more difficult than what KIPP seeks to do. (n.p.)

Kahlenberg's (2011a) detailing of KIPP attrition concerns led to a reply, interestingly from KIPP's Chief Research and Innovation Officer as well as the Public Affairs Officer. Cowan and Mancini (2011) challenged narrow claims by Kahlenberg, high attrition rates and student enrollment after sixth grade, and focused primarily on arguing that KIPP schools are evolving and improving:

> As KIPP continues to grow, moving from start-up to sustainability, we have seen significantly reduced attrition rates and had success enrolling students at all grade levels. We remain focused on continuing to improve in these areas so we can set ever more students on the path to college and a better future. (n.p.)

The rebuttal, then, does more to make both subtle and detailed arguments that allow KIPP to further promote itself through the media; in some ways, Kahlenberg's criticisms created a win-win for KIPP.

Similar to the CREDO/Hoxby debate about charters broadly (Thomas, 2010a), this mini-KIPP debate includes a response to the rebuttal. Kahlenberg (2011b) offers a solid and foundational clarification about how we must place KIPP evidence in the context of the larger education reform debate:

> KIPP schools are on the whole impressive, but they are often held up as proof that poverty and segregation are "excuses" for failure, rather than significant barriers to high student achievement. After all, most students in KIPP schools are poor and the schools are both economically and racially segregated. If KIPP can produce high levels of achievement, why can't regular public schools–through hard work, extended learning time, and a non-unionized workforce–achieve the same results? (n.p.)

Ultimately, this is the crux of the KIPP/charter school claim, leading Kahlenberg to offer Cowan and Mancini three further questions that end with—

> If KIPP wants to put the self-selection, attrition, and intake issues to rest, why doesn't it simply start taking over regular public schools, educating the students who happen to live nearby, including those who move in during the course of middle school? (Kahlenberg, 2011b, n.p.)

The answers to both can/does KIPP achieve what public schools can't and why doesn't KIPP simply take over public schools and do that under the same conditions as public schools are the knowledge that does lead to power, but that power is to unmask KIPP and charter schools as false prophets of miracles.

Ultimately, Miron, Urschel, and Saxton (2011) present some of the answers Kahlenberg requested of KIPP:

> To date, most research on KIPP has focused on outcomes (i.e., student achievement). This study does not question the body of evidence on student achievement gains made in KIPP schools. Instead of looking at outcomes,

this study examines two critical *inputs*: students and funding. Understanding more about these inputs allows for a better understanding of how KIPP works and whether the model can or should be replicated. (n.p.)

Part of the success of the public relations coming from KIPP has been the focus on simple outcomes, similar to the same success found by the new reformers who demonize U.S. public education by offering simplistic international test comparisons that rank the U.S. low (See Bracey, 2008; Riddile, 2010).

Setting aside the real and disturbing concerns I have for "no excuses" ideologies (which I will examine further below), that KIPP schools show improvements for students in certain types of outcomes is hard to debate, but a more important question seems to be how and why those outcomes look so impressive. Miron et al. (2011) offer three key reasons: "selective entry of students," "high rate of student attrition with nonreplacement," and "high levels of funding" (n.p.).

And this is important: If public schools are miserable failures due to some qualities within the control of those running those schools, and if charter schools such as KIPP have the answer to reform those public schools, then KIPP is potentially an ideal crucible for seeking the answers needed to serve better children from poverty in our country. But, Miron et al. (2011) reveal that KIPP's outcomes are strongly tied to controlling who attends the schools—which public schools cannot do—and additional private funding that reaches as much as $6,500 per student over state funding; these are conditions not possible in the public school system, leading Miron et al. (2011) to conclude:

> KIPP's only effort to take over a traditional public school—with a representative range of students and with the responsibility to serve all students who came and went during and between school years—ended in failure after only two years. This short-lived experiment with Cole Middle School in Denver speaks loudly about the viability of the KIPP model for public schools. (n.p.)

KIPP, like the HCZ, is no viable solution to broad public education reform—and certainly no miracle. If we fail to acknowledge this fact, we will miss the opportunity to use KIPP to focus on the weight of poverty instead of allowing the KIPP debate to once again reinforce ignoring poverty as a mere excuse.

THE (SHIFTING) TRUTH ABOUT CHARTER SCHOOLS

"There is no compelling evidence that investments in parenting classes, health services, nutritional programs, and community improvement in general have appreciable effects on student achievement in schools in the U.S.," concludes Whitehurst and Croft (2010) in their appraisal of Canada's HCZ, adding: "Indeed there is considerable evidence in addition to the results from the present study that questions the return on such investments for academic achievement" (n.p.).

Whitehurst and Croft's (2010) study for the Brown Center on Education Policy at Brookings prompted a *New York Times* article to reveal "Mr. Canada and his charter schools have struggled with the same difficulties faced by other urban schools, even as they outspend them" (Otterman, 2010). However, just about a year and half earlier, Brooks (2009), also writing in the *New York Times*, had sparked the claims of "miracle" surrounding Canada's HCZ which fueled a series of media outlets praising these charter schools, including "President Obama institut[ing] a Promise Neighborhoods Initiative intended to replicate the HCZ in 20 cities across the country. The program received a $10 million appropriation from Congress in 2010, under which 339 communities applied to the U.S. Department of Education for planning grants to create Promise Neighborhoods" (Whitehurst & Croft, 2010, n.p.).

From the President to Secretary of Education Duncan to Oprah and *60 Minutes* to the controversial *Waiting for "Superman"* and the media blitz surrounding that documentary, the charter movement has been experiencing an unprecedented level of support across the political and popular spectrum. Along with Whitehurst and Croft's (2010) cautions, however, other cracks in the move toward charter schools have been expressed, although not nearly as well publicized as the praise.

In an excerpt from the book, *Ohio's Education Reform Challenges: Lessons from the Front Lines*, included in *Education Next*, by Terry Ryan, Michael B. Lafferty, and Chester Finn Jr., Finn and Ryan (2010) admit:

> Sobered and a bit battered, Fordham continues as an authorizer of Ohio charter schools ... and a vigorous participant in the state's larger education-policy debates.... Meanwhile, we've learned a lot about how much harder it is to walk the walk of education reform than simply to talk the talk, and about how the most robust of theories are apt to soften and melt in the furnace of actual experience. (n.p.)

What, then, is the truth behind the shifting support for charter schools? The HCZ is a miracle or not? KIPP does what public schools can't for children in poverty or not?

- "Charter school" as a term and a concept has been co-opted by education reformers who support school choice and market forces over public education. The Whitehurst and Croft (2010) arguments against the HCZ being cost effective is framed against KIPP charter schools as an ideal: "There are 3 KIPP schools represented in the graph. All score higher than the HCZ Promise Academy" (n.p.). In short, charter schools of a certain kind, quasi-private schools that take tax funding and private donations to implement "no excuses" ideology, are welcomed *by the new reformers* as the next phase of school choice initiatives that have failed when promoting vouchers and tuition tax credits.

- Charter school advocacy is a mechanism for promoting the claims that schools alone can reform society, and thus a mechanism for discounting the impact of poverty on the learning and lives of children. Whitehurst and Croft (2010) proceed to discount efforts such as the HCZ and traditional federal programs such as Head Start: "In contrast to disappointing results for Broader, Bolder initiatives, there is a large and growing body of evidence that schools themselves can have significant impacts on student achievement" (n.p.). Corporate reformers are fully invested in branding public education as a failure while simultaneously arguing that schools can overcome social forces, despite evidence to the contrary (Krashen, 2010).

- Charter schools are often closely associated with alternatives to traditional teacher certification and an avenue to circumventing teachers unions. Teach for America (TfA) in charter schools is one such alliance, including being represented in *Waiting for "Superman"* and standing to reap significant boosts if federal policy helps fund and support more charter schools with faculties drawn largely from TfA recruits. Focusing on bad teachers and demonizing teachers unions as the status quo have roots in corporate agendas, not school reform (Hu, 2010).

- Charter schools also help promote "no excuses" ideology ("new paternalism" [Whitman, 2008; Landsberg, 2009]) and deficit perspectives of children living in poverty (Dudley-Marling, 2007) that perpetuate classist dynamics in the schools, thus exacerbating the inequities of children's lives in the schools themselves. These corrosive ideologies are further wrapped in compelling rhetoric such as the "soft bigotry of low expectations" (Skeels, 2011b, n.p.), despite the practices themselves institutionalizing racism, classism, and elitism.

By supporting charter school initiatives that reinforce corporate agendas that seek to hide social failures such as poverty, the Brookings Institution and the Thomas B. Fordham Institute are unwittingly exposing the mask that is charter school advocacy because their research and admissions about the complexity of educational reform confirm what we know to be the truth about charter schools—they are no better than public schools:

> And yet, this study [from CREDO] reveals in unmistakable terms that, in the aggregate, charter students are not faring as well as their TPS [traditional public school] counterparts. Further, tremendous variation in academic quality among charters is the norm, not the exception. The problem of quality is the most pressing issue that charter schools and their supporters face. (Center for Research on Education Outcomes [CREDO], 2009, n.p.)

THE GREAT CHARTER COMPROMISE

The two strongest voices in the educational reform debate—accountability advocates and competition advocates—have now overlapped after thirty years of tension by embracing charter schools. While that overlap could have signaled a powerful compromise that would have served children, schools, and society well, it actually highlights that both positions are flawed. And the apparent truce involving charter schools also reveals that the most powerful force in our economy and our government is corporate ideology.

The loudest voice in the popular discourse about schools remains the bureaucratic political force that runs public schools. Despite decades of their tired refrain—higher standards, more rigorous tests, greater accountability—the accountability advocates cannot admit that they are ignoring the true hurdles to better schools, poverty, and offering fruitless remedies to the historical failures of public education. However, few differences exist in the discourse or practices among the Obama administration and the previous four presidential administrations. For example, as I noted earlier, the blueprint for educational reform under Obama makes this compelling but misguided claim: "Of all the work that occurs at every level of our education system, the interaction between teacher and student is the primary determinant of student success" (U.S. Department of Education, 2010, n.p.).

The Obama administration, led by Duncan, has not wavered from focusing on teachers and schools as the sole avenue to social reform, the traditional bureaucratic approach to education reform, but their silver-bullet and false argument about the power of teachers is parallel to the equally compelling but flawed call for competition to cure the ills of educational attainment by all students. Yet, among choice and competition advocates, we have some evidence of hope because, unlike accountability advocates, the proponents of competition have begun to make concessions about the inherent weaknesses in their claims.

Recently, a long-time advocate of both accountability and competition, Diane Ravitch (2010a), rejected both as effective solutions to educational reform. Ravitch's change of perspective and the concessions made by Finn and Ryan on behalf of Fordham, noted above, expose the failure of ideology against evidence, but they also reveal the power of ideology among the new reformers who refuse to acknowledge any evidence that works against their agendas.

In 2010, the evidence clearly shows that neither accountability nor competition—specifically charter schools (CREDO, 2009)—fulfills in reality what their advocates claim in theory. What is missing from the two loudest voices in the educational debate? A nuanced and evidence-based perspective of poverty's primary influence on student achievement and solutions offered to address those social failures.

And while charter schools are currently being embraced by both camps—including Obama's administration endorsing the HCZ and think-tanks such as Fordham praising charter organizations such as KIPP—they are failing for the same reasons accountability and competition have been failing for decades. As the Fordham Foundation discovered, simply offering charter schools will not overcome the complex sources of educational failures. But, we do have a third voice that is rarely heard—a voice that calls for a recognition that social forces must be addressed along with school reform in order to provide more students with the opportunities that public schools can offer a free people.

Instead of advocacy, what we need is a nuanced understanding of education and educational reform in the context of social realities. Consider the conclusions we can draw about KIPP schools from the research that challenges the simplistic claim that a KIPP model could save public schools: KIPP, and other charter experiments, show some success, but some failures as well. In short, charter schools, private schools, and public schools all present a range of success and failure, most often tied to the socioeconomic status of the children.

When the Obama administration supports the HCZ while ignoring that those charter schools include virtually no special needs or ELL students, when think-tanks release advocacy reports that avoid and then fail basic peer-review, when accountability advocates and competition advocates repeatedly ignore the power of poverty to negatively impact the lives of children, including their academic achievement, we are doomed to failure as the status quo. Now, if the accountability reformers can discover the humility being embraced by some of the competition reformers, the calls to address social failures, poverty in the lives of children, may be heard once both corporate-driven advocacy camps stop talking and start listening.

SHIFTING TALKING POINTS AMONG SCHOOL CHOICE ADVOCATES

Few metaphors could be more appropriate than the "invisible hand" for free market forces, and the constantly shifting school choice movement over the past 30 years (paralleling the accountability era spurred by A Nation at Risk) reflects how choice advocates are driven by ideology and *faith* in market forces regardless of evidence. And what is expendable in that fervent pursuit of market forces? Those who have lost in the economic system advocates embrace—people trapped in poverty, especially the children living in poverty that cannot possibly be of their making.

As noted at the beginning of this chapter, Lubienski and Weitzel (2008) expose the shifting nature of school choice advocacy. In the 1980s and 1990s, before a substantial body of research had emerged, vouchers were heralded as the panacea for a failing public school system. Once the shine wore off those lofty claims—since research shows little to no academic gains driven by any choice initiatives—school choice advocates began to change claims and approaches, attempting to stay at least one step ahead of the evidence throughout the process.

The evolution of the school choice advocacy talking points has included the following, in roughly the order in which they surfaced in the advocacy reports by think tanks and the media from the 1980s until 2011:

- Public education is a failure because it is a monopoly, and market forces can and will eradicate the problems posed by a monopoly. Vouchers are the solution to public education failures because they will force public schools to compete with superior private schools. Subsequently, vouchers proved to be unpopular with the public, and private schools were revealed to be little different in effectiveness than public schools when student populations were taken into account (Braun, Jenkins, & Grigg, 2006; Lubienski & Lubienski, 2006; Wenglinsky, 2007).

- When the evidence mounted against vouchers, next in line was tuition tax credits. Tuition tax credits proved to be even less appealing than vouchers, so next was public school choice—a pale option but one that did help lay the groundwork for charter schools. Evidence from Milwaukee, Minnesota, and Florida shows that widespread choice and choice tied to accountability have neither raised achievement nor actually spurred any real competition (Belfield, 2006; Bell, 2005; Dodenhoff, 2007; Institute on Race and Poverty, 2008; Witte, Carlson, & Lavery, 2008).

- Then, how about charter schools? And let's be sure to address children and families in poverty. And parents really are happy when given choice. And choice might raise graduation rates. The choice refrains became more frantic and disjointed throughout the 1990s and 2000s.

- But vouchers/choice "do no harm!" (Lubienski & Weitzel, 2008).
- Currently, the argument is philosophical: Why would anyone want to deny choice to people in poverty, the same choice that middle- and upper-class people have?

That is where we currently stand in the school choice advocacy discourse that drives a substantial part of the new reformers' plans. The newest talking points are "do no harm" and that people opposing vouchers want to deny choice to people living in poverty. And throughout the school choice debate, ironically, the choice advocates shift back and forth about the validity of the research—think tank reports that are pro-choice and the leading school choice researchers tend to avoid peer-review and rail against peer-reviews (usually charging that the reviews are ideological and driven by their funding) while simultaneously using terms such as "objective," "empirical," and "econometrics" to give their reports and arguments the appearance of scholarship.

But, if anyone makes any effort to scratch beneath the surface of school choice advocacy reports, she/he will find some telling details:

> In education, readers should beware of research emanating from the Hoover Institution at Stanford University, the Heritage Foundation, the Manhattan Institute, the Heartland Institute, the Mackinac Center, the Center for Education Reform, the Thomas B. Fordham Foundation, the American Enterprise Institute, the Paul Peterson group at Harvard, and, soon, the Department of Education Reform at the University of Arkansas. Arkansas is home to the Walton family, and much Wal-Mart money has already made its way to the University of Arkansas, $300 million in 2002 alone. The new department, to be headed by Jay P. Greene, currently at the Manhattan Institute, will no doubt benefit from the Walton presence. The family's largesse was estimated to approach $1 billion per year (Hopkins 2004), and before his death in an airplane crash, John Walton was perhaps the nation's most energetic advocate of school vouchers. (Bracey, 2006, p. xvi)

School choice and charter schools may, in fact, hold some promises for reforming education since "choice" is central to human agency and empowerment. But the school choice/charter school movement and their advocates are the least likely avenues for us ever realizing what school choice has to offer because the advocates are primarily driven by ideology and funding coming from sources that have intentions that have little to do with universal public education for free and empowered people.

And the growing evidence that corporate charter schools as the latest choice mechanism *are causing harm*—in terms of segregation and stratification of student populations (Baker & Ferris, 2011; Frankenberg et al., 2011; Fuller, 2011; Miron & Urschel, 2010; Miron et al., 2010; Miron et al., 2011)—is reason for alarm for all people along the spectrum of school reform and school choice. If school choice/charter school advocates stick to the talking-points script and will not acknowledge the overwhelming evidence that out-of-school factors determine student outcomes, that evidence is mounting that choice stratifies schools, and that evidence on *how school is delivered* (public, private, charter) is mixed and similar among all types of schooling, then that advocacy isn't worth our time and isn't contributing to a vibrant and open debate that could help move us toward school reform that benefits each student and our larger society.

WHY ADVOCACY AND
MARKET FORCES FAIL EDUCATION REFORM

After a piece I wrote confronting Bill Gates and the market/corporate-based approach to education reform (Thomas, 2011i), I received several responses that are typical of the mainstream faith in market forces embraced among both conservatives and liberals, a faith that allows most market advocates to ignore the realities about poverty. One e-mail claimed the person had been swayed by my arguments against merit pay for teachers and charter schools, but offered further, "In many cases, schools do not see themselves as businesses."

I responded that education should not view itself as a business; in fact, the growing body of research on choice, competition, and market forces as tools for education reform shows that the market hypothesis fails in reality. Further, the rise in calls for charter schools as a panacea for ailing public education exposes another flaw in market reforms—advocacy. Recently, I completed and published a book confronting through a critical lens the idealized view of choice, specifically parental choice, because both the left and the right tend to be trapped within an idealized faith in parents as consumers. A close look at think tanks reveals that market-force advocacy is both powerful and resistant to evidence.

Nationally, The Friedman Foundation for Educational Choice states directly that the ideals of its founders, Milton and Rose Friedman, drive the foundation's entire education reform agenda: "They knew that when schools are forced to compete to keep the children they educate, all parties win" (2011, n.p.). In my home state of South Carolina, a consistent voice in the education debate is South Carolinians for Responsible Government (SCRG), an advocacy group that promotes school choice. Like The Foundation for Educational Choice, SCRG openly promotes its market-based agenda for school reform, but a careful look at the basis for their positions reveals that the evidence for their claims centers on a report from 2001—a decade of research ignored while the agenda still attempts the appearance of being research-based.

Think-tank advocacy focusing on education has increased over the past two decades, and although the think tanks have developed a strategy that involves creating the appearance of scholarship and research, the reality is that think tanks remain ideology-driven, not evidence-based (Welner et al., 2010). Consider the dynamics surrounding a comprehensive study of Milwaukee public school choice (Dodenhoff, 2007)—one of the largest and longest experiments in market forces for school reform in the country. The study comes from the Wisconsin Policy Research Institute (WPRI), which promotes itself as Wisconsin's free-market think tank.

When the study was released in 2007, WPRI fellow David Dodenhoff (2007) concluded:

> Taken as a whole, these numbers indicate significant limits on the capacity of public school choice and parental involvement to improve school quality and student performance within MPS [Milwaukee Public Schools]. Parents simply do not appear sufficiently engaged in available choice opportunities or their children's educational activities to ensure the desired outcomes.... Relying on public school choice and parental involvement to reclaim MPS may be a distraction from the hard work of fixing the district's schools. Recognizing this, the question is whether the district, its schools, and its supporters in Madison are prepared to embrace more radical reforms. Given the high stakes involved, district parents should insist on nothing less. (n.p.)

The media report was just as condemning of the evidence about parental choice and market forces fulfilling their promise of reforming public schools (and surprised about the source of that evidence):

> A study being released today suggests that school choice isn't a powerful tool for driving educational improvement in Milwaukee Public Schools. But more surprising than the conclusion is the organization issuing the study: the Wisconsin Policy Research Institute, a conservative think tank that has supported school choice for almost two decades, when Milwaukee became the nation's premier center for trying the idea. The institute is funded in large part by the Milwaukee-based Lynde and Harry Bradley Foundation, an advocate of school choice. (Borsuk, 2007, n.p.)

While, as I will examine below, the conclusion of this study should not be surprising since it matches what the growing evidence shows, it is key here to note the response by WPRI, both in the publishing of the research and in their press releases.

In the "Report from the Senior Fellow" prefacing Dodenhoff's study, George Lightbourne (2007) offers the following contradictory comments:

> The report you are reading did not yield the results we had hoped to find ... [Dodenhoff] discovered that there are realistic limits on the degree to which parental involvement can drive market-based reform in Milwaukee.... The message from the study is that educational leaders and policy makers must continue to strive to increase parental choice and parental involvement. (n.p.)

Further, on the WPRI web site, Lightbourne condemns the media's representation of the study—claiming that the evidence does not refute market forces because it addresses only public school choice—and makes this telling statement: "So that there is no misunderstanding, WPRI is unhesitant in supporting school choice. School choice is working and should be improved and expanded. School choice is good for Milwaukee's children" (2007, n.p.).

In short, regardless of the evidence, think tanks have advocacy agendas that are unwavering; they have a constituency that they *must speak to* and not confront. Many of those think tanks are committed to school reform through market-based policies; thus, the entire education reform debate is heavily biased toward market dynamics that are supported by ideology, but not necessarily by the weight of evidence.

Many think tanks, corporate leaders and politicians work within a market paradigm. Often, sensing the need to appear evidence-based, school choice advocates, like SCRG, cherry-pick data to give their advocacy the appearance of science. Most of that pro-choice evidence is selected from the 1990s and around 2000 or 2001, as the evidence was first building about school choice—evidence that was often created and promoted by think tanks advocating for vouchers. In the past decade, however, the patterns found in the data on choice of all types reinforce the skeptical conclusion drawn by Dodenhoff (2007) concerning Milwaukee's experiment with public school choice. Those patterns include the following:

- When parents are offered choice, they tend to make their choices based on concerns about issues other than academics, and they also often fail to participate at all in the choice offered. Choice appears to increase stratification of schools by socioeconomic factors without impacting academics positively (Bell, 2005; Bifulco, Ladd, & Ross, 2008; Cohen-Zada & Sander, 2007; d'Entremont, & Gulosino, 2008; Dodenhoff, 2007; Elaqua, 2005, 2006; Institute on Race and Poverty, 2008; Ladd, Fiske, & Ruijs, 2009; Watson & Ryan, 2009; Witte, Carlson, & Lavery, 2008).
- Although complicated and difficult to identify, choice does not appear to impact achievement positively, either for those students experiencing choice or for those students left in existing public

schools (Ballou, Teasley, & Zeidner, 2006; Belfield, 2006; Carr & Ritter, 2007; Chemsak, 2008; Elacqua, 2009; Esposito & Cobb, 2008; Gibbons, Machin, & Silva, 2006; Imberman, 2007; Lai, 2007; Ni, 2007; Rouse & Barrow, 2008; Wolf et al., 2009; Wylie, 2006; Zimmer & Buddin, 2005). In the most comprehensive consideration of the existing evidence on vouchers, Cecilia Elena Rouse and Lisa Barrow (2008) frame their conclusions as follows:

> Keeping ... limitations in mind, the best research to date finds relatively small achievement gains for students offered education vouchers, most of which are not statistically different from zero. Further, what little evidence exists about the likely impact of a large-scale voucher program on the students who remain in the public schools is at best mixed, and the research designs of these studies do not necessarily allow the researchers to attribute any observed positive gains solely to school vouchers and competitive forces. The evidence to date from other forms of school choice is not much more promising. As such, while there may be other reasons to implement school voucher programs, one should not anticipate large academic gains from this seemingly inexpensive reform. (p. 37)

• Choice fails to create competition for traditional public schools; therefore, choice and competition proponents may be able to point to this research as evidence that competition hasn't been shown to be ineffective, but that choice has failed to create competition (Buddin & Zimmer, 2005; Dodenhoff, 2007; Wylie, 2006).

These patterns are reflected in dozens and dozens of studies, most peer-reviewed and many coming from school choice advocates such as the work from Dodenhoff (2007) for a pro-choice think tank. With the evidence offering powerful reasons to place education reform outside of market dynamics, continued support for and shifting calls for market-based and corporate reform in a variety of forms suggest that market-based advocates for school reform are bound by ideology and not evidence—and as a result, their advocacy will continue to ignore poverty, marginalize those living in poverty, or both.

Market dynamics impose onto all institutions functioning within that paradigm the need for advocacy—building customers through promoting the institution, as is the case with the rising corporate charter school movement. Advocacy is often the enemy of transparency and truth; thus, some fields are best outside the market paradigm. Consider the field of medicine.

Throughout the 1970s, 1980s and 1990s, doctors prescribed greater and greater doses of antibiotics, rarely identifying whether the illness required those antibiotics or not (antibiotics work against bacteria, but not viruses such as the common cold). The result was an increase in the development of antibiotic-resistant bacteria, the most well known being methicillin-resistant staphylococcus aureus (MRSA). The dynamic at the heart of much of this problem was doctors allowing patients to behave as consumers. In other words, *doctors abdicated their expertise to the demands of the patients as consumers.*

Doctors found that patients gravitated to doctors who would indiscriminately prescribe antibiotics (patients with common colds wanted antibiotics after spending money on a doctor visit)—many thus acquiesced to that consumer pressure for the sake of keeping a vibrant (and profitable) practice. The medical profession has responded, issuing policies that warn against the misuse of antibiotics. Stuart Levy, in an introduction of a report on the use of antibiotics, explains:

> Increasing awareness of the problem of antibiotic resistance in the community and the threat that resistant bacteria may pose is a key first step in addressing this problem. Training health care practitioners to identify potential pathogens accurately and to treat them with effective agents and appropriate regimens are important additional steps. *Patient education is also crucial in ensuring that the public understands and participates in efforts to control the spread of antibiotic resistant bacteria* [emphasis added]. (DeBellis & Zdanawicz, 2000, p. 2)

The failure of the medical profession to maintain its expertise against the pressure of consumer/market forces reveals a central problem with applying market-based reform to education. Consumer-driven dynamics (think parental choice in school reform) allows the consumers to trump the expertise of any given field—regardless of the expertise of those consumers.

Further, once the consumer is recognized as the driving force in the field, those organizations wanting customers can distort the market through advocacy—regardless of the outcomes; note that the medical profession has attempted to regain its expertise for the good of all with limited success (Ong et al., 2007). The rise and damage done by the tobacco industry is another extreme but not uncommon example.

And here, we come face to face with the rise of corporate charter school advocacy as the newest version of school choice promoted by market force advocates—an advocacy that acknowledges poverty, but in so doing, places that poverty within a "no excuses" context against the invisible hand of market forces. In my home state, the news media carries consistent news stories and letters to the editor promoting the success of this or that charter school; the claims are often simplistic, suggesting causational relationships between charter schools and outcomes without the evidence of making such claims. The current evidence on charter schools showing charter schools failing to outperform public schools on balance and creating many equity and stratification problems remains mostly ignored (CREDO, 2009; Frankenberg, Siegel-Hawley, & Wang, 2011).

The think-tank advocacy process is chilling but effective: make claims through the media and move fast to the next thing before anyone has time to consider the evidence. Yes, the media is complicit here (see Chapter 3), because we know that think tanks and advocacy receive disproportionately more coverage without scholarly scrutiny when compared to university-based and peer-reviewed studies (Molnar, 2001; Yettick, 2009). Over the past two decades, market-based calls for school reform have moved from vouchers to public school choice to tuition tax credits and, now, to charter schools. The basic claim remains while the format shifts, but the evidence remains the same—in direct contrast to the ideology.

We have faced the "Texas Miracle," the "Chicago Miracle," and the "Harlem Miracle," all proving to be misleading advocacy and then fully deflated against the weight of evidence (evidence given less exposure in the media than the original claims of "miracle"). But the media and the public remain enamored with the promise of choice and competition despite the evidence to the contrary (Pontari & Rasmussen, 2009). So, throughout the Obama administration, we have been bombarded with *Waiting for "Superman"*-type media hype surrounding charter schools, the need to fire bad teachers and the scourge of teachers' unions on our schools. As well, *60 Minutes* entered the waters and presented a jumbled tribute to The Equity Project in Manhattan, which has received media attention for promises of paying teachers $125,000 a year. What was buried in the glitz and the praise?

> But then we get to the tough part. The actual outcomes after their first year in operation. "The results were disappointing. On average, other schools in the District scored better than TEP."
>
> Principal Vanderhoek responds, "We don't have a magic wand. We are not going to take kids who are scoring below grade level and bring them up in a year." (Cody, 2011a, n.p.)

Once again, the caution of evidence—*advocacy is the enemy of transparency and truth*. Like medicine, then, education and education reform will continue to fail if placed inside the corrosive dynamics of market forces that ignore and marginalize social inequity. Instead, the reform of education must include the expertise of educators who are not bound to advocating for customers, but encouraged, rewarded and praised for offering the public the transparent truth about what faces us and what outcomes are the result of any and every endeavor to provide children the opportunity to learn as a member of a free and empowered people.

Education "miracles" do not exist and market forces are neither perfect nor universal silver bullets for any problem—these are conclusions made when we are free of the limitations of advocacy and dedicated to the weight of evidence, even when it challenges our beliefs.

NO EXCUSES FOR "NO EXCUSES" CHARTER SCHOOLS

After game one of the 2011 NBA Finals, pundits began to clamor to reappraise the status of the Miami Heat, a team nearly equally loved and despised for the same reason—the acquisition of LeBron James. But in the closing seconds of game two, Dirk Nowitzki made a spinning, driving lay up with his splinted left hand to seal a huge fourth-quarter comeback, spurring Gregg Doyel (2011) at CBSSports.com to write a column titled "Heat return to their smug ways and Mavs make them pay." Consider some of Doyel's comments. Frame this about the Heat—"Ultimately, this was everything we have come to expect from these fascinating, infuriating Miami Heat: Hollywood as hell. Damn good. But a bit too full of themselves" (n.p.)—with this comment about Nowitzki:

> Dirk Nowitzki is the anti-Heat—a quiet, humble, mentally tough SOB. He played with a splint on the middle finger of his left hand, and for more than 45 minutes he didn't play well. But he scored Dallas' final nine points, seven in the last minute, four with his left hand. That game-winning layup? He created it, then finished it, with his left hand. It probably hurt, but Nowitzki had more important things to worry about than pain. He had a game to win. (Doyel, 2011, n.p.)

When I read this column, I immediately thought about a recent column by Dana Goldstein (2011), "Integration and the 'No Excuses' Charter School Movement." In her piece, she examines "no excuses" ideologies connected with the new charter school movement: "That said, there are some troubling questions about whether the most politically popular charter school model—the 'No Excuses' model popularized by KIPP and embraced by Moskowitz's Success Charter Network—is palatable to middle-class and affluent parents" (Goldstein, 2011, n.p.). Later in her essay, Goldstein (2011) makes one comment that continues to trouble me: "What seems clear is that the 'No Excuses' model is not for everyone, and presents particular challenges to parents who are accustomed to the schedules and social routines of high-quality neighborhood public schools" (n.p.).

It is the intersection of the column about game two of the 2011 NBA finals and Goldstein's article on "no excuses" charter schools that reveals the powerful influence of middle-class norms on every aspect of American society. Throughout the NBA playoffs this year, the story no one is talking about has been the narratives following Nowitzki and LeBron James.

Nowitzki, a German-born centerpiece of the Dallas Mavericks, has been repeatedly compared to Larry Bird, one of the NBA all-time greats who shares with Nowitzki an important quality—race—which appears to translate into a default assessment—working-class ethos, the ability to rise above limitations through hard work (the personification of middle-class myths).

James, while often championed as the "next Michael Jordan," has increasingly been compared to Magic Johnson, the arch-rival of Bird from an era decades in the past. Also like the Magic comparison, James now carries the "Hollywood" label—and that means too much talent and not enough humility, not enough effort.

And as the narratives about the Heat and the Mavericks (let's not ignore the coincidental symbolism in the team names and the geographical significance of Miami beach against Texas) continue to play out, we read the subtext of class and race that drives not what happens on the court but how the media and public craft those narratives as a response to the players.

Culturally, Americans *want* Nowitzki and the Mavericks to win because that proves American values right, the triumph of the middle-class norm. And we hope that a Nowitzki/Maverick win will go one step further by putting James and the Heat in their place, creating the ultimate personification of the middle-class norm—James's talent plus Nowitzki's humble working-class persona.

And this is what troubles me about Goldstein's (2011) sentence from above: "What seems clear is that the 'No Excuses' model is not for everyone" (n.p.). This leaves open an endorsement for continuing to champion "no excuses" schools as long as they target children of color, children trapped in poverty, and children struggling against being English language learners. Middle-class and affluent children don't need "no excuses" schools, the unspoken message goes, because they are already on board; they are a part of the normalization of middle-class myths of who people should be, what people should say, and how people should behave.

We should not be contemplating for whom "no excuses" schools are appropriate because "no excuses" schools are not appropriate for any children in a free society. "No excuses" schools are the worst type of classism, and they are the ultimate reduction of education to enculturation.

"No excuses" ideology denies human agency (Goodman, 2011), human dignity, perpetuating a Western caste system of knowing one's place. Yes, as a society, we want LeBron James, Dwayne Wade, and Chris Bosh to sit down and shut up, but we also want *some* children to learn this as well. The elite remain elite as long as the rest remain compliant.

As I have identified earlier, Rich (2001) fears that what is "rendered unspeakable, [is] thus unthinkable" (p. 150). And Ayers (2001) recognizes the silencing purposes of schools:

> In school, a high value is placed on quiet: "Is everything quiet?" the super-intendent asks the principal, and the principal the teacher, and the teacher the child. If everything is quiet, it is assumed that all is well. This is why many normal children—considering what kind of intelligence is expected and what will be rewarded here—become passive, quiet, obedient, dull. The environment practically demands it. (p. 51)

The "no excuses" miracle schools are no miracles at all. They are mirages carefully crafted to reinforce cultural myths. They are nightmares for childhood and the basic rights of life, liberty, and the pursuit of happiness. They are tragic examples of allowing the ends to justify the means.

If we are a people who embrace human freedom and agency, if we are a people who believe all people are created equal, if we are a people who trust the power of education as central to that freedom and equality, then there simply is no excuse for perpetuating "no excuses" charter schools that are designed to squelch the possibility of LeBron James-type agency among more people and throughout our society, and not just safely within the confines of a basketball court.

In Chapter 5, I turn to the new reformers' use of the "bad" teacher mantra to keep the education discussion away from poverty, but here, the rise of the corporate charter school movement as a tool to acknowledge poverty by marginalizing poverty is possibly one of the most insidious and corrosive strategies of corporate school reform and the corporate take-over of America.

KIPP and HCZ charter schools have commanded a tremendous amount of praise from the media and the political/corporate elite because of simplistic claims that these schools have produced student outcomes that public schools have failed to fulfill. These claims work because they speak to deep and powerful ideologies at the heart of middle-class America—regardless of the social class of any specific American: rugged individualism, pulling one's self up by the bootstraps, competition, choice, and deficit views of poverty and people living in poverty.

In her challenge to the myth of the charter school, Ravitch (2010c) concludes by addressing charter advocacy, poverty, international comparisons, and ultimately the enduring value of universal public education:

It bears mentioning that nations with high-performing school systems—whether Korea, Singapore, Finland, or Japan—have succeeded not by privatizing their schools or closing those with low scores, but by strengthening the education profession. They also have less poverty than we do. Fewer than 5 percent of children in Finland live in poverty, as compared to 20 percent in the United States. Those who insist that poverty doesn't matter, that only teachers matter, prefer to ignore such contrasts.... In the final moments of *Waiting for "Superman,"* the children and their parents assemble in auditoriums in New York City, Washington, D.C., Los Angeles, and Silicon Valley, waiting nervously to see if they will win the lottery.... First, I thought to myself that the charter operators were cynically using children as political pawns in their own campaign to promote their cause. (Gail Collins in *The New York Times* had a similar reaction and wondered why they couldn't just send the families a letter in the mail instead of subjecting them to public rejection.) Second, I felt an immense sense of gratitude to the much-maligned American public education system, where no one has to win a lottery to gain admission. (n.p.)

In the U.S., we are faced with the moral obligation to acknowledge and address the growing inequity in our society—an inequity that disproportionately impacts children—while also reforming our education system, not so that schools alone can change our culture but to insure that our school stop perpetuating the inequities of that society.

CHARTER SCHOOLS, POVERTY, AND RESEGREGATION: ANNOTATED BIBLIOGRAPHIES

The corporate charter school movement endorsed by the new reformers presents a complex picture about universal public education, poverty, race, and cultural commitments. To claim education "miracle" regarding any of these schools is misleading and careless; to ignore the new charter movement or to focus solely on student outcomes from these schools is inexcusable as well. With the rise of charter schools, we have a rise in scholarly commentary and research also.

Below is an initial listing of key works that help us identify what these charter schools are, who these schools enroll, and how those students and families are treated once children are accepted. Ultimately, for me, student outcomes do not justify the racial and socioeconomic stratification of these schools and the "no excuses"/"new paternalism" that these schools advocate.

- Baker, B. D., & Ferris, R. (2011). *Adding up the spending: Fiscal disparities and philanthropy among New York City charter schools.* Boulder, CO:

National Education Policy Center. Retrieved April 26, 2011 from http://nepc.colorado.edu/publication/NYC-charter-disparities

One contradiction of charter school advocacy is the claim that funding doesn't matter or is excessive at the public school level, but that many charter schools benefit from private donations or funding *in addition* to accepting tax dollars for running those charter schools. This study raises cautions about the wide variety of funding found in New York city charter schools. The authors warn about making careless comparisons and assuming that any charter schools are scalable as reform templates for public education reform.

- Center for Research on Education Outcomes (CREDO). (2009, June). Multiple choice: Charter school performance in 16 states. Stanford, CA: Center for Research on Education Outcomes. Retrieved November 2, 2009 from http://credo.stanford.edu/reports/MULTIPLE_CHOICE_CREDO.pdf

  This comprehensive study of charter schools, though not without controversy, presents a solid picture of the range of quality found in any education format. Charter schools appear to have about 17% high achieving, 46% average, and 37% low achieving characteristics when compared to public schools. This data help place in context claims of "high flying" charter schools as *all* or even most charter schools, but the study does not address key issues such as the ideology and practices of those schools.

- Frankenberg, E., Siegel-Hawley, G., & Wang, J. (2011). Choice without equity: Charter school segregation. *Educational Policy Analysis Archives, 19*(1). Retrieved April 26, 2011 from http://epaa.asu.edu/ojs/article/view/779

  We often fail to recognize the negative consequences of choice, but the charter school movement is exposing those consequences. This study concludes that charter schools "currently isolate students by race and class" and that charter schools may tend to under-serve English language learners and the extreme low end of poverty.

- Fuller, E. (2011, April 25). Characteristics of students enrolling in high-performing charter high schools. A "Fuller" Look at Education Issues [Web log post]. Retrieved April 26, 2011 from http://fullerlook.wordpress.com/2011/04/25/hp-charter-high-schools/

  The choice dynamic of charter schools necessarily creates a student population unlike the community-based traditional public schools. In order to understand if and how charter schools in fact provide some evidence for reforming public schools, the populations of charters schools must be fully examined and understood. Fuller begins to examine the characteristics of students in charter schools labelled "high-performing" and identifies many disparities including special education students served, achievement characteristics among high-poverty students in both charter and public schools, and at-risk students, concluding:

> This suggests that HP charter high schools do not serve the same types of students as the regular neighborhood schools. Now, granted, the HP charter high schools do enroll a greater percentage of students participating in the free- and reduced-price lunch program and in the free lunch program, but these economically disadvantaged students are not the same as the economically disadvantaged students in the regular neighborhood schools! (Fuller, 2011, n.p.)

- Garcia, D. (2011). Review of "Going Exponential: Growing the Charter School Sector's Best." Boulder, CO: National Education Policy Center. Retrieved April 26, 2011 from http://nepc.colorado.edu/thinktank/review-going-exponential

  Garcia debunks think tank advocacy for expanding rapidly charter schools. This review is important for remaining skeptical about charter schools and for continuing to be vigilant about distinguishing between advocacy dressed as research and credible conclusions drawn from scholarship and research.

- Miron, G. (2011). Review of "Charter Schools: A Report on Rethinking the Federal Role in Education." Boulder, CO: National Education Policy Center. Retrieved April 26, 2011 from http://nepc.colorado.edu/thinktank/review-charter-federal

  Miron presents a mixed view of a report from the Brown Center on Education Policy of the Brookings Institution. The Brown Center report represents a growing endorsement of a federal role in promoting the expansion of charter schools. Miron argues for a tempered position on expanding charter schools and for using this report as just one initial piece of evidence in forming policy.

- Miron, G. & Urschel, J. L. (2010). *Equal or fair? A study of revenues and expenditure in American charter schools.* Boulder, CO and Tempe, AZ: Education and the Public Interest Center & Education Policy Research Unit. Retrieved April 26, 2011, from http://epicpolicy.org/publication/charter-school-finance

  Funding and how funding is distributed lie at the center of much of the charter school and public school reform debates. This study details the complexity of how charter schools are funding and how that compares to public school funding. Key in this study is a call for more research on charter funding along with greater and fuller disclosure of charter funding, since charter schools tend to receive less per-pupil funding than public school but additional private funding that is not disclosed. As well, public schools remain likely to offer services that charters do not provide, distorting further any comparisons of funding equity.

- Miron, G., Urschel, J. L., Mathis, W, J., & Tornquist, E. (2010). *Schools without Diversity: Education management organizations, charter schools and the demographic stratification of the American school system.* Boulder, CO and Tempe, AZ: Education and the Public Interest Center & Education Policy Research Unit. Retrieved April 26, 2011 from http://epicpolicy.org/publication/schools-without-diversity

   This study draws a disturbing pattern being uncovered about the charter school movement: "The analysis found that, as compared with the public school district in which the charter school resided, the charter schools were substantially more segregated by race, wealth, disabling condition, and language" (n.p.).

- Miron, G., Urschel, J. L., & Saxton, N. (2011, March). *What makes KIPP work?: A study of student characteristics, attrition, and school finance.* Teachers College, Columbia University. National Center for the Study of Privatization in Education. Retrieved April 26, 2011 from http://www.ncspe.org/readrel.php?set=pub&cat=253

   Focusing on inputs instead of student outcomes, this study examines KIPP schools and finds that KIPP schools do enroll high-poverty students but under-serve special needs students and English language learners. The study also raises questions about student attrition and about the apparent inequity in funding that KIPP schools receive when all funding is examined, totaling about $6,500 more per pupil than public schools in the area. Combined, this evidence challenges the KIPP model as scalable.

- Ravitch, D. (2010c). The myth of charter schools. *The New York Review of Books.* Retrieved March 11, 2011 from http://www.nybooks.com/articles/archives/2010/nov/11/myth-charter-schools/

   Ravitch's scholarly commentary is important because of her credibility as a scholar and historian, along with her recent shift in positions concerning accountability/testing and school choice. This detailed discussion confronts the media-driven claims of "miracle" charter schools.

CHAPTER 5

THE TEACHING PROFESSION AS A SERVICE INDUSTRY

The central character, George Falconer, of Christopher Isherwood's *A Single Man* is often discussed for his most provocative characteristics—a gay man in 1960s America struggling against his dual life and the nearly overwhelming loss of his lover in an accident before the action of the novel. But central to the character and the narrative of this compelling novel, also adapted into film with some significant changes, is that George is a professor, a teacher, and it is here that I want to begin a chapter on the public discourse about teachers in the early twenty-first century—when American leaders, the media, and the public have decided to accept and perpetuate a damning narrative about teachers central to the uncritical acceptance of Davis Guggenheim's documentary *Waiting for "Superman."*

First, let's consider how teacher quality and evaluation (including the rising concern for merit pay for teachers and the need to fire "bad" teachers) fit into a discussion of ignoring poverty in the U.S. *Waiting for "Superman"* has expressed and thus exposed among the broader U.S. public a few narratives that are both compelling (these claims resonate because people believe them at the intuitive level) and factually inaccurate, including the following:

- U.S. public education is an overwhelming failure—primarily based on simplistic international comparisons of test scores such as PISA (see Riddile, 2010, for the flawed reasoning), *and* public education is the single source for addressing the plight of poverty in children's lives (see Berliner, 2009; Hirsch, 2007; Rothstein, 2010; and Traub, 2000 for evidence to the contrary as well as the speeches of Secretary Duncan examined in previous chapters).

- Public education is a failure primarily for two connected reasons—too many "bad" teachers (see Bessie, 2010a for an examination of this narrative) and the teachers' unions who make firing "bad" teachers nearly impossible through traditional structures such as tenure.

- To resurrect our public school system, then, we need to expand charter schools (see Chapter Four), especially the "no excuses" corporate model found in KIPP and HCZ, and invest in a fresh teacher core such as Teach for America, which recruits top students, forgoes traditional teacher education, and commits recruits to teaching in the most challenging schools, notably urban schools with high poverty and disproportionate populations of ELL students.

And this pattern of claims has a cultural myth at its core—do not allow poverty to be an excuse for any failures for anyone, even children, because rugged individuals *do* rise out of poverty, and education is often the key to that success. This chapter, then, examines the growing teacher quality mantra being used by the new education reformers (corporate reformers) that masks addressing poverty in a parallel way to the impact of claims of "miracle" charter schools discussed in Chapter Four. So how does Isherwood's novel fit our education reform debate?

As a teacher, I have often been sensitive to how literature, film, and TV shows portray teachers; and those portrayals are often quite distorted. But George in *A Single Man* presents for us a place to pause and consider the assumptions underneath the popularity of *Waiting for "Superman"* claims: What are the characteristics of an effective teacher? Just what influence can a teacher have on her/his students? What role does content and curriculum play in that influence? And, ultimately, we must tease out the difference between "can" and "should"—What are the ethical parameters of the teacher/student relationship within the narrow consideration of *knowledge*?

In *A Single Man*, George is depicted in front of his classroom teaching, specifically addressing Aldous Huxley's *After Many a Summer Dies the Swan*, and having casual interactions with a student, conversations that raise tension in the reader about the complex and varied dynamic between a teacher and student. Throughout the novel, I was profoundly aware of George as a *human being*—complex, flawed, brilliant, hopeful, burdened, and passionate. I also found the student compelling for many of the same reasons. This novel, then, highlights for us that teaching and learning are *human endeavors*, also complex and resistant to simple characterizations.

George as a professor may and does have many qualities related to his expertise of his field, experience with that field and the teaching of that field, and his *intentions* with that expertise, but all of his abilities as a professor are filtered through the *perspectives and abilities of each student*. To place teaching in a post-modern perspective, if any teacher or professor has before her or him, for example, 25 students, there exists 26 separate realities of that teaching and learning in addition to the one community experience of the 26 people involved. As I confront more fully below, those new reformers and the general public who view teaching as an *objective* and simple transfer of a fixed body of knowledge from one teacher to passive and receptive students are trapped within the reductive "banking concept" of education (Freire, 1993) that accepts the possibility of politically neutral knowledge and transfer of that knowledge.

As readers encounter George before his class and especially as readers consider George talking with his student about his teaching and their learning, readers can confront fully the failures of mechanistic and reductive views of teachers, teaching, students, and learning. In short, that we *can* quantify student learning and then hold teachers directly accountable for that data point doesn't justify that we do such—and it also exposes our willingness to fail the concept of accountability by ignoring the myriad influences on any student's life and learning, again hiding the power of poverty behind the seemingly safe veneer of numbers. As I will continue to examine, political, corporate, and public assumptions about teaching tend to fail basic considerations of causation while also creating criteria of evaluation that normalize outliers—thus, the irony of calling for statistical (and claimed "objective") accountability for teachers while simultaneously committing basic statistical errors of reasoning.

Yet, during the Obama administration, the U.S. public has had reinforced disturbingly simplistic characterizations of who teachers are and should be, what teachers can and should accomplish, and how students matter (or not) in the teaching/learning dynamic. Isherwood's novel shows us that George makes political decisions through what he says to his students, what he doesn't say, what text he brings to the class, and what persona, ultimately, he takes in front of students both in and out of the class setting—even if and when any teacher takes the pose of objectivity or scholarly disinterest (which is the cultural norm we expect of teachers). But the novel also reveals that the student is a powerful element in what is learned, the ultimate agent of learning that involves that student's background, that student's willingness to learn, and that student's ability to learn (both biological and environmental).

To remain trapped in the *Waiting for "Superman"* narratives is to deny the complexity of the teaching/learning dynamic, to discount the humanity of teachers and students, and to ignore the cultural dynamics guiding

all human behaviors, specifically cultural facts about the privilege of affluence and the burden of poverty. Like George, every teacher is a part of a
community and a myriad of cultural norms. We are simultaneously considered a failure and brilliant by different students in the same class. For
public discourse, however, it seems most compelling and possibly more
manageable to confront a *person* (the teacher) instead of an abstraction
(poverty), and as a result, we have chosen to cast stones at teachers while
continuing to ignore the poverty that defines many children's lives.

THE NORMS OF TEACHING AND BEING A TEACHER

Teacher education is an ideal point to begin for any consideration of
teaching. Education as a field of study has suffered a second-class existence that remains; many in higher education are conflicted at best about
the validity of education as a credible field. Education departments are
often marginalized, teacher education is typically seen as "easy" or "soft"
(perpetuated by inaccurate claims that education majors are themselves
academically weak), and majors in education are viewed as less weighty
than content areas such as the sciences because the major is preparing
candidates directly for a career (oddly as a culture we both assume education is preparation for work and discredit any education that directly pre-
pares students for work).

That teacher educators are teaching candidates to be teachers helps
highlight how often we fail to acknowledge our working definitions for
"teacher," "teaching," "student," and "learning." To make claims about
teacher quality and the possibility of teachers to *cause* student outcomes
that rise above the influence of children's lives requires that we define
these terms up front.

What, then, are the norms of being a teacher and teaching that lie
beneath the surface of the public and political discourse calling for the
removal of "bad" teachers, the end to tenure and teachers' unions, and
the direct and sole teacher accountability for student outcomes?

Yeigh, Cunningham, and Shagoury (2011) offered some insight into
this question when they decided to take the gate-keeping standardized
test that determines if teaching candidates can be certified as reading
specialists:

> As we took the Praxis test, a disturbing subtext emerged from the questions.
> The exam implied that the main function of a reading specialist is to do the
> bidding of the building administrator and the school district—that the posi-
> tion is not one of decision-making but of implementation and enforcement.
> Test questions communicated no expectation that reading specialists and

literacy coaches should rely on their own understanding of the reading process or look to students in making decisions. (n.p.)

A complex and hidden pattern is exposed here, one at the heart of focusing on teacher quality in order to mask the need to address childhood poverty—and that pattern has *authority* at its core along with a view that knowledge is easily identified capital.

The norms that should be contested but instead drive the call for greater teacher accountability include the following:

- *Objectivity* is possible and preferred, particularly the objectivity inherent in content (again as neutral capital) and the objectivity expected of teachers as dispensers of that content.
- The teaching/learning dynamic is simple *transference*—both sequential and linear, thus the justification for holding one teacher solely accountable for any student's learning.
- Learning is easily measurable and quantifiable, resulting in a historical and powerful faith in testing (again, standardized testing that has garnered the necessary credibility of being "objective").
- A free people can and should be educated in a hierarchical and authoritarian system that codifies the curriculum (what is to be learned) through the authoritative bureaucracy of government and is then transferred dutifully by teachers, under the supervision of administrators, to passive students. (All of this must be placed in the context of the accountability era starting in 1983 that initiated the standards/testing/accountability paradigm at the state level that has gradually been moved to the federal level with NCLB and looks to be further intensified with the Obama administration's call for common core national standards and the likely rise of national tests for that common set of standards.)

These norms are mechanistic, viewing people as cogs in a sterile and apolitical process. Yet, teaching and learning are human endeavors, not easily captured, defined, or controlled. These norms of teaching are what work against human agency, ironically. In order to hold any person accountable ethically, we must address what that person has agency to control. For example, we often find ourselves frustrated by meteorologists and weather reporters because it seems they miss their predictions too often. Our frustration is embedded in our failure to recognize that they are primarily describing weather patterns and then using those patterns to predict and to acknowledge and clarify that ultimately they are not the cause agents in the weather; in short, we blur holding them accountable for their predictions versus holding them accountable for causing the weather.

And as I will examine more closely throughout this chapter, in order to reform our schools for the benefit of all children regardless of their lives outside of school, we must acknowledge the power of poverty but also address directly the qualities best suited for teachers in that school system, along with re-examining our assumptions about teaching and learning. Before we can reform education by addressing teacher quality, however, we must recognize that our current assumptions about both teacher quality and evaluating teachers are more likely to do harm than good.

AN ENDURING, BUT FLAWED, PATTERN OF EFFICIENCY: TEACHER AS COG?

"The formula is simple: Highly effective teachers equal student academic success. Yet, the physics of American education is anything but. Thus, the question facing education reformers is how can teacher effectiveness be accurately measured in order to improve the teacher workforce?" explains Goldhaber (2010, n.p.), revealing the sweeping assumptions at the heart of intensifying the spotlight on teacher quality in order to keep poverty in the shadows. The formula is *simple*?

The formula is not simple and neither is the assumption that teacher quality is at the center of student academic success. But this claim is rarely challenged because it rests on a cultural faith in efficiency. Decades ago, however, Callahan (1962) recognized the corrosive impact of efficiency on attitudes toward the teaching profession—attitudes that have resulted in praise for scripted curriculum, attacks on teacher quality, and calls for increasing class sizes:

> The whole development produced men who did not understand education or scholarship. Thus they could and did approach education in a business-like, mechanical, organizational way. They saw nothing wrong with impos-ing impossible loads on high school teachers, because they were not students or scholars and did not understand the need for time for study and preparation. (p. 247)

Setting aside Callahan's sexist language, his description fits perfectly the current new reformer movement including Secretary Duncan, Gates, Rhee, and Canada—all of whom have no or very little experience and expertise in education but speak in a "businesslike, mechanical, organiza-tional way."

Goldhaber (2010) immediately qualifies his opening comment from above with: "There is a growing body of quantitative research showing teaching ability to be the most important school-based factor influencing student performance" (n.p.). But many of the new reformers fail to distinguish in-school from out-of-school influences, and nearly all of the attacks on teacher quality fail to identify a truly important fact: Out-of-school factors dwarf the in-school importance of teacher quality, which accounts for only about 13-17% of student outcomes (Hanushek, 2010; Hirsch, 2007). Which should lead us to say, that if the formula is in fact simple (ironically, not what Goldhaber means)—teacher quality is less than 80% of measurable student outcomes—why don't we put more of the discourse and policies toward that 80%?

The answer is clear, but complicated. First, political leaders like Duncan, entrepreneur hobbyists like Gates and Canada, and career self-promoters like Rhee are completely committed to and rewarded by a corporate/mechanistic view of everything. They allow no criticism of corporate assumptions and therefore are driven by their own self-acknowledged success to believe they have the answers for everything. Consider this from Duncan:

> "This is about a call to service.... Our ability to attract and retain teachers will shape the future of education in the next 25 to 30 years," he said to Brokaw. "If you want to have an impact, this is the civil rights issue of our generation. I'm very optimistic because we know what works. *We* are the answers: Great teachers, great principals, great schools will strengthen our economy and give children the chance to fulfill their potential. If young kids can help us to fight for social justice, it'll last for generations to come." (Barseghian, 2010)

This is typical of Duncan—soaring rhetoric (often tied to progressive causes such as civil rights), sweeping claims with no evidence, and no mention or recognition of poverty or out-of-school factors.

While Duncan has been pushing the refrain that teacher quality is central to student achievement, Rhee gained fame and notoriety for dismissing large numbers of teachers in Washington DC and creating both support for and rejections of linking teacher evaluations and retention on student test scores. Eventually, Rhee was dismissed after an election shifted support away from her much-heralded run as an iron-fisted school chancellor, but most of the push-back against Rhee has been from educators, not from the public, and certainly not from the corporate and political elite. Rhee, in fact, has ridden a high tide of media coverage, secured positions advising politicians, and established her own education-related organization, Students First (http://www.studentsfirst.org/).

While Rhee has exhibited an effective ability for impressing the media, courting political and corporate support, and promoting herself as an education expert (despite her Teach for America background and experience as more bureaucrat than educator), the most powerful force in the teacher bashing cycle under Secretary Duncan has been Gates, whose public speeches and commentaries along with his philanthropic organization have secured momentum for focusing on teacher quality and linking teacher evaluations/retention to student test scores (Obama and Duncan's Race to the Top, a centerpiece of Obama's education agenda, directly ties federal funding to states' adopting teacher evaluation systems linked to student outcomes). The Gates influence like Race to the Top reveals the power of money to trump evidence.

As I examined in Chapter 3, the power of think tanks to drive policy despite their not being peer-reviewed is real and disturbing. This power is not lost on the Bill and Melinda Gates Foundation. Part of the push from Gates concerning education reforms includes teacher quality. Gates has endorsed firing "bad" teachers (and ending tenure), replacing traditional teacher pay scales for merit-based systems, and even identifying the best teachers and then asking them to teach increased class size loads. But ultimately, Gates's focus on teacher quality has proven to be more ideology (corporate assumptions) than evidence-based policy, including the report from the foundation on teacher quality and merit pay, which offers this in the conclusion:

> The evidence of wide differences in student achievement gains in different teachers' classrooms is like a colossal divining rod, pointing at the ground, saying, "Dig here." Dig here if you want to learn what great teaching looks like. Dig here if you want to better understand what teachers do to help students learn. This is where you will learn about ways to generate dramatically different results for kids.... The public debate over measuring teacher effectiveness usually portrays only two options: the status quo (where there is no meaningful feedback for teachers) and a seemingly extreme world where tests scores alone determine a teacher's fate. Our results suggest that's a false choice. (Learning about teaching, n.d., n.p.)

And the implications—teacher quality is central to student outcomes, demonizing the "status quo"—drive the ultimate conclusion that value-added methods should be used to evaluate, retain/remove, and reward teachers.

The report is a professional looking document, with footnotes and citations that give the report the look of quality research, but that look is misleading. First, a review of the Gates report concludes:

> The MET Project is assembling an unprecedented database of teacher practice measures that promises to greatly improve our understanding of teacher performance. Even the preliminary analyses in this report expand the boundaries of our knowledge, pointing, for example, to student percep-

tions as a potentially valuable source of information. Unfortunately, however, the analyses do not support the report's conclusions. Interpreted correctly, they undermine rather than validate value-added-based approaches to teacher evaluation. (J. Rothstein, 2011, n.p.)

Most considerations of value-added methods (VAM) and merit pay, in fact, find that teachers do not want merit pay and that the merit-pay process is ineffective (Au, 2010; Baker et al., 2010; Quintero, 2011):

> Merit pay ... is one of those incentive schemes that sounds good but never works. The most rigorous evaluation of merit pay was published last fall by Vanderbilt University, which found that a possible bonus of $15,000 for higher test scores produced no results. The teachers who were not eligible for the bonus got the same test scores as those who were eligible.
>
> Worse than being ineffective, merit pay damages the culture of the school by destroying teamwork and collaboration. Teachers in successful schools agree that the fundamental elements of school improvement are trust and collaboration, not competition for monetary rewards. (Ravitch, 2011d)

Yet, the calls for and trust in simplistic faith in the value of teacher quality and our ability to identify easily the best and worst teachers are enduring. As just one example, however, the problems with mechanistic and merit-based approaches to teacher evaluation are clear in a review of a proposal in Massachusetts (Guisbond & King, 2011). The plan in Massachusetts exposes five basic flaws with evaluation systems linked heavily to test scores:

- Test-based teacher accountability often codifies standardized assessments for purposes beyond the intent of those tests. All states now implement testing as part of the accountability and standards movement, but these tests were never intended to produce data regarding teacher quality. This is the same flaw seen with using the SAT—a test designed solely to predict freshman college success—to judge the quality of schools or entire state's education systems. Simply put, test validity and reliability are directly linked to the purpose of any assessment; using a test for something beyond its design immediately jeopardizes its reliability and validity.
- Shifting teacher evaluation to test-based methods will increase the amount and cost of testing for any district or state implementing such a program. The 30 years of accountability, standards, and testing have failed to produce promised results for student outcomes (Hout & Elliott, 2011) so expecting the same failed process to raise teacher quality is foolish. The use of tests to evaluate teachers is more problematic and expensive since most calls for this process

are seeking a pre- and post-test model that appears to show the impact of one teacher on one set of students (although that simplistic model is deceptive itself).

- As noted above, we already have data on test-based teacher evaluation, and those data reveal more problems with the process than supporters will admit.

- Increased high-stakes dynamics create tension among all of the stakeholders in the process, building the likelihood that relationships between teachers and students as well as among teachers will be negatively impacted by holding teachers accountable for the outcomes of their students—outcomes that are out of the teachers' control as well as often out of the control of students.

- The call for teacher evaluations based on test scores and increased accountability ultimately fails for the same reason the push for national standards is flawed: The call assumes we don't already know what to do. Many systems and processes exist for evaluating and supporting teacher growth effectively; the fields of teacher education and professional development are being ignored and marginalized by a corporate and bureaucratic elite who appear hell bent on reform without regard to the professional and scholarly knowledge base of the field they are reforming.

Gardner (2011) frames the current teacher evaluation debate well:

I understand the appeal of the business model. There is intense frustration over the admittedly slow pace of school reform. When it reaches a certain level, anything that is presented as a solution is seized upon. That's because desperate people embrace desperate measures. But before assuming that anything is better than what exists at present, it's vital to ask a hard question: To what extent is ideology used in place of evidence? (n.p.)

And, ironically, the evidence is that ideology is trumping evidence—bureaucracy and corporate assumptions are driving a call for raising expectations for teachers that will do more harm than good, just like the current accountability movement for student outcomes. The business model based on technocratic methods, hierarchies of power, and competition are ill suited for education, as Gardner adds:

I consider the Gates report to be another step in reducing teachers to labor under the heel of principals who function as management. If reform is ever to be successful, teachers and principals must work as partners. An adversarial system may work in the courtroom, but it has no place in the classroom. (n.p.)

The teacher-as-cog metaphor lies at the heart of the call for teacher evaluations based on test scores, but that metaphor is also at the center of the move toward embracing Teach for America while dismantling traditional teacher certification, schools of education, and teachers' unions.

TEACH FOR AMERICAN CORPORATIONS

Central to the narrative of *Waiting for "Superman"* is a persuasive masking of poverty's influence on the lives of children by demonizing teachers and idealizing charter schools. Within the teacher bashing is an equally insidious claim that bad teachers supported by teachers' unions are the primary source of school failure, but that the entrepreneurial spirit of Teach for America (TfA)—which counts among its alumni Michelle Rhee—is, like charter schools, the course for resurrecting the teacher corps in the U.S.

Similar to claims about miracle charter schools, praising TfA as a powerful or even effective process for recruiting and placing teachers into the education system is based mostly on public relations since the data behind such claims doesn't exist (Heilig & Jez, 2010; Ravitch, 2011a). Heilig and Jez concluded, in fact:

> Thus, a simple answer to the question of TFA teachers' relative effectiveness cannot be conclusively drawn from the research; many factors are involved in any comparison. The lack of a consistent impact, however, should indicate to policy-makers that TFA is likely not the panacea that will reduce disparities in educational outcomes. (n.p.)

Despite the evidence against the program, Levy (2011b) captures the rise of the TfA brand:

> Although Teach For America began twenty years ago as a well-intentioned band-aid, it has morphed into what is essentially a jobs program for the privileged, funded by taxpayers and wealthy individuals. TFA was originally designed it to serve a specific need: fill positions in high-poverty schools where there are teacher shortages. A non-profit organization that recruits college seniors primarily from elite institutions to teach for two-year stints in high-poverty schools, preceded by five weeks of training. TFA has grown from 500 teachers to more than 8,000 teachers in thirty-nine rural and urban areas. As TFA is expanding, it is no longer just filling positions in shortage areas; rather, it's replacing experienced and traditionally educated teachers. To justify this encroachment, TFA claims that their teachers are more effective than more experienced and qualified teachers, and that training and experience are not factors in effective teaching. (n.p.)

While I believe the evidence suggests that TfA has many problems as a mechanism for recruiting and maintaining teachers in the U.S., I want to focus here primarily on how embracing TfA reflects the historical pattern of ignoring poverty while demonizing schools and de-professionalizing teachers. First, TfA represents a cultural belief that anyone can teach since TfA recruits elite college students who are not education majors/certifiers and provides them only weeks of training before placing them in high-poverty schools—the most challenging situations any teacher can face. The evidence on teacher quality supports the effectiveness of teacher education and experience (Darling-Hammond, 2002), but that evidence is overshadowed by the cultural belief in teaching being easy, or something anyone can do. TfA depends on that misconception as part of the public relations aimed at securing more and more of the public education pie.

Further, the TfA mythology parallels our faith in the miracle powers of schools and concurrent faith in miracle charter schools—again against the grain of evidence to the contrary. The best-and-brightest argument for staffing our teaching core resonates with a public that believes in the rugged individual and the allure of the elite. Teachers have been mischaracterized as lazy and academically weak for most of the modern era, leading the public to reach common sense conclusions that elite students must make elite teachers.

But the most damning aspect of TfA as the proposed savior of an ailing teacher corps in the U.S. is the nature of the program itself, which requires only two years commitment, that targets high-poverty schools. Currently, one of the primary failures of the U.S. public education system is that high-poverty students, ELL students, and students of color disproportionately sit in classrooms taught by un- and under-certified teachers with the least experience (Peske & Haycock, 2006). *TfA is proposing the exact dynamic we need to change—uncertified new teachers placed in the classrooms with the students most in need of quality teachers.*

The ultimate conclusion, then, that we can draw about the new reformers' push for increasing the role of TfA in the workforce of U.S. public education is that TfA serves some sort of corporate function. And the function is twofold—eradicating unions and reducing teaching to an inexpensive service industry. In other words, TfA is a mechanism for reducing labor costs, not a revolutionary process for bringing the best and brightest into an important profession.

THE TEACHING PROFESSION AS A SERVICE INDUSTRY

Walt Gardner (2010e), writing in his *Education Week* blog, concluded:

> The latest reminder that freedom of speech for teachers in K-12 is an illusion came from the U.S. Court of Appeals for the 6th Circuit in Cincinnati

on Oct. 21. In *Evans-Marshall v. Board of Education of the Tipp City Exempted Village School District,* the court ruled that teachers cannot make their own curricular decisions. (n.p.)

This significant court case revolved around an English teacher asking her students to choose among often banned books, to read the chosen books, and then to examine why the books were banned. Many would consider this assignment a rich and engaging lesson ideal for high school students.

But this ruling comes amid an unmatched season for examining teachers and teaching. Not long after Obama and Duncan began focusing on teachers and teacher quality as the central component of school reform, the media followed with a similar theme. *Waiting for "Superman"* premiered with a great deal of fanfare and support, including an episode of *Oprah* and a week-long focus on education at NBC.

In August of 2010, as well, the teacher assault was raised even higher when the *Los Angeles Times* published teacher quality analyses based on value-added methods (VAM) (Felch, Song, & Smith, 2010). The charges against teacher quality and teachers' unions initiated several stringent rejections, but most challenges came from educators themselves—and received little media coverage (Baker et al., 2010; DiCarlo, 2010; Gardner, 2010a).

Eventually, the narrative added that our teaching core is weak because "countries with the best-performing school systems largely recruit teachers from the top third of high school and college graduates, while the United States has difficulty attracting its top students to the profession, a new report finds" (Heitin, 2010, n.p.). Auguste, Kihn, and Miller (2010) promoted education reform based on recruiting top students into teaching:

> Our research makes a compelling case for exploring top third+ strategies with pilots in high-needs districts or in a state, perhaps via a new "Race to the Top Third" grant competition, or through collaborating among school systems, philanthropic institutions, and other education stakeholders.... In more than 50 countries, we have never seen an education system achieve or sustain world-class status without top talent in its teaching profession. If the U.S. is to close its achievement gap with the world's best education systems—and ease its own socio-economic disparities—a top third+ strategy for the teaching profession must be part of the debate. (pp. 7-8)

This direct and complex claim combines several assumptions that have little to support them, notably a sweeping comment about the "world's best education systems" without noting that international comparisons that consider poverty put the U.S. above most of the countries this claim implies (Finland, for example; See Riddile, 2010). The call for increasing teacher quality, again, ignores the role of poverty and rests on ideology instead of evidence.

The teacher bashing formula grew complex, but there was a pattern: (a) Usurp teachers' union control and fire bad teachers, and then (b) restock depleted teacher core with recruits from the top students in the U.S.— which sounds compelling until you consider the great contradictions of all of this and even more recent news: Let's return to teachers' autonomy as professionals: " 'Teachers are not everyday citizens,' the panel wrote, adding that the school board had the right to control teachers' curricular choices and in-class speech" (Hudson, 2010, n.p.). "Teachers have no First Amendment free-speech protection for curricular decisions they make in the classroom," Walsh (2010, n.p.) explained in *Education Week*.

And also consider that during the first weeks of the 2010 NFL season, three players were fined for excessively violent hits during several games on the same Sunday. The fines? $75,000 and $50,000—well above the average salaries for teachers across the U.S.

So let's step back from all of the separate but connected claims about teachers, teacher quality, and teachers' unions because if we look at them together we discover that two powerfully contradictory messages are existing simultaneously in the larger public discourse without anyone trying to address the contradiction.

Political and corporate leaders are seeking to speak about teaching as if it is a profession while expecting those professionals to function as a service industry. In the narratives offered by Obama and Duncan, *Waiting for "Superman,"* and organizations such as KIPP and Teach for America, we need the best and the brightest to implement mandated common core standards so that their students can take national tests for which those teachers will be held accountable—all with those teachers having no first amendments rights, no right to due process, and salaries that are less than a common NFL fine.

Beneath the political and corporate veneer espousing teaching as a profession lurks a simple fact: Corporate and political elites want teaching to be a service industry. Yet, if public education is ever to fulfill its promise as a central element in the pursuit of free and empowered people living in a thriving democracy, we must seek teaching as a profession—a quest that flies in the face of the contradictory messages dominating public discourse today.

BILLIONAIRES VERSUS MILLIONAIRES: WHAT ELSE THE NFL CAN TEACH US ABOUT TEACHER BASHING

In 2011, management and labor were hurtling toward an impasse, and a work stoppage occurred. Workers were seeking public support by emphasizing the importance of benefits for workers, specifically long-term healthcare for conditions caused by the profession that do not appear until later in life. This scenario may trigger for many the possibility of a teachers' strike fueled by a powerful teachers' union, and if this were a teachers' strike, in 2011, we could anticipate little support for those teachers—in part because of the propaganda created by the media and the rise of a new crop of education reformers.

However, above, I am speaking about the threat of an NFL strike, a struggle between billionaires and millionaires that indirectly shines an important light on the rise of teacher and teacher union bashing in the U.S. Bessie (2010a) identifies how the myth of the bad teacher has evolved:

> In this political season of faux anti-establishment anger born of very real economic desperation, public educators have become the villain du jour, their reputations collateral damage in the war against "big government." In a remarkable sleight of hand, the super rich who imploded the economy, manufacturing the recession which now enrages the public, have successfully misdirected the public's justifiable anger away from them and toward teachers. (n.p.)

While some people demonized and criticized either the billionaire owners or the millionaire players (represented by a union) in the NFL, the education reform landscape is built on a false premise, blaming teachers and unions for school failures, that lacks credibility and masks the overwhelming source of education failures—poverty.

Ironically, the new push against teachers' unions cloaked in discourse about the damage done by "bad" teachers comes from Democrats under Obama and Secretary Duncan. But the political attacks on teachers and unions that come from both the Left and the Right would likely not resonate as they have if not for the celebrity tour fueled by the media and perpetuated by celebrity reformers. Two of the celebrity reformers, Gates and Canada, share an entrepreneur status that suggests expertise on everything simply because they are wealthy (possibly what protects NFL owners and players from social ridicule in their fight). Both also use the media to promote their unsupported claims.

Ultimately, the public relations campaign by corporate and political leaders is effective, but it remains inaccurate. Teacher quality is only a small percent of achievement, and there is little evidence that teacher quality is the biggest or even one of the main problems with student achievement in public schools. But a provable problem with teacher quality is teacher assignment (Peske & Haycock, 2006), something rarely addressed in calls for reform since teacher assignments expose the inequities of the school system that mirrors the inequities of the society. Of course, teacher quality does matter in terms of what happens once students are within the walls of schools, but we seem blind to the long standing tradition of assigning the most experienced and best qualified teachers to the elite students, who are already experiencing advantages in their full lives outside of school.

That the evidence-based inequity of teacher assignment is ignored, while the myth of the bad teacher is perpetuated, is evidence of the motivation behind the new reformers—a commitment to the status quo of inequity driven by America's consumer culture that benefits the exact people making charges against teachers and unions. And the rants against unions are just as suspect as the claims that bad teachers are crippling schools. Two examples expose the flaws in union bashing.

First, the new reformers hold up Finland as the model for education reform (Thomas, 2010y)—while failing to identify that Finland has low childhood poverty (about 3-4% compared to over 20% in the U.S.) and that Finland's teachers are nearly 100% unionized.

Next, in the U.S., consider South Carolina, a high-poverty state with a reputation as a weak education system. South Carolina joined the accountability era at the beginning, taking A Nation at Risk seriously and implementing standards, testing, and accountability in 1984. Despite nearly three decades of the exact process supported by the new reformers, South Carolina finds itself ranked still at the bottom of education in the U.S. Important in this dynamic is that South Carolina remains a high-poverty state—the real source of the low test scores—but also that South Carolina is a non-union state, with no union contracts for teachers and no tenure.

So let's return to the 2011 NFL dispute with a players' union in the middle. Corporate, political, and public sentiment is against teachers' unions, framing unions as the source of all that ails public education. But virtually no one has cried foul concerning unionized labor struggles of millionaire NFL players pitted against billionaire team owners. While this seems contradictory, I believe it is not.

Corporate America (and thus political America) benefits from the NFL thriving *and* from the de-professionalizing of teaching. The truth is that the union element is coincidental. Outcries of bad teachers and corrupt teachers' unions are not about educational reform, but about guaranteeing that teaching will become permanently a service industry and schools will be reduced exclusively to producing compliant workers.

"A QUESTION OF POWER": OF ACCOUNTABILITY AND TEACHING BY NUMBERS

The speaker in Adrienne Rich's "Diving into the Wreck" confronts the contrast between land and sea—"the sea is another story/ the sea is not a question of power"—leaving the clear message that our world *is* "a question of power." Over the past 30 years, the education reform debate and the rising calls for education reform have exposed themselves as a question of power. The education reform debate is a mask for the powerful to maintain their power at the expense of marginalized groups, primarily people trapped in poverty. The first 3 years of the Obama administration have evolved into intense clashes about policy and commitments in the field of education, exposing that the education reform debate is about more than our schools; it is a question of power. Unless the sleeping giant—the voice of educators—is awakened, the power will remain in the hands of the inexpert.

As many ignored or marginalized the rallies in Wisconsin about teachers' rights and the role of unions in our public education system, a role that is not nearly as unified as the public believes since many states are non-union (Larkin, 2011), the corporate and political elite continued to speak from positions of celebrity and authority that lack expertise and fly above the accountability that they champion:

"Well, it's a dereliction of duty on behalf of the Democrat state senators in Wisconsin," Bachmann said. "There was an election in 2010. The people spoke clearly in Wisconsin. They elected a new senator, Ron Johnson to replace Russ Feingold, a new governor, Scott Walker. And then they elected Republicans to run both the House and the Senate. This was a change election in Wisconsin. People wanted to get their fiscal house in order. That's exactly what Gov. Walker and the House and Senate are trying to do, and now the Democrats are trying to thwart the will of the people by leaving the state? This is outrageous. And, plus, we have the president of the United States also weighing in with his campaign organization busing 25,000 protesters into Madison? It's outrageous." (Poor, 2011, n.p.)

During the rising calls for bureaucratic education reform, revamping teacher evaluations and pay, and the Wisconsin teacher protests, former Secretary of Education Margaret Spellings (2011) weighed in about reauthorizing NCLB: "However, any new law must be a step toward stronger, more precise accountability" (n.p.). And her audacity here is even bolder than what the new reformers have been perpetuating through film and popular media.

During President George W. Bush's tenure, NCLB was a corner stone of his agenda, and when then-Secretary Spellings announced that test scores were proving NCLB a success, Gerald Bracey and Stephen Krashen (2006) exposed one of two possible problems with the data. Spellings either did not understand basic statistics or was misleading for political gain. Krashen detailed the deception or ineptitude by showing that the gain Spellings noted did occur from 1999 to 2005, a change of seven points. But he also revealed that the scores rose as follows: 1999 = 212; 2000 = 213; 2002 = 219; 2003 = 218; 2005 = 219. The jump Spellings used to promote NCLB and Reading First occurred from 2000 to 2002, *before the implementation of Reading First*. Krashen (2006) notes even more problems with claiming success for NCLB and Reading First, including:

> Bracey (2006) also notes that it is very unlikely that many Reading First children were included in the NAEP assessments in 2004 (and even 2005). NAEP is given to nine year olds, but RF is directed at grade three and lower. Many RF programs did not begin until late in 2003; in fact, Bracey notes that the application package for RF was not available until April, 2002. (n.p.)

And for this, how was Spellings held accountable? Not at all, as the contradiction and misinformation were primarily ignored by the mainstream media.

And herein lies the problem with the accountability demands coming from the new reformers and not being challenged by the media or the public. The premise that our schools are failing is a distortion, especially when based on further misuse of data such as international comparisons (Riddile, 2010), but the claim that education is failing because of "bad" teachers and powerful teachers' unions is more disturbing since no one ever offers any evidence, even manipulated evidence, to show that the most pressing education reform needed is teacher quality and disbanding unions. In fact, the entire course of the current accountability era has been destined to fail because the reforms are never couched in clearly defined problems. Instead, solutions are driven by ideology and cultural myths.

Calls for higher standards and greater accountability suggest that educational failure grows from a lack of standards and accountability—but where is the evidence those are the sources? Calls for changing teacher pay scales and implementing merit pay suggest that current pay scales and a lack of a merit pay system are somehow causing educational failures—but where is the evidence those are the sources? Charges against union influence and claimed protection of "bad" teachers also suggest that unionization of teachers has caused educational failure—but where is the evidence those are the sources?

The truth is that the new reformers are attacking teachers and unions because this is a question of power—maintaining power with the corporate and political elite at the expense of the ever-widening gap between them and the swelling workforce that is losing ground in wages and rights (Noah, 2010). De-professionalized teachers stripped of the collective bargaining are the path to a cheap and compliant workforce, paralleling the allure of TfA as a cheap, recycling teacher pool—an essential element in replacing the universal public education system with a corporate charter school and privatized education system. From the perspective of the new reformers' corporate lens for education, there is money to be made, of course, but better yet, the corporate takeover of education helps solidify the use of schools to generate compliant and minimally skilled workers.

In Ralph Ellison's (1952) *Invisible Man*, the unnamed main character finds himself in a hellish nightmare after being kicked out of college and sent on a cruel quest for work in New York. He then turns to a paint manufacturing plant for employment:

KEEP AMERICA PURE

WITH

LIBERTY PAINTS. (p. 196)

The exchange between the main character and his supervisor, Kimbro, when the main character is first learning his job is important at this moment in the history of U.S. public education and the rising tide against unions:

> "Now get this straight," Kimbro said gruffily. "This is a busy department and I don't have time to repeat things. You have to follow instructions and you're going to do things you don't understand, so get your orders the first time and get them right! I won't have time to stop and explain everything. You have to catch on by doing exactly what I tell you. You got that?" (p. 199)

What follows is the main character being told by Kimbro that Liberty Paints' prize item, white paint, requires 10 drops of black. The process makes no sense on many levels to the main character, but he is chastised for questioning doing his job as told: "'That's it. That's all you have to do,' [Kimbro] said. 'Never mind how it looks. That's my worry. You just do what you're told and don't try to think about it'" (p. 200).

The scenes that follow include the main character being reprimanded for a decision although the compared paint samples *look* identical—the only difference being one is the result of his choice and the other is the work of the supervisor. (Later, Ellison examines the role of unions at the plant, also sections valuable to the debates today.) But here, I want to emphasize that this scene from *Invisible Man* is little different from the accountability dynamic begun in the early 1980s. For nearly three decades, teachers have been mandated to implement standards and to prepare students for tests that those teachers did not create and often do not endorse. Like the main character in *Invisible Man*, they are told daily,

"'You just do what you're told and don't try to think about it'" (Ellison, 1952, p. 200).

And like the main character above, they are now being held accountable for the results—disregarding the power structure that mandates the standards and the tests, disregarding the weight of evidence that shows test scores are more strongly aligned with poverty than teacher or school quality. The question of power in the U.S. is that *voice*, thus power, comes from wealth and status. As I considered earlier, would anyone listen to Bill Gates about education if he had no money? (Thomas, 2011i).

At the end of his ordeal, the main character in *Invisible Man* has been rendered not only *silent* but also *invisible*. He hibernates and fights a covert battle with the Monopolated Light & Power company by living surrounded by 1,369 lights. His story is a question of power, a struggle to bring the truth to light. In the second decade of the twenty-first century, teachers, educators, scholars, and everyone concerned about democracy and freedom must reject the urge to hibernate and wage silent battles. Instead, voices must be raised against the powerful who have now set their sights on teachers, schools, students, and ultimately the majority of us standing on the other side of the widening gap between the haves (who have their voices amplified) and the have nots (who are silenced, invisible).

The focus on teacher quality is a political struggle over power, one that benefits the corporate and political elite as long as the public remains blind to social inequity and poverty.

HOW DO TEACHERS MATTER?
NOT AS CAUSE AGENTS BUT AS LEARNING OPPORTUNITIES

Lost in the exaggerated claims of "bad" teachers being at the core of all that ails education and the concurrent calls for greater teacher accountability, often linked to student test scores, is a careful consideration of why we have universal public education in a free society and what the role of the teacher is within that purpose. Debates about teacher quality and education reform are doomed to fail if we do not first place *both* within our purposes for and beliefs about education, human nature, and our culture. Universal public education, in its essence, must rest upon a commitment to human agency and autonomy as well as a full and complex faith in and support for democratic principles. Our perception of and expectations for teachers must also include an honest awareness of the impact of poverty—not a masking of poverty—and a much more complex view of how any teacher addresses students from a wide variety of backgrounds and abilities (see Chapter Seven for a complete examination of addressing children living in poverty).

Once we embrace human agency and autonomy—everyone is born equal, including the rights of life, liberty, and the pursuit of happiness regardless of social class—we have chosen a definition of "education" that rejects indoctrination and enculturation, although *these two purposes have dominated how and why our schools have functioned for over a century* (Thomas, 2011z). A people who believe in individual freedom must cherish the empowerment of every human mind. To distrust human autonomy is to reject freedom and to call for some authority to determine the lives of others—and thus either to diminish each person's access to education or to reduce a system of schooling to oppression through indoctrination and enculturation (the goal of "no excuses" ideology). The role of the teacher and the school must be sacred as well for all children regardless of their home lives.

If, then, we are truly a people who believe in human freedom and thus appreciate the role of universal public education as an opportunity for individual empowerment, agency, and autonomy, we must acknowledge the complex and important role of a teacher within a commitment to individual freedom and democracy. Let me clarify here that I have been a teacher from the middle school level through graduate education for 29 years now. In that time, I have taught thousands of students of nearly every possible ability, background, and level of commitment. For the record, I have not caused a single one of those students to learn: *Teachers in an education system designed for a free society and people are not cause agents but mechanisms for designing, providing, and enhancing learning experiences for every student regardless of that student's station in life. Ultimately, a student who is free is the sole determinant of whether or not learning occurs—as long as that student's life allows that choice.*

Calls for teacher accountability tied to student outcomes, such as tests, distort the role of a teacher in a free society. Few people take the time to consider that viewing a teacher as a cause agent (holding a teacher accountable for the behavior of a separate free human) and viewing learning as the mere transmission of knowledge from a teacher-authority to a passive class of students are *antithetical to our beliefs in individual freedom and democracy.* Bureaucratic and mechanistic plans for teacher accountability for student outcomes are as oppressive as the conditions of poverty in the lives of children; thus, the teacher accountability plans of new reformers are perpetuating a stratified culture through our schools instead of reforming our schools to address social inequity.

Can a teacher through coercion, threat, bribe, or force of personality demand from a student a behavior that appears to match a learning outcome? Of course. But that is indoctrination/enculturation—not education. It denies the dignity and humanity of the teacher and the student; it rejects the sacred faith in individual freedom and democratic principles.

And as long as we use education reform debates and mandates to ignore poverty as well as social inequity, we will continue to perpetuate a public school machine that fulfills the worst of government education—enculturation—since that enculturation fails to confront the status quo which has created and maintained an unjust society.

Teachers of free people cannot and should not *cause* learning to happen; thus, we must focus our concern for teacher quality exclusively on the characteristics of that teacher and the quality of the learning opportunities that teacher provides. (As well, the pursuit of teacher quality must be situated appropriately in the larger picture of what influences impact student learning, acknowledging that the quality of the teacher is a small percentage of those influences that are dominated by factors beyond the walls and control of the teacher or the school.)

So, how do teachers matter, and how should we seek higher quality teachers, holding them accountable for providing every child access to the learning opportunities all humans deserve at birth?

Teachers must possess *and* constantly enhance their knowledge base— the content they teach, their pedagogy, and their understanding of human beings as biological, social, and cultural beings—by being lifelong learners in formal classroom settings, such as graduate courses and degrees, and by being scholars, actively engaged with the fields that they teach (the first is typical of K-12 educators and the latter, of professors, but both should be elements of all teachers).

Teachers must be reflective and transparent practitioners of their craft, and here is a key element of the debate about teacher quality that we are consistently failing to recognize. Teacher quality is not revealed in student outcomes; in fact, *student outcomes tend to mask and distort the quality and role of the teacher.* Teacher quality is best revealed in the *act of teaching itself*— although complicated and time consuming to capture and evaluate, the act of teaching is the single best evidence of the opportunities a teacher provides for all students. And those opportunities are the only rightful outcomes for which teachers can and should be held accountable because it is the act of teaching and creating learning opportunities that is within the teacher's power to control.

Rightful accountability, then, must be limited to that which a person controls—all other accountability is unethical, oppressive, and corrosive. All other accountability is a perpetuation of the status quo, a masking of social inequities and a denial of poverty as a condition tolerated at best and manipulated at worst by the ruling elite. But every child deserves a high quality teacher, one who is in a constant process of growth as a teacher and not fixed at a moment in coming to know the profession. One truism that should guide how we evaluate teacher quality is seeking ways to determine the difference between a teacher who teaches 1 year 20 times and a teacher who teaches 20 concurrent years that build one upon the other, informed by an equal commitment to being a scholar.

Focusing on prescriptive and external data points (student test scores) works to insure that we create and reward the worst sort of teachers—fixed at a point in their growth, teaching 1 year 20 times. Teacher accountability linked to student outcomes reduces teacher quality to raising test scores—a misleading and minimal expectation for teacher quality in a free society. Bureaucratic, evaluative, and punitive teacher accountability drives any teacher's focus away from the child and toward scripts (Schmidt & Thomas, 2009) and data. That shift erases the lives of children from the teaching/learning dynamic; it creates a false belief in standard children, standard learning, and standard human outcomes—all dehumanizing, oppressive, and wedded to an unjust status quo that serves those already in power.

Teacher quality matters, and we can identify and foster better teachers. But that process, if we truly value individual freedom and democracy, must exist in a spirit of community and with a commitment to human dignity and empowerment—for both the teacher and students. A system of self-evaluation, peer-evaluation, and supervisor-based evaluation—designed to support and not punish or reward—that addresses teacher competence (content and pedagogy) and, above all else, the quality of the educational opportunities offered to students regardless of their background is the sort of teacher accountability and education reform we must seek.

However, *any* commitment to teacher quality and education reform for individual freedom and democracy will not produce the results we seek for our children if we continue to see raising teacher and school quality as a silver bullet and as a singular avenue to social reform. Social reform must precede or occur simultaneously with proper care for teacher quality or we will persist in our greatest failure of all—pointing an accusatory finger at teachers and schools while many children and their families lie beneath the rubble of poverty that we fail to acknowledge.

"THE BUREAUCRATIZING OF THE MIND": TEACHER CERTIFICATION AND ACCREDITATION

As I have discussed throughout this chapter, the current and even historical focus on teacher quality, teacher preparation, and teacher professional development tends to work against placing the role of teachers within a social context and against the possibility of teachers as change agents. Yeigh, Cunningham, and Shagoury (2011) exposed the connection between credentialing and reinforcing the status quo of teachers as passive mechanisms for perpetuating a bureaucratic educational system dedicated to producing compliant workers. If we place their confrontation of testing teachers as part of the credentialing process within Freire's "bureaucratizing of the mind" (1998, p. 111), we begin to see that teachers are more often reduced to pawns within a corporate view of schooling than they are supported in their own professional empowerment that leads to their potential to do exactly what the new reformers claim education can accomplish—challenge and change the social dynamics that trapped a growing number of children and their families in poverty.

Historically, teachers enter the public school workforce through colleges and departments of education that award both degrees in education and certification linked to state departments of education. These bureaucratic processes have gradually evolved away from the domain of the state and toward a national process, paralleling the accountability era's move in the early 1980s from state-driven standards and testing to the Obama administration promoting a common core set of standards and even more testing that is centralized.

The bureaucratic and administrative players in this move to a national certification and accreditation of teachers have included The National Board for Professional Teaching Standards (NBPTS, http://www.nbpts.org/), and The National Council for Accreditation of Teacher Education (NCATE, http://www.ncate.org/Default.aspx); as well, the momentum toward a national call for higher expectations for teachers and more rigorous avenues to teaching has seen NCATE merge with Teacher Education Accreditation Council (TEAC, http://www.teac.org/) to form Council for the Accreditation of Educator Preparation (CAEP, http://www.caepsite.org/) and the more recent National Council on Teacher Quality (NCTQ, http://www.nctq.org/p/).

Just as political leaders and the national debate on education have ignored the role of poverty in student outcomes—resulting in a relentless call for high standards, increased testing, and more intense accountability in order to raise student achievement—this same pattern has now enveloped how we view and prepare teachers. Briefly, I want to highlight just two examples of how the evidence on this process is ignored and what we should be pursuing instead if we truly want elite teachers and an improved public education system. Let's consider NBPTS and NCTQ.

NBPTS was formed in 1987, but throughout the 2000s, it gained momentum alongside the rising accountability era boosted by NCLB. States throughout the country began reimbursing teachers for going through the NBPTS process, leading to significant stipends for those teachers once they attained certification. NBPTS was viewed as a commitment to high-quality teachers and as an avenue of empowerment for those teachers seeking to grow as educators. The assumptions about teacher quality, teacher impact on student achievement, student achievement, and research are embedded in the media coverage of NBPTS as well as NBPTS's own public relations machine.

"Schools looking to hire teachers should keep an eye out for those with national board certification," reads the lead to a June 11, 2008, article in *USA Today* with the headline: "Board-certified teachers boost student scores." Why such a claim?: "Students taught by educators certified by the National Board for Professional Teaching Standards make bigger gains on standardized tests than students taught by other teachers, finds a National Research Council report out Wednesday" (Board-certified, 2008, n.p.).

This news report about a study addressing board certification of teachers confirmed political and public trust that certification equates with quality, and the report also feeds the claim that teachers are the most important element in student outcomes. But the problem buried beneath the news article is disturbing.

Despite what the news headlines claim, the study does not show that board certified teachers *cause* higher student achievement. The study (Hakel, Koenig, & Elliott, 2008) does show a *correlation* in that students in classes taught by board certified teachers scored higher than students in classes with teachers not board certified. The details of this distinction tend to be buried (or ignored) in news accounts:

> "The NBPTS has the potential to make a valuable contribution to efforts to improve teacher quality, together with other reforms intended to create a more effective environment for teaching and learning in schools, increase the supply of high-quality entrants into the profession, and improve career opportunities for teachers," the report concludes. "Our review of the research, however, suggests that there is not yet compelling evidence that the existence of the certification program has had a significant impact on the field, teachers, students, or the education system," it says. (Viadero & Honawar, 2008, n.p.)

The study clarifies that the research cannot distinguish between whether or not board certification attracts more effective teachers or creates more effective teachers (Hakel, Koenig, & Elliott, p. 6).

And we must not simply blame the media for failing to report the crucial distinction between correlation and causation because NBPTS feels no shame in a creating press release proclaiming: "In the most comprehensive study to date of National Board Certification, the NRC's extensive, multi-year report formally affirmed the National Board's positive impact on student achievement, teacher retention and professional development" (Aguerrebere, 2008, n.p.).

As I have discussed in Chapter 3, the media fails the discourse about education because the media lacks a critical perspective and works to maintain the status quo that in turn insures the media's existence, but the role of advocacy is central here as well since NBPTS depends on promoting itself to maintain its existence. If no one plans to call them on it, NBPTS will continue to make claims that are misleading at best and self-serving at worst. NBPTS, however, may prove to be less important in our consideration of certification and accreditation dynamics as masks for addressing poverty than NCTQ.

Welner (2010) provides a foundation for considering the role of bureaucracy in teacher preparation and certification:

> Reformers appeal to the urgency of confronting "failing schools," but the logic of their argument leads inevitably to students' dependence upon parents who know how to maneuver within the system to gain private advantage. This is an abandonment of the goal of a comprehensive public sector that provides equitable, universal opportunities. Such consequences are anathema to progressives when free-market ideas are applied to health care; there is no reason they should be welcome when applied to the education of the nation's children (in Skeels, 2011a). (n.p.)

Bureaucracy, mechanistic credentialing, and hierarchical policies are driven by market and corporate assumptions—assumptions that in fact work against the ideals of many public institutions such as education.

Skeels (2011a) addresses that behind NCTQ's press releases and slick reports, we discover that their work is not peer-reviewed and that their claims are distorted. In short, NCTQ has an agenda that has little to do with teacher quality:

> NCTQ is a right of center think tank immersed in neoliberal policy promotion. While not as reactionary or as far to the right as say The Heritage Foundation, The Cato Institute, or the Manhattan Institute, they are nevertheless ideologically charged and strongly biased. NCTQ releasing an unreviewed paper like the one on LAUSD has all the legitimacy of a policy analysis recommending the repeal of all civil rights legislation by The John Birch Society. (Skeels, n.p.)

And that agenda is funded by Bill Gates and includes connections and support among the rising class of new reformers such as Rhee, Rick Hess, and Joel Klein. NCTQ, like Secretary Duncan, includes direct and subtle connections to civil rights organizations, suggesting that NCTQ cares about teacher quality in order to address social inequity, but these connections are as misleading as NCTQ's claims about education failures and teacher quality:

A clear picture should be beginning to emerge. All of these so-called civil rights groups are right-leaning astroturf organizations funded by the same corporate backers of corporate school reform. School privatization propagandists pushing policy under the guise of civil rights is nothing new. The illustrious Brian Jones, of *The Inconvenient Truth Behind Waiting for Superman* fame, deals with this phenomenon in two powerful articles, Charter Schools and Civil Rights: What Kind of 'Movement' is This? and Using "civil rights" to sell charter schools. (Skeels, n.p.)

The irony? NCTQ is a recent but not atypical bureaucratic approach to teacher preparation and certification that creates a silenced and powerless teacher workforce that is trained to be compliant and *not* to be political—by covert organizations such as NCTQ that are themselves being *political*. And here is where we must confront the failure of certification and accreditation of teachers in the name of higher teacher quality.

If we want independent and thoughtful young people, the standards/testing-driven accountability paradigm can only fail us since it is prone to scripted classrooms and silenced students (Schmidt & Thomas, 2009). If we truly want and believe in public education as a revolutionary institution for change capable of eradicating poverty, then increasing our historical commitment to bureaucratic teacher preparation is antithetical to that cause and belief.

The alphabet soup that is NCATE, TEAC, CAEP, NBPTS, and NCTQ isn't child's play, but a corrosive reflection of neoliberal norms masked as high expectations democratic commitments, and genuine concern for civil rights. Instead, we need education degrees and all avenues to the teaching profession to seek the empowerment of teachers as change agents, not agents of the status quo silenced by the cultural norm of unbiased teaching.

POVERTY AND EDUCATION:
QUESTIONS RAISED, QUESTIONS IGNORED

In Room for Debate in the *New York Times*, I argued that focusing on test scores to evaluate teacher quality (something NCTQ endorses, for example) allows politicians and the public to ignore poverty as the overwhelming source of educational problems (Thomas, 2011r). While this stance is well supported by evidence and many leading scholars in education, sociology, and economics, the questions my response elicited online as well as the questions that were not raised provide an ideal opportunity to examine the many misconceptions around education reform and teacher quality.

First, many people have trouble accepting an irrefutable fact: Single data points (such as test scores) are overwhelmingly most highly correlated with any student's out-of-school circumstances. For one easily accessible example, the wealth of data on the SAT provided by the College Board reveals that scores have been most strongly and directly correlated with "Family Income" and "Highest Level of Parental Education" every year the test has been administered. This pattern of out-of-school factors being the greatest influence on test scores has been found in virtually all testing situations, but with the SAT, this evidence is extremely important because the pool of students taking the SAT are uniquely elite compared to all students, meaning this pool of students is enrolled in the most challenging courses and learning from the most qualified and experienced teachers (see Peske and Haycock, 2006, which reveals that children of color, children in poverty, and ELL students are disproportionately taught by teachers who are un- or under-qualified and least experienced).

Test scores, then, are poor evidence for teacher quality because those scores mask what impact teacher quality does have on the lives and learning of children. But this remains ignored by many political leaders, education reformers, and the general public, leading to three very common retorts to any recognition that poverty overwhelms the impact of schools and teachers: (1) Poverty should not be used as an excuse; (2) if some exceptional schools (often charters) can produce high test scores, then why can't they all?; and (3) just test students at the beginning and end of each year to factor out the home conditions of the children.

Those of us identifying that poverty overwhelms the impact of schools and teachers that is captured in test scores are not suggesting that this is evidence of poverty being fatalistic. In fact, our position is a call to address poverty in both society (see Berliner, 2009) and in schools (again, consider evidence that school perpetuates the inequities found in society through teacher assignment)—instead of repeating the same failed test-and-accountability paradigm we have tried for over 30 years.

Next, many people have fallen into the trap of believing the repeated claims of education "miracles"—found in the "Texas miracle," "the Chicago miracle," and the "Harlem miracle"; the popular embracing of the recent documentary *Waiting for "Superman"* has helped reinforce a common flaw in popular belief: Making the exceptional normal. But more damning than asking everyone to match the characteristics of outliers is that every media-created education miracle I have ever witnessed has been found later to be no miracle at all (Ravitch, 2011c; also see the miracleschools wiki: http://miracleschools.wikispaces.com/).

The third question—why not just pre- and post-test each year—is incredibly compelling because examples such as the SAT are addressing single-test situations that seem more likely impacted by external factors.

But the evidence on value-added methods (what lay people are usually calling for) shows that a teacher identified as excellent one year may be identified as poor the next; in short, the method is highly volatile.

Part of the problem with any quantified system of evaluating teachers based on student outcomes is that students spend most of their lives outside of school—and any score a child ever produces on a test is the culmination of that child's whole life. *To isolate and identify direct causational relationships between any teacher and any student would be far too costly in time and money to justify the effort.*

While the challenges above elicited by acknowledging the powerful influence of children's lives on their educational outcomes are persistent, they may not be as important as what we are not asking. While identifying and rewarding teacher quality based in part or entirely on measurable student outcomes is ultimately flawed, we rarely consider that any such system is based on competition—identifying a limited pool of resources for teacher quality and requiring teachers to compete for that pool.

And this may be what is most wrong about pursing test scores to identify teacher quality because education and students always lose when learning is reduced to competition for resources. Teachers and students will thrive in a cooperative and collaborative community of learners; basing teacher quality on student outcomes will pit teacher against teacher, teacher against student with everyone losing.

Education reform is needed, and addressing teacher quality is clearly an important element of that reform. But neither will achieve what we are seeking unless we commit to address poverty in the lives of children while reforming our schools to insure that once in the classroom, we stop perpetuating the exact inequities we claim education can overcome.

TEACHER AS RADICAL, TEACHER AS CHANGE AGENT

If the new education reformers such as Secretary Duncan, Gates, and Rhee were genuinely committed to teacher quality because they have faith that public education is *the* institution of change they claim it to be, then the discourse about teachers and the calls for reform would look much differently than they do—Gates funding NCTQ, Duncan promoting Race to the Top as a lever to force states to replace teacher pay and promotion policies with VAM-based systems that usurp tenure.

Howard Zinn (1994), as teacher and historian, represents the radical imperative of change agent that personifies the type of teachers the U.S. needs if public education can be an institution of social reconstruction. But Zinn's embracing the praxis of radical as both teacher and historian worked against the cultural expectations for both and placed him in jeopardy of losing his status within each field. His memoir speaks to the *risk* inherent in confronting the norms of the status quo, and while his life's story is inspiring, it also can be read as a cautionary tale for teachers today—those working under union contracts and the relative safety of tenure as well as those working in non-union circumstances.

The same forces calling for higher teacher standards are also working to dismantle tenure—opening the gate to removing academic freedom and due process from the exact profession the new reformers claim needs a high level of professionalism. Historically and currently, teachers are safe when they take a claimed neutral stance of objectivity and perpetuate the norms of the U.S. culture; historically and currently, teachers risk all sorts of negative consequences if they speak against any norms of being.

Calls for reforming teacher quality that acknowledge and address the weight of poverty in the U.S. would instead embrace the following:

- A focus on teaching as a major and substantive content area, rich in history, philosophy, theory, and praxis. Teacher education has been driven by certification guidelines at the expense of the weight of the content of the field. If we want high quality teachers, we need teachers to be scholars, not students who comply within a series of mandates listed on a checklist. Certification has decontextualized teachers; teachers as scholars and activists must be placed within the full social fabric of life if we expect education to be transformative.

- A recognition that teachers have informed positions that must be at the core of who that teacher is in front of students. We must reject the mask of objectivity as counter to the qualities well-educated people exhibit. Teacher-as-scholar is not being capricious with positions or oppressive, but a central aspect of creating an atmosphere conducive to students discovering and embracing their own empowerment. As Kohn (2003b) warns:

  > But a number of critics over the last century have contended that it is futile, and therefore disingenuous, to pretend that social science can ever be value-free. Some have noted that there are political consequences to that charade: when you take pains to avoid making a value judgment, you end up tacitly accepting the values of the status quo. "Research rooted in the dominant values of the society is less likely to be questioned about its scientific objectivity and yet more likely to suffer from the lack of it," observed Herbert Kelman (1968, p. 72). (n.p.)

- A trust in teaching and learning as politically contested spaces. All human interactions involve the negotiation of power, including the classroom. To mask that reality is to insure a static hegemony; to expose that reality allows the possibility of confronting inequities.

• Identifying the role of the teacher as teacher-student and the role of the student as student-teacher (Freire, 1993). To be a change agent dedicated to social justice and human agency is to avoid the direct causational relationship between an oppressor and the oppressed. Teachers as radicals can create *opportunities*, but they must not impose their authority onto any students, regardless of the intent. The classroom becomes a community shared by the teacher-student and student-teacher for the pursuit of all that is good for both each student and the collective class (and collective society beyond the walls of the classroom).

• Recognizing teaching, learning, and assessment as collaborative/communal and recursive. Traditional assumptions frame the teacher as an agent doing something *to* students instead of *with* students, and the teaching/learning process is defined as analytic and linear instead of an organic condition.

• Reimagining and confronting our social and educational assumptions about poverty, class, and the human condition within privilege and poverty. I will examine this more fully in Chapter 7, but both social and educational assumptions about poverty and people living in poverty are driven by deficit perspectives that measure people against middle-class norms that become standards of being fully human. Teachers must challenge and rise above these normative assumptions in their own belief system and in their praxis as teachers, scholars, and activists—again, if education is to be transformative

Here, I have examined the complex and often contradictory concern for teacher quality in the education reform debates in the twenty-first century. The new reformers argue that poverty is not an excuse for weak student achievement, that teachers are the most powerful influence on that achievement, and that strict bureaucratic avenues to teacher preparation and certification are needed to achieve the promise that our schools can alone overcome the social inequities that plague more and more people in the U.S.

These refrains, however, are all false albeit powerful claims that prove to be yet more evidence that the political and corporate elite are using the education debate to distract the public from social inequity and injustice that are both within the power of those elite to address—although to do so, the elite would have to risk their own status.

I find it unlikely that the ruling elite will ever make that decision. Thus, today more than ever, then, the role of the teacher as change agent is imperative if education can support a cultural commitment to social justice and individual autonomy. In Chapter 6, I turn to what education can and cannot do—in terms of what how we frame the purposes against the weight of social realities such as poverty.

CHAPTER 6

"IF EDUCATION CANNOT DO EVERYTHING ..."

Education as Communal Praxis

The refrain I have weaved throughout this discussion—the U.S. ignores poverty in its political leadership, its cultural discourse, and its institutions—challenges the cultural narratives and myths that create the fabric of the American Ideal. The tension that exists between what the U.S. claims to be and what the U.S. *is* exists vividly in the universal public education system, an institution trapped between the utopian claim that education can create social reform and the reality that schools are a reflection of society (including its inequities in the lives of children).

In the final two chapters, I intend to shift somewhat away from the argument that public education reflects and perpetuates the masking of poverty and toward a re-envisioning what education can achieve (Chapter 6) and that poverty and privilege must be redefined and reconsidered (Chapter 7). Utopian expectations for public schools and deficit views of poverty and people trapped in poverty are ultimately corrosive narratives that destroy, ironically, the possibility of social justice that lies beneath the ideals that Americans claim to embrace.

Let me return to a key idea I have cited in the introduction: "If education cannot do everything, there is something fundamental that it can do. In other words, if education is not the key to social transformation, neither is it simply meant to reproduce the dominant ideology" (Freire,

Ignoring Poverty in the U.S.: The Corporate Takeover of Public Education, pp. 155–180
Copyright © 2012 by Information Age Publishing
All rights of reproduction in any form reserved.

1998, p. 110). One part of Freire's claim directly challenges the repeated argument by Secretary Duncan and other new reformers—education is the key to overcoming all of society's ills, including poverty—and the final point by Freire brings us to the critical heart of my call for education reform—education committing to equity once any students enter a school.

What, then, can education achieve as a social institution? And how do the assumptions about the purposes of education impact the larger public debate about education and education reform?

PUBLIC DISCOURSE ABOUT PUBLIC DISCOURSE: TALKING EDUCATION REFORM

Common among writers is the occasional (or frequent) distrust of the value of words against the possibility of action. William Shakespeare embedded in his works this angst, powerfully and with humor in *A Midsummers Night's Dream*. In one of my poems, I examined this tension between words and actions, drawing on two works of literature—Shakespeare's *Hamlet* and William Faulkner's *As I Lay Dying*. The education debate is bound to that same tension between rhetoric and action—between what leaders espouse in their discourse and what conditions they perpetuate and tolerate.

In *Hamlet*, Polonius is taunted by the troubled Prince when Polonius asks, "What do you read, my lord?" Hamlet responds with "Words, words, words" (Shakespeare, Act II, scene ii, 190-191). For Faulkner's (1930/1990) Addie in *As I Lay Dying*, the message is much darker and direct: "That was when I learned that words are no good; that words dont [sic] ever fit even what they are trying to say at" (p. 171).

These literary truths bode poorly for politicians, pundits, and scholars/academics because they all share one quality—the proclivity to function in the world of ideas as expressed through the medium of *words*, spoken and written. The education reform debate that has developed during the Obama administration has entered an Ouroboros stage—public debate about the public debate. While the symbolism of the snake eating its own tail can have positive implications, I fear that this self-consuming debate about education reform is likely to keep everyone entertained by words-as-sideshow while our education system and the children that it serves remain ignored and outside the tent with the teachers.

And so I am trapped, myself an academic compelled to add words to the smoldering fire, prompted by Michael J. Petrilli's (2011) discussion of the Diane Ravitch/Jonathan Alter/Secretary of Education Arne Duncan battle of words as well as Rick Hess's (2011) two-cents about a debate between Deborah Meier and Terry Moe.

In Petrilli's (2011) response to the Ravitch/Alter debate, Petrilli appears to step out of his ideological camp on the right to side (somewhat) with Ravitch and take issue with Alter's discrediting of Ravitch and reformers who stress the impact of poverty on education outcomes. Petrilli takes issue with the new reformers like Alter who insist on a "no excuses" ideology about poverty that suggests scholars like Ravitch are preaching "defeatism" (a qualification offered by Petrilli). About Alter's argument, Petrilli (2011) rebuts:

> That would be swell. But it's not exactly true. Remember the old adage, actions speak louder than words? The No Child Left Behind act is still the law of the land, and it most definitely rests on the principle that poverty is "no excuse" for low achievement. And it absolutely punishes schools for bad test scores alone. (n.p.)

This endorsement of Ravitch—"Diane is on firm ground"—appears to reflect in Petrilli a willingness to set aside ideological partisanship and rise above the flaws of debating about debates. Until we look closely at the rest of his discussion.

While Petrilli (2011) should be commended for confronting and discounting the corrosive nature of codifying 100% proficiency among school children entirely under the jurisdiction of the public school system, his olive branch offered instead must raise additional concern: "Rather than get defensive at Diane's defeatism, we reformers should clarify the ends that education reform can achieve. If not 100 percent proficiency, then what?" (n.p.). As we should expect, Petrilli's solutions include a laundry list of assumptions that are nothing new, and more troubling, these reform measures have almost thirty years of evidence showing that they simply do not and cannot work.

Instead of 100% proficiency goals, Petrilli (2011) offers more *reasonable* goals, discounting that federal or state mandates do not make anything happen merely by codifying a goal. As well, to suggest that a reasonable goal—seeking "9 percent instead of 4 percent," for example—is the solution again falls into the trap of believing that words equal action while also ignoring that placing a goal on one group of students based on a *different* population of students inherently discounts the very real flaw of comparing apples to oranges (4% for population A, for example, may have been truly exceptional while 9% for population B may be an utter failure, but comparing B to A gives the appearance that A is a failure and B is a success—the perfect picture of why words fail us if we ignore reality).

The error here—the simplistic faith in goals and numbers out of context that speaks to public assumptions instead of solid evidence—is recurring over and over in the media. Consider this misleading, yet again, international comparison, this time Germany. Leonhardt (2011) references Eric Hanushek who claims Germany is succeeding in education reform because they focus on PISA. But, the facts concerning Germany and PISA are not what the article claims since both Germany's raw PISA scores and scores adjusted for poverty (Riddile, 2010) fall *below* the U.S. The decontextualized claim about Germany falls apart once Germany's test scores are placed against the scores of the U.S. and within the influence of poverty. In short, Hanushek's claim and the narrative of the article by Leonhardt are false.

More broadly, and this is where at least one portion of the education debate seems deaf and blind, Petrilli (2011) maintains the new reformers' focus on in-school reform *only*. His concession to out-of-school factors is brief (mere words, words, words) and absent in his reasonable reform alternatives. On balance, however, I believe Petrilli's (2011) big picture here is commendable, especially his closing comment:

> Is this making you uncomfortable? Good. If we are to get beyond the "100 percent proficiency" or "all students college and career ready" rhetoric, these are the conversations we need to have. And if we're not willing to do so, don't complain when Diane Ravitch and her armies of angry teachers say that we are asking them to perform miracles. (n.p.)

If the new reformers listen to *this*, then we may be hopeful about the debate-about-the-debate moving from words to actions. But the Hess (2011) blog about Meier and Moe suggests any hope gained here must be tempered.

While Ravitch and Alter sparred over poverty and education, the Meier/Moe debate focused on teachers' unions prompting Hess (2011) to blog: "To me, it looked like two key fault lines ran through the discussion. One was the notion of 'reform unionism' and professional voice. The second was how to judge whether schools or teachers were doing well" (n.p.). Hess's work has been inspected recently as concern has grown about Gates's influence on the education reform debate—influence through his words and his enormous wealth (Horn, 2011). This debate about *how the debate is shaped* is central to the characteristics of Hess's blog about Meire, Moe, and teachers' unions.

First, to suggest a simple duality of positions as personified by Meire and Moe (or Ravitch and Alter) is to ignore a central warning from John Dewey (1938/1997) about either/or thinking. But dualistic public discourse about education reform reveals a pattern—epitomized by Fox News and its claim to "fair and balanced"—of masking imbalance as balance.

This is hard to grasp and it certainly causes discomfort in a free society that claims to embrace democracy and freedom of speech, but *some times, only one position in a debate is credible.* There may be two or more sides to debates about the Holocaust or slavery in the U.S., for example, and while all sides have the right to voice their positions, *one side remains credible while other claims remain flawed, unethical, and unsubstantiated by the evidence.* And this is the case in education reform debate as well.

Hess (2011) has every right to portray Meier and Moe as "equals" in the debate over unions, but, on balance, I find accepting Moe's stances as credible impossible:

> Yesterday, Moe sketched the book's argument, saying, "Teacher unions are the most powerful force in American education... from the bottom up and the top down." He said that fully understanding this dynamic is essential to making sense of why education policy "has been such a disappointment for a quarter century," because schools are organized like they are largely due to the pressures exerted by teacher unions. (n.p.)

Hess will never fully confront the corporate challenge to unionization because Hess has an abiding faith in market dynamics, but to place Moe's arguments in an equal context with Meier's here is, again, to suggest that all perspectives are credible, and Moe's isn't.

U.S. public education has been criticized as a failure for over a century, from at least the 1890s and the work of The Committee of Ten. Unions have been the root cause of that failure all that time?

More damning to the anti-union drumbeat, however, is a much more obvious fact: States most often identified as typical of the failures we associate with our public schools are non-union, right-to-work states where teachers do not have tenure and teacher working conditions and contracts are not negotiated by unions (South Carolina, for example, my home state and a perennial target of the "worst schools in the country" mantra). If teacher's unions are "the most powerful force in American education," as Moe (and *Waiting for "Superman"*) claims (Hess, 2011), then how are these non-union states among the proclaimed worst-of-the-worst?

And this, like a snake eating its own tail, circles back to the same issue uncovered in the Ravitch/Alter debate: The most powerful force in American education is poverty. And why do we have more than 20% of children living in poverty in the U.S.? Because the ruling elite, at best, tolerate it, and at worst, want it.

This is not an excuse, but a fact. And this is not defeatism or an endorsement of the status quo. We need real education reform and we need it now. But not without serious social reform that addresses poverty in the lives of children and their families. And the school reform can't be statistical goals, mere words and numbers (Bryant, 2011), but must be actions taken to ensure that our schools stop reflecting the inequities in our society and directly model for our children and our country the equity that every human deserves in a country honoring words such as "freedom" and "justice." Otherwise, we are left with Addie's lament: "Words dont [sic] ever fit even what they are trying to say at" (Faulkner, 1930/1990, p. 171).

SMELLS LIKE ... ANOTHER STRAWMAN ARGUMENT

Discussing the purposes of education and debating needed educational reform are often built on unbending ideology and flawed reasoning—as I examined above. But the ability to make compelling arguments often depends on the strategies chosen by all sides in the debate. In the education debate occurring under the Obama administration, making unwarranted claims is often just the tip of the iceberg of careless argumentation.

Genuine dialogue feeds the essence of a free and democratic society as well as a classroom dedicated to human agency and democratic principles. But this foundational principle veers away from its fertile possibilities and toward corrosive results when the voices driving the dialogue stop being informed and slip into predictable patterns that fail all sides of the debate. As a *New York Times* columnist, David Brooks (2011) is the steward of a privilege held by few, which makes his column on Diane Ravitch's role in the education reform debate even more troubling.

Brooks is often eager to join the education market place of ideas, having spurred the robust charter school miracle narrative (Brooks, 2009; Thomas, 2010e) that is mostly ideology and public relations. Like his hasty and inaccurate claims of "miracle," Brooks' rebuttal of Ravitch fails for a recurring reliance on the strawman argument as well as sweeping and simplistic claims not supported by evidence.

Early in his confrontation of Ravitch, Brooks (2011) lets the reader know more about himself than Ravitch:

> She picks and chooses what studies to cite, even beyond the normal standards of people who are trying to make a point.
> She has come to adopt the party-line view of the most change-averse elements of the teachers' unions: There is no education crisis. Poverty is the real issue, not bad schools. We don't need fundamental reform; we mainly need to give teachers more money and job security. (n.p.)

Mixed in with his condescending tone, according to Brooks, Ravitch is not offering evidence-based commentary on education; she is simply a mouth-piece for the unions (a weak swipe for a journalist of his stature akin to putting babies and kittens in a TV commercial), a cherry-picker posing as a scholar, and a defender of the status quo that wants us to pay teachers more without asking for any school reform. This ad hominem attack suggests that Brooks may be less able to argue the topic than his authoritative commentaries want to reveal.

If any of his claims were accurate, Brooks (2011) would have captured the entire argument well in the characterization of Ravitch, but the truth is a bit more complicated—primarily because he establishes a complex strawman in the above assault on Ravitch in order to have an argument. Setting aside the people involved in the education debate, Brooks is voicing the powerful but false talking points now driving the education debate:

- *False claim: Anyone disagreeing with Bill Gates, Arne Duncan, Michelle Rhee, and company is a defender of the status quo.* The truth is that many passionate educators and scholars both disagree with the new reformers *and* are calling for significant and radical education reform (Thomas, 2011c). The us-versus-them strategy is a signal that Brooks (2011) and other new reformers such as Duncan, Gates, Rhee, and Canada have little expertise or experience to stand on.

- *False claim: Anyone acknowledging the primary influence on the lives and educational outcomes of children—poverty—is a shill for teachers' unions and those hordes of greedy teachers draining the U.S. as we speak.* Yet, a basic knowledge of the history of education reveals that public education has been demonized and under the weight of "crisis" discourse since the mid-1900s (Thomas, 2010q). And despite the persistent evidence that poverty outweighs teacher quality in student outcomes, the political elite have committed to refrains of educational "crisis" while ignoring the weight or even fact of poverty in U.S. society and schools.

- *False claim: Public education is clearly a failure because we can identify charter schools that excel despite serving high-poverty populations.* This is a powerful claim, unless we consider the evidence that exposes that charter schools—like private schools—produce a wide range of quality, just as public schools do (CREDO, 2009). And, a rising rebuttal to claims of "miracle" schools is showing that essentially no claims of "miracle" hold up under scrutiny (Miracleschools, 2011; Ravitch, 2009b, 2010c, 2011b, 2011c).

These talking points about education reform resonate with an uninformed public and have become powerful tools for our political leaders to keep anyone from considering deep education or social reform—radical reform that would confront the role the ruling elite has played in both the inequities of our society and our education system. And we cannot discount the role of the media (Welner et al., 2010)—including commentators such as Brooks—in perpetuating the status quo while claiming to be speaking against it, in speaking against ideology and the shoddy use of evidence while being ideological and careless with claims of evidence.

Brooks has every right to challenge Ravitch; in fact, such weighty conflicts of personas and ideas have the potential to raise the debate and help insure that at some point we truly address social inequity and education failures. But we need Brooks and other commentators to be expert in their topics before we accept their claims.

Do accountability, standards, and testing produce the educational reform and outcomes we are seeking? No, and we have decades of evidence to show the accountability premise is a failure (Hout & Elliott, 2011).

Further, are Hoxby's and CREDO's work on charters as simple and clear as Brooks (2011) claims? Hoxby's work presents more questions, possibly, than solutions:

> As a result of the flaws in the report's statistical analysis, it likely overstates the effects of New York City charter schools on students' cumulative achievement, though it is not possible—given the information missing from the report—to precisely quantify the extent of overestimation. It may be that New York City's charter schools do indeed have positive effects on student achievement, but those effects are likely smaller than the report claims. Policymakers, educators, and parents should not rely on the report's conclusions regarding charter school effects in grades 4-12 until these issues have been fully investigated and the analysis has undergone rigorous peer review. (Reardon, 2009, n.p.)

While Brooks (2011) appears to have committed to the talking points coming from Duncan, Gates, and Rhee, we must give him credit for some abrupt and convoluted ingenuity toward the end of his piece on Ravitch: "If your school teaches to the test, it's not the test's fault. It's the leaders of your school" (n.p.). If we set aside the many careless errors in reasoning and evidence Brooks offers throughout his commentary, we must pause at this final comment and recognize that, again, Brooks is telling us way more about himself than Ravitch.

And what do we discover?

Like the entire crew of new reformers in education, Brooks (2011) fails this debate because he appears incapable of even imagining the life of educators who rise each morning and walk into real schools with real children and have to choose between doing what they know those children want and need or fulfilling state and federal mandates that promise only one thing—to label every person in every school a failure. Like the entire crew of new reformers in education, Brooks fails this debate because he appears incapable of even imagining the life of anyone not benefiting from the life of privilege that he and the reformers themselves enjoy.

Poverty is no excuse, and teaching to the test is the work of shoddy administrators—who could have imagined it was all so simple?

RUGGED INDIVIDUALISM

One of the most powerful aspects of the American mythos is the enduring faith in the rugged individual, a cultural narrative at the heart of the work ethic behind our labor force and how we encourage children to "try harder" in school. We are especially quick to tell children not to fall back on any excuses, including their home lives beyond their control.

Americans pay little attention to the sport of cycling except for the exploits of Lance Armstrong in the Tour de France, but the spring Classics of 2010 offered a notable feat by Fabian Cancellara that speaks to much we should consider as a culture and as a people often seeking better schools. In eight days of early April 2010, Cancellara, a Swiss cyclist riding then for Saxo Bank, powered away from an entire professional field of elite cyclists to win the prized Tour of Flanders and Paris Roubaix—mythic cycling events that are followed with more interest in their countries than the Super Bowl in the U.S.

Cancellara, like Armstrong, likely triggers in the American psyche our affinity for the rugged individual—that person who succeeds by rising above all sorts of adversity, whether it be Armstrong's fight with cancer or forces we speak of in the abstract like poverty. Yes, in the U.S., we believe the rugged individual myth, and we also regularly evoke the rugged individual as not just possible, but the ideal for all people to achieve. This narrative is central to many of the message we send children, especially in our schools.

While many consider this ideal a central tenet of the wider American Myth, we would all benefit from recognizing that the rugged individual simply doesn't exist and promoting the myth as both possible and ideal causes each of us more harm than good—especially as it impacts how we think about and practice education. That our public schools perpetuate a corrosive myth exposes what education can do (indoctrination) as well as providing an opportunity for genuine education reform that seeks individual agency and social justice.

On April 4 and 11, 2010, I watched Cancellara win two of the most inspiring races I have ever watched as an avid cyclist and fan, and I consider his feats some of the best athletic performances I have ever witnessed. And while he did cross the finish lines by himself, it is careless and naïve to suggest that he did so solely of his own determination and ability. Cancellara did not "pull himself up by the bootstraps"; in fact, Cancellara's singular accomplishments were not possible without dozens of other people, including those against whom he competed.

Despite what many think, cycling is a team sport, and winning a bicycle race often means one rider receives help in a variety of ways from several other riders (who *succeed* by sacrificing themselves for the good of the team and one other teammate) and dozens of support staff along the course. In one of his victories, in fact, Cancellara had to dismount his bicycle and swap it for another—all of which had to be orchestrated by his team support nearly perfectly for him to succeed.

French writer and philosopher Albert Camus (1955) offered his view of the human condition by envisioning the mythical Sisyphus, not as the rugged individual, but as the individual bound to the context of his being—social, cultural, natural. Sisyphus was condemned to pushing a rock over and over up a mountain only to have the rock roll each time back to the base of that hill. Camus examined two important points about what many would see as a torturous existence, a hell on earth. First, Camus asks us to consider Sisyphus *happy* because it is struggling that is our human condition. And next, and I think this is key, Camus (1995) explains, "All Sisyphus' silent joy is contained therein. His fate belongs to him. His rock is his thing" (p. 91).

We as a central element of being human are, I believe, defined by our context—by the people, places, events, and obstacles that surround us. Nothing failed and nothing achieved by a human is done so in a vacuum or alone, including teaching and learning that are also not themselves bound solely to the school room. Now what do Fabian Cancellara and Albert Camus have to do with education?

Echoing John Donne's poetic claim that no person is an island, Hillary Clinton was criticized and satirized (Boaz, 1997) all along the political spectrum for her "it takes a village," a call by Clinton about the lives and futures of children. Why? Clinton's message works against our commitment to rugged individualism as both possible and an ideal. We are prone to see success and failure as inherent only in the effort of each person, a message we send time and again to children about their own lots in life.

Yet, no child learns in a vacuum, no teacher teaches in a vacuum. And no child leaves her/his life behind simply by walking into a classroom.

Education is a complex and community-based journey that has no finish line or boundaries. When we suggest and outright proclaim that students simply need to work harder, that teachers simply need to work harder (both within the "no excuses" ideology), we are speaking to a deforming myth of individualism that helps neither the individual nor the society. In Cancellara's victories, he was defined by his adversaries (competition), he was blessed with elite ability (genetics), he was afforded the equipment and training opportunities few people ever experience (collaboration), and he was assisted by other riders who placed his individual success at the finish above theirs (sacrifice). He is no rugged individual, but the culmination of a human in the context of others and other forces.

For children facing a wide variety of rocks and mountains in the *lives not of their creation or choosing*, the rugged individualism myth is not only misleading, it is overwhelming, especially for children who start their lives under the burden of poverty. Do perseverance, determination, and self-sufficiency matter? Of course. But asking a child to lift herself or himself up by the bootstraps alone is a self-defeating ideology that ignores the value of collaboration and sacrifice—among many of the complex aspects of living and learning that are ignored when our mythologies cloud the realities of being fully human, when our mythologies are built on ignoring realities such as poverty.

WHAT THE SAT TEACHES US

At the end of George W. Bush's presidency, the U.S. and the world experienced an economic downturn that has persisted into the Obama administration. Throughout the history of the U.S., while the economy has fluctuated, one constant has remained since the early decades of the twentieth century—a faith and misuse of the SAT.

Each year, the media uses the release of SAT data to do exactly what the College Board warns we should not do with that data by ranking and evaluating the quality of schools across the U.S. (The College Board, 2002). The SAT has one purpose, predict college freshman success, but SAT scores are routinely used for dozens of purposes for which the test was not designed. I tend to reject any value in using the SAT—notably since SAT scores are still less effective for their sole purpose than GPA data (Kobrin, Patterson, Shaw, Mattern, & Barbuti, 2008)—but there are some valuable conclusions we can reach about education purposes and education reform based on the SAT.

Despite ample evidence against using the SAT as a gate-keeping data point for many aspects of education, we persist in those practices and continue to encourage more and more students to take the test. This has led to two unintended consequences. First, the SAT is at the center of the rise in teaching-to-the-test dynamics that ask less of students and teachers and funnel inordinate amounts of time and money toward test-prep materials and instructional practices (including students enrolling in SAT test-prep courses during the school day). Second, using SAT scores to judge our education system combined with requiring more and more students to take the test insures only one thing—lower average SAT scores[1] that will create greater and greater unfounded claims of low educational quality.

The statistical problem created by increasing the pool of students taking the SAT is the exact reason the College Board recentered the test in 1995: When you move a unique and elite population toward the normal distribution by increasing that population, the statistical average must move toward the middle, thus down. But that statistical fact then creates an ethical problem: Raising an average score while shifting an elite population toward a normal distribution can occur only by corrupting the data (through test-prep, for example, which also distorts the validity of the data in terms of reflecting student ability).

Beyond the contradiction of our SAT goals—increasing both the pool of students taking the test and the overall SAT averages—a wealth of evidence shows that the test is not worth the expense of time and money invested by our public schools:

- Schools across the U.S. have dedicated large amounts of financial resources and school time to the SAT during the parallel growth of accountability mandates, yet SAT scores have dropped (consider the warning above) along with a widening of the achievement gap on the test during the accountability era (Stagnant, 2010). In short, SAT goals and school reform goals are also conflicting agendas because focusing on testing reduces the validity of that test data, increases the role of test-prep at the expense of authentic teaching and learning, and ironically tends to lower the raw data thus creating a complicated but ultimately unfounded pubic perception that public schools are failing when in fact it is the focus on testing that is failing.

- The College Board's own research has shown as recently as 2008 that SAT scores are less effective than GPA for predicting freshman grades, the only purpose of the SAT (Kobrin et al., 2008). Rarely do we examine the economic agenda of test companies; the SAT needs the public trust in the value of the test itself despite the evidence exposing a free data point, GPA, being more effective for the purpose of the SAT.

- A 2010 Harvard study has confirmed a 2003 study that the SAT is inherently biased against minority students; the SAT also works against our efforts to address life and educational inequities for all students (Santelices & Wilson, 2010). Testing remains biased against class, race, and even gender (Spelke, 2005)—all of which discounts focusing on testing in an education system designed to address social inequity.

- The College Board (2002) issued a statement denouncing the historical and flawed use of SAT average scores to judge and rank schools and state educational systems. Since the media and political leaders persist in ignoring this warning, states should remove the misleading data from the debate.

Before discarding the SAT, however, we should consider the key powerful lesson that the test has provided year after year. Let's start with the facts of who takes the SAT. The pool of students taking the SAT is more elite academically and financially than the general population of students. As they are college-bound and elite, these students are also enrolled in more challenging courses than the general population of students. Those students taking the more challenging courses, then, are also enrolled in the classes of the most experienced and highly qualified teachers.

The lesson? Despite the relative affluence of students taking the SAT, despite their rigorous course loads, despite the high quality of their teachers, what are the strongest correlations with their scores? SAT scores are now and have always been most strongly correlated with the income level of the parents and the educational background of the parents (see The College Board, 2005, and note the influence of out-of-school factors linked with gender).

Instead of chasing contradictory SAT goals, the entire U.S. should reignite the charge against the SAT begun a decade ago in California. If the U.S. would now commit to becoming SAT-free, we would be seeking an outcome that is both achievable and in the best interest of our students and our nation.

SPEND ENERGY ON STUDENTS, NOT TESTS: LESSONS IN EDUCATION FROM SOUTH CAROLINA

Historian and education scholar Diane Ravitch (2010d) has made a bold claim regarding another sacred test, NAEP:

> The reading and math scores for 12th grade students on the National Assessment of Education (NAEP) were just released, and they are unimpressive. Scores are no better than they were in the early 1990s. The achievement gap is unchanged. I can hear the gnashing of teeth, the cries for more accountability, more charters, more this or more that. But not to worry. In fact, the 12th grade scores don't mean much. They probably mean nothing at all. (n.p.)

Soon after Ravitch's claim, I was interviewed about the most recent state assessment scores in my home state of South Carolina. I made a similar comment to Ravitch's—that test scores don't really mean much. But I have found that few people respond well to such claims.

Since A Nation at Risk in 1983, under President Reagan, the U.S. has invested a great deal of time and money in identifying standards, testing students, and labeling schools. SC was at the front edge of the commitment to the accountability era and has participated in most of the reform initiatives championed today; thus, evidence from SC provides an ideal crucible for considering the efficacy of continuing to pursue educational goals driven by standards, testing, and accountability while maintaining a "no excuses" ideology regarding poverty:

- SC has historically characterized itself and been characterized from the outside as ranking last, or near the bottom, of education throughout the nation. Part of that ranking rests on the flawed practice of ranking states by SAT averages. As a result of the charges of "last in education," SC has pursued three decades of accountability, standards, and testing (begun nearly two decades before No Child Left Behind) along with implementing education policy and funding that support increasing the number of students taking the SAT and providing in the schools extensive SAT preparation coursework and technology/software.

- SC has also stood at the leading edge in terms of teacher quality with several phases of state-wide teacher assessment/evaluation programs and one of the most aggressive campaigns for teachers to achieve NBPTS certification (see Chapter Five), including the state providing fee reimbursement for the board certification process and rewarding board certified teachers with a yearly supplement of $7,500.

- As reflected in a court case and resulting documentary, *Corridor of Shame*, SC has wrestled with pockets of poverty impacting schools negatively across the state, particularly along the I-95 corridor. Again, SC has been proactive by creating several programs offering teachers incentives to teach in high poverty schools; concurrently, the state has implemented an aggressive accountability system, identifying schools quality through report cards and intervening where reform appeared ineffective.

- While SC has resisted powerful efforts to bring school choice to the state, SC's largest school district has practiced public school choice for many years, presenting a snapshot of choice dynamics, which resulted in greater stratification, pockets of affluence and poverty.

- And SC has experimented with a number of reforms being championed today: charter schools, single-gender education, on-line schools.

Since I have been a public school teacher (eighteen years) and teacher educator (nine years) in SC for almost three decades as of 2011, I can attest that the people leading these policies and reforms have overwhelmingly been sincere, and while education reform has often been contentious throughout the past 30 years, many bright and dedicated people have worked tirelessly to improve the schools of SC. So as we enter the second decade of the twenty-first century, what has been the result of three decades of high accountability?

SC continues to lament low SAT scores, and is faced each testing season with scores that do not attain the goals the state has established. In fact, in each election season, both major parties portray SC schools, once again, as failures.

It is time that we all set aside our preoccupation with test scores as the central goal and evaluation tool of public schools. We should not bemoan scores that are too low, and we must not praise scores that appear successful. Instead of standards and tests, our energy should be spent on children, students who are much more than any test scores. And our focus on these children in the care of our schools must not be just inside school walls. The great irony is that test scores do not mean what we claim (the quality of learning in our schools), but they are a mirror to something worth noticing, something that we continue to ignore—the fact of many children's lives outside of school.

Test scores are yet one more marker of the inequities of our society, and while not one more second or dollar should be spent chasing higher test scores, we should find the courage to face and address the plight of poverty that makes learning impossible for children struggling to live.

TEST-BASED ACCOUNTABILITY IN EDUCATION AND INTERNATIONAL COMPARISONS

The historical and current focus on test-based accountability to drive education evaluation and reform is often situated within another historical and current approach to judging U.S. public education—international comparisons. Just as we tend to misuse test data, specifically the SAT, to rank and label the quality of schools and state education systems, we do the same with international comparisons.

"A century ago, the United States was among the most eager benchmarkers in the world," opens Tucker (2011), leading to the focus of his report: "In this paper, we stand on the shoulders of giants, asking what education policy might look like in the United States if it was based on the experience of our most successful competitors" (p. 1). Tucker notes that the report's goal also stands on the claims by Secretary Duncan that U.S. education is lagging behind other countries.

Tucker (2011) also establishes early the evidence supporting the U.S.'s slipping status among the world in terms of education when placed against GDP per capita. According to the four charts offered by Tucker (pp. 3-4), the U.S. sits far ahead of other countries in GDP (including a massive quadrupling of Shanghai and over $11,000 ahead of Finland), but sits well behind other nations in reading, math, and science scores on Program for International Student Assessment (PISA), specifically Shanghai, Finland, Singapore, Canada, and Japan. The charts and the message are compelling because political leaders and the public believe strongly several assumptions about education: (1) the primary purpose of education is to ready students for the workforce, either directly after high school or through college-readiness that also leads to the workforce, (2) there is a powerful and direct relationship between the quality of any country's education system (as measured by tests) and that country's economic well being, and (3) U.S. education has always been weak, especially when compared internationally (even though the same people who claim this also simultaneously claim that the U.S. once was at the top).

To understand fully, then, the purposes for education—what education can and cannot accomplish as a foundational institution of a free society—we must unpack the assumptions and claims we commonly make about education and compare those to the evidence. Since political and public discourse about education seamlessly and haphazardly intertwines claims about education, economics, international comparisons, and testing, these claims are complex and, thus, difficult to separate and address accurately, but let's look here at many of the claims placed against the evidence:

- Is there a powerful and direct relationship between test-based assessments of educational quality and strength of economies internationally? Bracey (2004, 2008) offers a careful refuting of this robust but flawed claim. In short, Bracey (2008) explains:

  > First, comparing nations on average scores is a pretty silly idea. It's like ranking runners based on average shoe size or evaluating the high school football team on the basis of how fast the average senior can run the 40-yard dash. Not much link to reality.... Second, test scores, at least average test scores, don't seem to be related to anything important to a national economy. Japan's kids have always done well, but the economy sank into the Pacific in 1990 and has never

recovered. The two Swiss-based organizations that rank nations on global competitiveness, the Institute for Management Development and the World Economic Forum, both rank the U.S. #1 and have for a number of years. (n.p.)

Thus, the faith the U.S. has in education as a central institution for driving an internationally competitive economy is "not ... link[ed] to reality." Likely, political and corporate leaders *need* the public to believe their claim in order to keep public schools focused on producing a compliant workforce, instead of allowing public education to fulfill its role in supporting human agency and democratic ideals.

- Even if the relationship between education quality and economic strength is not supported by the evidence, isn't the U.S. education system, as measured by PISA, lagging behind other nations, notably nations with much lower GDP? The basic charts offered by Tucker (2011) appear damning, but as Bracey (2008) warns, simple ranking of average test scores from single data points cannot offer a fair or accurate picture of much of anything of value concerning the quality of education in an entire country—particularly if we decontextualize that data from one important factor, poverty. Riddile (2010) presents a more nuanced analysis of PISA that compares apples to apples internationally by considering childhood poverty rates along with PISA data (see Table 6.1). The result shows that the U.S. sits at the top of ranking when poverty is considered:

Riddile also notes more problems with simplistic international comparisons by addressing Shanghai (Zhao, 2010):

Shanghai, China topped the list with 556 but is not included in this analysis because Shanghai is a city not a country and because only 35% of Chinese students ever enter high school and because "when you spend all your time preparing for tests, and when students are selected based on their test-taking abilities, you get outstanding test scores." (n.p.)

The two most repeated and compelling claims about education in the U.S., then, are factually inaccurate; thus, we have to be skeptical at best about Tucker (2011) pursuing an extended discussion of the U.S. adopting practices from other countries in order to reform education—even if we maintain the tenuous and distorting assumption that the primary purpose of education is to prepare students as future workers. But Tucker's central goal for his report, to suggest how the U.S. can and should model education reform on successful international comparisons, does provide further evi-

Table 6.1.   International Comparisons of PISA Scores Relative to Poverty Rates in Each Country (Riddile, 2010)

Country	Poverty Rate	PISA Score
United States	<10%	**551**
Finland	3.4%	536
Netherlands	9.0%	508
Belgium	6.7%	506
United States	10%-24.9%	**527**
Canada	13.6%	524
New Zealand	16.3%	521
Japan	14.3%	520
Australia	11.6%	515
Poland	14.5%	500
Germany	10.9%	497

Source: Riddle (2010).

dence that we have misguided assumptions about the purpose of education, and thus are prone to continue pursuing flawed policies for reform.

The first focus offered by Tucker (2011) is addressing quality, primarily teacher quality. While this has been the central argument for the "no excuses" segment of the new reformers led by Secretary Duncan and Gates, the claim has some serious problems. First, discussions of teacher quality suffer the similar fate that international comparisons experience, oversimplification. Teacher quality is difficult to measure, just as student learning is, but assuming that the best students make the best teachers is at least debatable (Sears et al., 1994). Further, the argument that teacher quality must be increased to reform education rests on another flawed assumption—the impact of teacher quality on student outcomes. Sawchuk (2011) details the current understanding of teacher quality and student outcomes, concluding:

> Research has shown that the variation in student achievement is predominantly a product of individual and family background characteristics. Of the school factors that have been isolated for study, teachers are probably the most important determinants of how students will perform on standardized tests [original in italics]. (n.p.)

The in-school influence of teachers on student outcomes is considerably small—about 14% (Hirsch, 2007) or 13%-17% (Hanushek, 2010). Thus, even if we accept that elite students make elite teachers, and thus we need to recruit high-achieving students into the teaching profession, we are tinkering with a very small measurable influence on the exact data we are using to evaluate schools.

What Tucker (2011) approaches but never fully addresses within the larger and misleading call to focus on teacher quality is how many countries he labels superior to the U.S. do treat, educate, and pay teachers. For one example, let's consider Finland—where teachers are required to complete a publicly-funded masters degree, where teachers are universally unionized, where teachers are not held accountable for standards or test scores (Horn, 2010b). While Tucker's echoing of Duncan and Gates the need for greater teacher quality is refuted by evidence, it seems likely that the U.S. could benefit from reconsidering how we treat, educate, and pay teachers, but the details of that consideration works against many of the commitments of corporate reformers.

Equity, the second focus presented by Tucker (2011), appears justified by, ironically, the flaws inherent in his initial premise based on raw comparisons of PISA data. While the argument for equity focuses on in-school equity without considering the need to address social inequity—the primary reform needed in the U.S.—Tucker raises important questions about stratified course offerings (tracking), teacher assignments (students coming from poverty tend to have least experienced and un- or under-qualified teachers), and the potential for schools to address high-poverty students more effectively than we currently do in the U.S.

While the equity section from Tucker (2011) has the most potential for being valuable in the education reform debate, we should note, again, that out-of-school equity is essentially ignored and that this section is dwarfed by the other two sections, the teacher quality section being seven times in length and the final section being just a bit more than double the equity section. Yes, equity matters, but Tucker's discussion helps highlight that most new reformers persist in undervaluing the impact of social inequity as well as the greatest flaw in public education—that school perpetuates the inequity children experience in their lives outside formal education.

The final section, productivity, reveals the corporate commitments driving the report. Tucker (2011) endorses the business model for reforming and running schools, accountability, and merit-based incentives for teachers and schools to perform. Again, even if we remain within the assumptions about international comparisons, test scores, and the relationship between education and economies, Tucker's third focus is not based on evidence. Hout and Elliott (2011), using test scores and international comparisons, conclude that the current and prolonged accountability era driven by standards, testing, and high accountability "have not increased student achievement enough to bring the United States close to the levels of the highest achieving countries" (p. S-3). What we should insert here is that nearly three decades of focusing on high accountability in order to raise U.S. test scores in order to compete internationally has produced two conclusions the new reformers will not acknowledge: (1) Test scores remain most strongly connected to out-of-school factors, and (2) accountability paradigms do not work.

Accountability has never worked, but neither has merit-based incentive programs. Kohn (2003a) has discredited merit pay at both the corporate and education levels, concluding about merit pay for teachers:

> So how should we reward teachers? We shouldn't. They're not pets. Rather, teachers should be paid well, freed from misguided mandates, treated with respect, and provided with the support they need to help their students become increasingly proficient and enthusiastic learners. (n.p.)

As well, the merit pay argument fails for the same reason international comparisons based on test scores fail—test scores and linking those scores to teacher quality are unstable, misleading, and corrosive to the teaching/learning dynamic (Baker et al., 2010).

The historical and current education reform movement, then, is doomed to fail (yet again) as long as leaders persist in placing tests at the center of determining education quality, international comparisons, and recruiting, preparing, and paying teachers. The reform movement is also futile as long as schools remain primarily to train a compliant workforce, as long as schools are managed like businesses, and as long as accountability drives that reform regardless of decades of evidence that standards, testing, and accountability do not work.

Finally, and most importantly, education reform will always fail students and our society if we fail to learn the lessons taught by international comparisons and testing—the weight and impact of a child's life is the central issue of equity our culture must address as we also commit fully to equitable schools. To maintain tunnel vision on schools and simplistic use of data serves only the privileged at the expense of everyone else.

WHY THE ACHIEVEMENT GAP MATTERS AND WILL REMAIN

Education Week featured a story that is a typical crisis report on education in the U.S. that has been repeated for decades, although the current crisis has expanded beyond African American students to include Hispanic students: "Study Finds Gaps Remain Large for Hispanic Students":

> While growing numbers of Hispanic students have changed the face of American education over the past two decades, the gap between them and their white classmates in math and reading remains as wide as it was in the

1990s, according to a new federal study. (Sparks, 2011, n.p.; see Hemphill, Vanneman, & Rahman, 2011)

The hand wringing over the white/Hispanic achievement gap, however, exposes more about the failure of political, media, and public discourse as well as current and historic patterns of education reform than about the quality of the U.S. education system. With a little care, we can unravel the inherent flaws in both our assumptions about the achievement gap and the misguided approaches to addressing it in our schools.

First, and this is the most important aspect of the topic, the achievement gap is primarily a reflection of the equity gap that exists in the lives of children (Berliner, 2009) and only secondarily a reflection of school quality and practices. This is central to any effective commitments to addressing inequity for children, but this fact exposes why the *Education Week* headline is unlikely ever to be any different as long as we persist in addressing only in-school dynamics and focus on the narrowest forms of student outcomes, test scores, as I have discussed above.

While politicians and the media misrepresent the achievement gap in order to demonize schools and teachers, we have ample evidence that addressing the whole life of the child is the only avenue to closing an achievement gap. After years of examining the achievement gap, Barton and Coley (2007, 2009) have crafted a plan to address reform targeting schools, children's homes, and the complex mix of any child's community and wider society, concluding:

> The bottom line is that gaps exist in the correlates of achievement. Some gaps have narrowed, some gaps have widened, but more often there was little or no change. The stark fact remains, then, that gaps in the life and school experiences of minority group and low-income children—all correlated with school achievement—mirror the achievement gaps in school, just as they did five years ago. (2007, p. 4)

But the political, corporate, and media elite—who are using the "achievement gap" refrain to mask their true commitments to maintaining the current status quo of privilege and inequity—reject all evidence-based calls for addressing social forces as using poverty for an excuse:

> In the early days of the education-reform movement, a decade or so ago, you'd often hear from reformers a powerful rallying cry: "No excuses." For too long, they said, poverty had been used as an excuse by complacent educators and bureaucrats who refused to believe that poor students could achieve at high levels. Reform-minded school leaders took the opposite approach, insisting that students in the South Bronx should be held to the same standards as kids in Scarsdale. (Tough, 2011)

Yet, the persistent result that in-school-only reform has achieved over the past half century is to ensure, as the newest report (Hemphill et al., 2011) shows (just as all studies have shown), that the gap remains. Tough, who supports Canada's Harlem Children's Zone because it addresses the whole life of children, comes to a nuanced conclusion about the "no excuses" ideology and the new reformers' claim that those acknowledging the impact of poverty are using poverty as an excuse:

> The reformers' policy goals are, in most cases, quite worthy.... But these changes are not nearly sufficient. As Paul Reville, the Massachusetts secretary of education, wrote recently in *Education Week*, traditional reform strategies "will not, on average, enable us to overcome the barriers to student learning posed by the conditions of poverty." Reformers also need to take concrete steps to address the whole range of factors that hold poor students back. That doesn't mean sitting around hoping for utopian social change. It means supplementing classroom strategies with targeted, evidence-based interventions outside the classroom. (n.p.)

And this first point—that the achievement gap is a reflection of the social equity gap—leads to a key failure in logic that is the second point, as Walt Gardner (2010b) has succinctly explained: "Don't forget that advantaged children are not standing still in the interim. They continue to benefit from travel and other enriching learning experiences. As a result, the gap will persist" (n.p.). This second point is a simple failure in logic. If we start with a solid premise (the lives of children outside of school contribute about 80% of measurable student outcomes), and then implement inequitable in-school policies (testing, labeling, and stratifying students in order to ask less of those labeled most in need), we should expect only one outcome—a persistent achievement gap.

Historically and currently, we claim that test scores fairly represent learning, we claim that schools alone determine student outcomes, we implement inequitable school policies that we label as reform addressing the gap, we pretend that lives of inequity and lives of privilege somehow pause while we implement these policies, and then we express disbelief that the achievement gap persists. And this is the cruel irony of political and bureaucratic approaches to the achievement gap—an irony that is a damning rebuttal to the intent of the rhetoric each time a political or corporate leader speaks to that gap.

A few key shifts in both how we discuss the achievement gap and address that gap would show a genuine concern for closing that gap, for empowering education reform, and for democracy and human agency:

- We must replace the phrase "achievement gap" with "equity gap"— clearly expressing that many aspects of children's lives reflect the persistent facts of privilege and inequity in our culture. Since children have little autonomy and no political power, children remain the starkest mirrors of who we are as people and a culture.

- We must address inequity in the lives of children and their families—and confront our cultural habit of masking those inequities behind our myths claiming freedom and equality for all. If we indeed embrace the ideal of human agency and equity, then we must also be willing to admit that this *ideal* has yet to be achieved. We have historically embraced the myth to the exclusion of confronting we have work left to do.

- We must focus all school reform on ending traditional and bureaucratic approaches to education that perpetuate the inequity and privilege students bring to school from their lives: standardized testing that is highly correlated with students' home characteristics, stratified courses and gate-keeping policies for those courses, inequitable teacher assignments and class sizes (privileged students sit in classrooms with the most experienced and highly qualified teachers as well as the smallest student-to-teacher ratios), and a community-based school resources model that allows each school to reflect the coincidence of every child's birth to determine her/his access to education.

The political and corporate elites benefit from a constant state of education crisis because that perception allows them to point at the schools and distract the public from their own failure to address the conditions of inequity that insure their privilege. *People living in poverty and trapped in a cycle of social inequity—specifically children—are not the agents of that inequity.* The powerful determine the conditions of any society, and schools reflect and too often maintain those conditions.

A persistent achievement gap is an accurate indictment of our schools as mechanisms of perpetuating inequity and privilege, but it is a greater indictment of the power of the cultural elite to maintain their privilege while claiming to seek equity.

EMANCIPATORY EDUCATION IN A MECHANISTIC AGE

The education reform movement that has blossomed and flourished under Obama has presented a debilitating contradiction of idealism and policy. Secretary Duncan has personified a commitment to education as the sole institutional force promising social reform, specifically the elimination of poverty, and within that claim, Duncan has also established that teacher quality is the primary area of need in order for schools to achieve

their utopian goal of social reconstruction. These ideologies have mani-
fested themselves in federal policy, such as Race to the Top, but have also
fueled other education reformers both inside and outside the field of education—Bill Gates, Michelle Rhee, and Geoffrey Canada, most notably.

The foundational ideology, then, running through the discourse and
policies among the new reformers is "no excuses"—a belief system that
marginalizes and silences acknowledging the influence of poverty on the
lives and learning of children, a group that is increasingly suffering the
burden of poverty while having no political voice or power. The inherent
contradiction of the ideology and policies is best exposed by the call to
address teacher quality within a call for national standards and increased
standardized testing. *Teachers are being deprofessionalized and classrooms are
being more directly scripted in direct contrast to teachers and schools being agents
of social change.*

Scripted curriculum and test-based accountability are necessarily culturally bound, likely to perpetuate cultural norms instead of encouraging
teachers and students to expose and act against deforming cultural
dynamics—such as poverty, the sources of poverty, and the forces denying
the agency needed to overcome and eradicate poverty. The contradictory
nature of the reform movement on the cusp of the second decade of the
twenty-first century has its roots in foundational commitments to education that occurred in the early decades of the twentieth century.

Kliebard (1995) identifies four ideological trends that represent what
America pursued as the basis for what schools can and should contribute
in a capitalistic democracy, but two of those ideologies represent well how
the U.S. maintains an ideology—social meliorism—that contrasts with
policy—social efficiency. Since the policy constitutes the reality of what
schools do and how schools perform, the ideology becomes little more
than rhetoric. In short, political discourse uses language dedicated to
social reform in order to maintain a narrowly scientific and bureaucratic
approach to schooling that ironically guarantees the status quo of inequity
remains intact.

Thus, we are left with the lingering issue of what schools can accomplish and what they should accomplish. The rhetorical power of schools as
vehicles for social reform suggests that this ideology is where we should be
focusing our reform efforts, setting aside our corrupting fascination for
measurement, labeling, and accountability. Kliebard (1995) explains:

> According to the social meliorists, the new social conditions did not demand
> an obsessional fixation on the child and on child psychology; nor did the
> solution lie in simply ironing out the inefficiencies in the existing social
> order. The answer lay in the power of the schools to create a new social
> vision. (p. 25)

What, then, would education reform involve if we place the goals of universal public education within a genuine social equity agenda?

- Social justice must become a central narrative that drives public policy, and that public policy must be evaluated in terms of its impact on social justice. The cultural mythology must balance individual with community; the role of public institutions must also be re-examined against the shift toward privatization. Public education as a public institution charged with social reform must be placed within the broader need to address social inequity through other institutions as well, such as health care, housing, and justice.

- Schools must be redesigned as models for egalitarian communities, including ending traditional commitments to standardized testing, labeling and sorting students, stratified course offerings, and inequitable class sizes and teacher assignments. Currently and historically, schools have reflected our society; if we are committed to social justice, schools must practice the equity we envision for the wider society. At the center of the failure of education to reject social inequity has been the use of and faith in standardized testing, which remains primarily a reflection of class, race, and gender instead of genuine achievement.

- Teachers must be allowed their professional autonomy, instead of being reduced to mechanism for imposing the state curriculum onto passive students. Within that professionalism, teachers must be re-imagined as change agents, setting aside silencing norms of "objectivity" imposed on teachers traditionally. Teachers should be supported for having scholarly transparency and warned against indoctrination. The inherently political nature of teaching as change agent has to be endorsed and embraced by the culture if education is to achieve its role in social reform.

- The role of students must change as well, shifting from passive receptacles for facts to critical agents of confronting and creating their own worlds. Students must be invited into engaging and authentic examinations of curriculum that supports their own pursuit of coming to know social justice, challenging the norms of their world, and exploring their role as agents of change and of their own lives.

- Teaching and learning must be released from the mechanistic assumptions that have evolved from the social efficiency movement of the early twentieth century (Kliebard, 1995). Instead of isolated and transmissional relationships, teaching and learning (including assessment) must be recognized as social, recursive, and constructivistic.

As Kohn (2004) acknowledges, the in-school changes needed for schools dedicated to social justice are nearly as daunting as addressing social inequities themselves:

> To suggest that teachers relinquish the comfortable position of authority over students is to ask a lot, especially if most of *their* teachers, from pre-school to graduate school, haven't set a particularly daring example. For that matter, any change that entails rethinking basic questions about the teacher/student relationship and the objectives of schooling is more likely to take hold if, as a matter of policy, teachers are treated as professionals and trusted to use their judgment. They need to feel safe about taking risks in order to create classrooms where students can feel the same way; it's hard to give others what you, yourself, don't have. A teacher who has been deluged with directives and intimidated into following orders is rarely able to help students find the courage to dissent. (n.p.)

The current and traditional climate of schools and society includes a harsh punitive message underneath the cultural faith in individual accountability, but this authoritarian dynamic squelches the possibility for authentic learning, human agency, and social justice. Instead, we must encourage and celebrate risk and confrontation—a dramatic shift away from schools that breed compliance among the teachers and the students.

Compliance is the life-blood of the status quo; it masks and silences, and ensures that our culture continues to ignore poverty by marginalizing and demonizing it and those trapped in its vices.

As we confront what universal public education can and cannot do, and as we place those considerations in the context of the interplay between social status and education, we must also examine how we view poverty and people living in poverty. Chapter 7 concludes this book as a challenge to the deficit perspective that sits beneath many of the traditional practices central to public schooling as well as the cultural norms that drive our society.

NOTE

1.   One statistical fact is important here. The SAT has historically been taken by a uniquely elite population of students. Once that population is increased and becomes more like the entire population of students, the statistical average score must decrease. Any lower SAT data will result in the misinformed conclusion that schools are underperforming.

CHAPTER 7

CONFRONTING POVERTY AGAIN FOR THE FIRST TIME

Rising Above Deficit Perspectives

In a letter written to reviewers about the draft of his novel *American Gods*, Neil Gaiman (2001) explains the focus of his narrative:

> If *Neverwhere* was about the London underneath, this [*American Gods*] would be about the America between, and on-top-of, and around. It's an America with strange mythic depths. Ones that can hurt you. Or kill you. Or make you mad.... It's about the soul of America, really. What people brought to America; what found them when they came; and the things that lie sleeping beneath it all. (n.p.)

Gaiman's work of fiction speaks to a truth, however, about the essence of America—the unexamined power of myth. The rugged individual myth drives the narrative of the U.S. to the exclusion of the community. In America, competition trumps cooperation.

And within these cultural narratives, much is never spoken or acknowledged, especially in terms of class and the forces behind the stratification of people. Giroux (2011b) makes this observation about class, quoting Lawrence Grossberg:

> The working and middle classes have been condemned to a new form of neoliberal tyranny "in which there can be only one kind of value, market

Ignoring Poverty in the U.S.: The Corporate Takeover of Public Education, pp. 181–211

value; one kind of success, profit; one kind of existence, commodities; and one kind of social relationship, markets" (n.p.)

And beneath this new—or at least intensified—reality lie those people trapped in poverty who have been lured into *aspiring* to that neoliberal tyranny, an aspiration fostered so those same oppressed would never look closely at their own oppression or their oppressors—the privileged who experience that privilege at the expense of others. We are a people in the U.S. enamored with affluence, at any cost, and determined to believe that each of us has the life he or she deserves. Wealth and success come from simply sucking it up and trying harder, and poverty is a reflection of sloth (or more damning to our myths, the inherent flaws of gender, race, or self). But, as Giroux (2011b) concludes, there exists a permanent and powerful link between capitalism and stratification of humans that works against democracy and human agency:

> Of course, this form of economic Darwinism is not enforced simply through the use of a government in the hands of right-wing corporate extremists, a conservative Supreme Court or reliance upon the police and other repressive apparatuses; it is also endlessly reproduced through the cultural apparatuses of the new and old media, *public and higher education, as well as through the thousands of messages and narratives we are exposed to daily in multiple commercial spheres* [emphasis added]. In this discourse, the economic order is either sanctioned by God or exists simply as an extension of nature. In other words, the tyranny and suffering that is produced through the neoliberal theater of cruelty is coded as unquestionable, as unmovable as an urban skyscraper. (n.p.)

As I have been discussing throughout the previous chapters, the U.S. political and corporate elite have insured that the public ignores poverty even when addressing it. Here, in this last chapter, I examine how we view poverty through a deficit lens that impacts greatly why we continue to ignore poverty in our public policy and perpetuate stratification of children through our public education system in direct contrast to our claimed commitment to democracy and human agency.

LABOR AND LEISURE:
POVERTY AND PRIVILEGE IN A CLASSLESS SOCIETY

The story of America is a fabric woven of the real and the mythologized (Zinn, 2003), but central to those narratives stands a firm belief in class, including a pride for middle-class work ethics, an aspiration for upper-class privilege, and an implication of lower-class laziness. One of the most puzzling aspects of American views of class is who we tend to ascribe causational power to in terms of that class's status—somehow, it appears, those in the lower class are responsible for poverty. The cycle of poverty is a self-perpetuating thing that could be brought to a halt if those people in that cycle simply took advantage of the opportunity afforded everyone in the U.S.—or so goes the myth.

Before discussing the role of poverty in education—both how we view children and families in poverty and how we teach children coming from poverty—I want to consider how framing class as lower, middle, and upper helps distort and mask a genuine and critical consideration of class as well as the forces creating a stratified society. Let me begin by placing this in the context of my avocation, cycling.

I have been an avid cyclist for nearly as long as I have been a teacher, writer, and scholar, approaching 30 years. And I have noticed something that I understand is anecdotal, but to me, it is powerful all the same. Cycling prompts a wide range of reactions from people when we are out on the roads in packs; one pattern to those reactions has now convinced me that those reactions reflect a more authentic representation of class than our traditional use of lower-, middle-, and upper-class.

In the U.S., cycling as a recreation is a hobby among the privileged—those with disposable income, leisure time, and safety nets such as insurance and job security. The people who tend to shout at us in anger, drive their cars far too close when they pass, and offer us hand gestures and exaggerated scowls are most often from that same privilege as we are. But when we pass laborers on the side of the road—crouched in ditches, repairing fences, roofing other people's houses, patching potholes in the road—they often smile, wave, nod, and make sure that we can pass safely.

This distinction has become unnerving to me—not because of the misplaced derision of the leisure class at those of us investing our time and money in recreation, not because of the genuine kindness found among the labor class, but because of the normative dynamic behind both. The cultural narrative in the U.S. has replaced the natural human need for agency with the allure of leisure—rendering the labor class certain they deserve their roles as laborers (roles that allow the leisure of others), certain that the leisure class deserve their privilege, and certain that if those in labor work hard enough, they too will attain that leisure.

In the U.S., the labor class has their entire lives, their entire self-worth invested in their labor—their income, their insurance, their ability to maintain a home, their ability to secure food (the least expensive and most unhealthy meals), and their never-ending quest to attain the material goods that will allow them to deny their labor class. The people in labor class more often than not begin their lives in labor, within families of the labor class, through no decision or effort of their own. The leisure class, then, includes those who have begun to attain some gap between their labor and their self-worth through, in some cases, the genuine sweat of the their brow, but many in the leisure class have been awarded leisure by the privilege of their birth; and all people in the leisure class are enjoying the fruits of leisure because there exists a labor class.

Privilege and leisure are not class conditions that exist in a vacuum. As well, privilege and leisure spring from the effectiveness of capitalism and consumerism to suppress natural human tendencies toward agency, community, and sustainability. Everyone in the labor class works in order to live, with their lives often along some spectrum of surviving. The leisure class includes those who work in order to have that leisure as well as those who use their leisure and privilege to secure work that is also their livelihood.

And here is where my life as a scholar concerned with poverty and education collides with my life of leisure and privilege—a life lived as a scholar, teacher, and writer just as fulfilling as a life lived as a cyclist (a hobby that drains a significant amount of disposable income that is the life-blood of the exact consumer culture I blame for oppressing the labor class). The current stratified class system in the U.S.—one that is portrayed as natural, a just shaking out of status based on merit because of the invisible hand of the free market—creates a perverse balance of labor and leisure that allows scholars to live in leisure and privilege and study poverty and labor.

It is against the paradox of privilege and leisure that I work as a scholar and a teacher genuinely concerned about the oppressive nature of consumerism as it impacts both the labor and leisure classes with a pooling of leisure and privilege among the increasingly small number of elites who drive both the consumer culture and the narratives that insure its power. And this leads to considering the ways people living in poverty—aspiring to the labor class as a lever into the leisure class—are portrayed in the narratives at the center of American mythology. Further, the role of education as an idealized mechanism for achieving the leisure class stands against an education system that perpetuates the marginalization of those in poverty by implementing a deficit perspective of teaching and learning broadly and poverty more narrowly.

One of the most powerful and corrosive ideologies at the heart of the new education reform movement is the "no excuses" discourse among reformers and ideology driving the rise of corporate charter schools.

"NO EXCUSE"?—INEXCUSABLE

"By the time youngsters reach high school in the United States, the achievement gap is immense" Whitman (2008, n.p.), explains in the opening sentence of a piece summarizing *Sweating the Small Stuff: Inner-city Schools and the New Paternalism* published by the Thomas B. Fordham Institute. As their on-line mission statement reveals, Fordham has strong ideological commitments:

> We promote policies that strengthen accountability and expand education options for parents and families. Our reports examine issues such as the No Child Left Behind Act, school choice and teacher quality. Our sister non-profit, the Thomas B. Fordham Foundation, sponsors charter schools in Ohio. (n.p.) (http://www.edexcellence.net/about-us/)

Here, the premise of Whitman's endorsing a new paternalism, which is parallel to the "no excuses" ideology, is couched both in an uncritical acceptance of the achievement gap (see Chapter Six) and a conservative political stance wedded to rugged individualism, market forces, and charter schools.

Whitman (2008) embraces schools that implement the "new paternalism":

> They are *paternalistic* [emphasis in original] institutions. By paternalistic I mean that each of the six schools is a highly prescriptive institution that teaches students not just how to think, but also *how to act according to what are commonly termed traditional, middle-class values* [emphasis added]. These paternalistic schools go beyond just teaching values as abstractions: the schools tell students exactly how they are expected to behave, and their behavior is closely monitored, with real rewards for compliance and penalties for noncompliance. Unlike the often-forbidding paternalistic institutions of the past, these schools are prescriptive yet warm; teachers and principals, who sometimes serve in loco parentis, are both authoritative and caring figures. Teachers laugh with and cajole students, in addition to frequently directing them to stay on task. (n.p.)

For Whitman, the classist and authoritarian characteristics of "new paternalism" is completely justified because "the new breed of paternalistic schools appears to be the single most effective way of closing the achievement gap" (n.p.). Again, the achievement gap is portrayed as decontextualized from the equity gap in society and as within the purview of schools to close alone. Beyond these broad and largely unsupported (or even challenged) claims, Whitman also represents "new paternalism" as outside the mainstream (ironically, since paternalistic stances are at the core of tradition): "But while these 'no excuses' schools have demonstrated remarkable results, the notion of reintroducing paternalism in inner-city schools is deeply at odds with the conventional wisdom of the K-12 education establishment" (n.p.).

Throughout the decade after NCLB was enacted, "no excuses" ideology and charter schools appeared to be elements of the conservative movement in the U.S. with President George W. Bush the face on bureaucratic school reform. With the election of Obama, the shift was not away from "no excuses" and charter schools, but toward an even more pronounced embracing of both. "No excuses" ideology as practiced in KIPP charter schools and HCZ schools became the foundation for the school reform promoted by Obama and Secretary Duncan.

While the corporate charter school movement gained momentum—notably with the media hype surrounding *Waiting for "Superman"*—educators and scholars tended to push back against the glorification of charters combined with the demonizing of public schools (Ravtich, 2010c). But the message that resonated was that charter schools could do what public schools could not—address the achievement gap for children living in poverty and children of color. While that narrative was factually false, few people addressed *how* those charter schools conducted school and the educational purposes of those charter schools. Again, note Whitman's direct admission that "no excuses" schools impose middle-class values on the students as part of the school's mission to educate.

Paul Tough (2011), an advocate for Canada's HCZ, eventually took what many considered a bold step and confronted the "no excuses" reformers themselves:

> To point out the obvious: These are excuses. In fact, they are the very same excuses for failure that the education-reform movement was founded to oppose. (If early reformers believed in anything, it was that every student is an apple.) And not only are they excuses; they aren't even particularly persuasive ones.... So why are some reformers resorting to excuses? Most likely for the same reason that urban educators from an earlier generation made excuses: successfully educating large numbers of low-income kids is very, very hard. But it is not impossible, as reformers have repeatedly demonstrated on a small scale. To achieve system-wide success, though, we need a shift in strategy. (n.p.)

But Tough's challenge to the hypocrisy of the new reformers and their "no excuses" ideology never confronts, again, *how* children are treated, *what* children are indoctrinated to accept, and *why* the "no excuses" ideology ultimately fails education in a free society.

As is the emerging pattern of education discourse in the twenty-first century (see Chapter 6), DiCarlo (2011) entered the discussion of "no excuses" schools by examining Tough (2011):

> In an article in this week's *New York Times Magazine*, author Paul Tough notifies supporters of market-based reform that they cannot simply dismiss the

"no excuses" maxim when it is convenient. He cites two recent examples of charter schools (the Bruce Randolph School in Denver, CO, and the Urban Prep Academy in Chicago) that were criticized for their low overall performance. Both schools have been defended publicly by "pro-reform" types (the former by Jonathan Alter; the latter by the school's founder, Tim King), arguing that comparisons of school performance must be valid—that is, the schools' test scores must be compared with those of similar neighborhood schools. (n.p.)

DiCarlo calls Tough's stance "noble," and then does the same about "no excuses":

> Look, "no excuses" is a noble philosophy, but in this extreme form, it assumes an ideological character that borders on the absurd.... If a school's founder cannot point out that his low pass rates are comparable to those of similar schools in his area, then we have reached a point in our education debate where most of how we assess performance, and the great empirical research that does so, is founded on tolerating failure. Those who endorse this perspective must think three times before they use any of the research studies—of charter schools, teacher effectiveness, and so on—to advocate for their policy preferences. (n.p.)

Like Tough, DiCarlo offers little resistance to the inherent flaws in "no excuses" ideology, only conceding some problems with an "extreme form." While DiCarlo makes a solid point at the end of the piece— "there's a difference between excuses and explanations"—and supports the educators and scholars calling for a recognition and addressing of social inequity, he shares with Tough a missed opportunity to confront how we view people in poverty against the norms of an idealized middle-class calculation.

On balance and in their essence, then, Whitman (2008), Tough (2011), and DiCarlo (2011) share a basic and uncritical acceptance of "no excuses" ideology that ignores the classist underpinnings of the perspective. In "no excuses" settings, the middle-class norm is embraced and endorsed; in short, children are inculcated into that norm.

TWENTY-FIRST CENTURY SEGREGATION: INVERTING KING'S DREAM

Brian Jones (2011) asked us to pause during the 2011 MLK Day to consider King's reaction to the achievement gap that persists well into the twenty-first century, suggesting that education policy begun under George W. Bush, NCLB, and accelerated under Obama works against King's dream. As Jones mentions, political leaders are apt to quote King selectively, focusing on King's words that serve their political and ideological purposes—Republican and Democrats alike. I agree with Jones, and suggest we spend more time and energy on the challenges from King in 1967 that Jones recommends. I also recommend that we place King's messages in the context of today's public claims coming from the new reformers, including Secretary Duncan (2010c), who persistently claims education alone can overcome poverty. How would King respond to the utopian expectations coming from the same educational leaders who regularly characterize our public schools and their teachers as failures?

In "Final Words of Advice," King (1967) asserted directly:

> I am now convinced that the simplest approach will prove to be the most effective—the solution to poverty is to abolish it directly by a now widely discussed measure: the guaranteed income.... We are likely to find that the problems of housing and education, instead of preceding the elimination of poverty, will themselves be affected if poverty is first abolished. (n.p.)

In the past 40 years, the evidence is overwhelming that King was right *then*, and that Duncan is wrong *now*. This is a sobering civil rights and social justice message to face in the twenty-first century when we honor the work of Dr. King, but the evidence is clear that the U.S. and all countries must address the plight of poverty directly through a variety of social commitments, recognizing that the education system is part of the solution but not the source of miracles that political leaders and the media claim.

Like Jones (2011), I wonder further how King would respond to the education policies coming from the Obama administration, which seems committed to the new reformers' corporate model for public schools—notably the great charter compromise among all political ideologies. The original charter school movement focused on relieving public schools of bureaucratic mandates, creating real-world laboratories for experimentation in order to benefit all public schools. But the charter school movement endorsed and perpetuated by Obama and the new reformers is a corporate model, characterized by KIPP and Canada's HCZ.

While much of the charter school debate has focused on "no excuses" ideology and student achievement (CREDO, 2009), often absent in the public discourse is the impact of charter schools and all aspects of school choice on student populations (race, income, special needs, ELL) and most importantly on segregation. In my own work examining school choice (Thomas, 2010a), I identified some basic patterns among school choice options. One important fact of choice is that while choice is rarely taken when offered, parents tend to choose for non-academic reasons, *creating stratification* and thus working against one of the central tenants of King's civil rights agenda—desegregation.

And while we can only speculate about King's response to the corporate charter school movement as it reflects our social concern for and view of people living in poverty, we now have some valuable evidence of what his reaction might be. Frankenberg, Siegel-Hawley, and Wang (2011) present a sobering picture of the segregating impact that charter movement is having on children (from the abstract):

> Our findings suggest that charters currently isolate students by race and class. This analysis of recent data finds that charter schools are more racially isolated than traditional public schools in virtually every state and large metropolitan area in the nation. In some regions, white students are over-represented in charter schools while in other charter schools, minority students have little exposure to white students. Data about the extent to which charter schools serve low-income and English learner students is incomplete, but suggest that a substantial share of charter schools may not enroll such students. As charters represent an increasing share of our public schools, they influence the level of segregation experienced by all of our nation's school children. (n.p.)

While promising utopian results from public education is also promising failure, we can begin to state with a good deal of certainty that the new reformers' endorsement of corporate charter schools is inverting King's dream of racial and economic harmony.

Yet, questions remain, and I cannot improve upon King's (1967) similar charge from "Where Do We Go from Here?":

> I want to say to you as I move to my conclusion, as we talk about "Where do we go from here," that we honestly face the fact that the Movement must address itself to the question of restructuring the whole of American society. There are forty million poor people here. And one day we must ask the question, "Why are there forty million poor people in America?" And when you begin to ask that question, you are raising questions about the economic system, about a broader distribution of wealth. When you ask that question, you begin to question the capitalistic economy. And I'm simply saying that more and more, we've got to begin to ask questions about the whole society. We are called upon to help the discouraged beggars in life's market place. But one day we must come to see that an edifice which produces beggars needs restructuring. It means that questions must be raised. You see, my friends, when you deal with this,
>
>   You begin to ask the question, "Who owns the oil?"
>   You begin to ask the question, "Who owns the iron ore?"
>   You begin to ask the question, "Why is it that people have to pay water bills in a world that is two thirds water?"
>   These are questions that must be asked. (n.p.)

To create an authentic honoring of King, the U.S. must reframe how we view people living in poverty and the condition of poverty itself—rejecting deficit views of those people and students struggling in school under the weight of lives in poverty.

OUR FAITH IN A "CULTURE OF POVERTY" NEVER LEFT

Writing in *The New York Times*, Patricia Cohen (2010), in a piece titled "'Culture of Poverty' Makes a Comeback," announced: "Now, after decades of silence, these scholars are speaking openly about you-know-what [the 'culture of poverty'], conceding that culture and persistent poverty are enmeshed" (n.p.) While Cohen's article accurately reflects a scholarly move to examine and support claims that a culture of poverty exists, and to revive support for the 1965 Moynihan report, announcing that the U.S. public's faith in a "culture of poverty" is somehow making a comeback masks that it never left.

And nowhere is this more evident than powerful and disturbing trends in education that began mid-decade under President Bush, but have received unprecedented support under President Obama—deficit approaches to poverty as embodied in the work of Ruby Payne and the rise of "no excuses" charter schools such as KIPP and the HCZ. Since 2005, Ruby Payne's workbook- and workshop-focused "framework" has spread throughout U.S. public schools scrambling to address the achievement gap as mandated by NCLB. A rising number of scholars have detailed not only the amount of Payne's influence but also that her ideology resonates with our popular assumptions concerning people and children living and learning in poverty (Baker, Ng, & Rury, 2006; Bohn, 2006; Bomer, Dworin, May, & Semingson, 2008, 2009; Dudley-Marling, 2007; Dudley-Marling & Lucas, 2009; Dworin & Bomer, 2008; Gorski, 2006a, 2006b, 2006c, 2008a, 2008b; Howley, Howley, Howley, & Howley, 2006; Howley, Howley, & Huber, 2005; Ng & Rury, 2006a, 2006b, 2009; Osei-Kofi, 2005; Sato & Lensmire, 2009; Thomas, 2009, 2010b; Valencia, 2010; Weiderspan & Danziger, 2009):

> Arguably, one of today's most conspicuous speakers on issues of poverty and education is Dr. Ruby Payne, president of a company called "Aha Process, Inc." and author of a self-published book titled *A Framework for Understanding Poverty*, currently in its fourth revised edition (2005). Payne has sold more than half a million copies of her book since 1996 as well as related workbook materials, and her organization conducts workshops and training sessions for tens of thousands of educators, administrators, and other human-service professionals across the country and abroad. A principal

thrust of these activities is teaching people about poverty and working with
poor children in school settings. (Ng & Rury, 2006a, n.p.)

U.S. popular narratives have established and reinforced middle class
norms as the bare minimum requirements for being fully American or
even human, and within that norm is a powerful embracing of societal
myths—rugged individualism, upward mobility, and an idealizing of
wealth and material possessions. Implicit in those myths is a negative and
deficit perspective of people living in poverty.

Payne's work reinforces social assumptions about a "culture of poverty,"
and as a result, people and children living in poverty become characterized by all that they do not have when measured against middle class
norms—and the implications are overwhelming. The "culture of poverty"
narrative implies this: People and children living in poverty lack the rugged individualism needed to be upwardly mobile into the essential middle class and especially the cherished upper class. And into that deficit
perspective stepped a rise in "no excuses" charter schools discussed earlier. Corporate charter schools embrace a "new paternalism," championed by Whitman (2008) and flaunted in the *Los Angeles Times*:
"Conservatives, including columnist George Will, adore the American
Indian schools, which they see as models of a 'new paternalism' that could
close the gap between the haves and have-nots in American education"
(Landsberg, 2009, n.p.).

By 2011, the policies and speeches of President Obama and Secretary
Duncan, the media blitz surrounding *Waiting for "Superman"* (NBC spe-
cials, Oprah, John Legend on Bill Maher's *Real Time*), and the continuing
social narrative about failing public education, all shifted toward the new
savior—"no excuses" charter schools that embody American rugged individualism. Charter schools with "no excuses" practices establish contrac-
tual demands of parents and students. When either parents or students
fail to fulfill the contracts, the norm of the rugged individual, the students
are dismissed, thus ostensibly denied access to upward mobility, to conforming to the middle-class minimum or the upper-class ideal:

> Importantly, Miron is also not saying that the KIPP schools do poorly.
> Those schools provide about 50% more instructional time and place rigor-
> ous demands on students and their families. "We have every reason to
> believe that KIPP likely does a great job with the low-income students of
> color who wish to attend and who have relatively supportive parents who
> can do things like drive them to Saturday school," Miron says. But he does
> question whether this is a viable model for larger numbers of students, and
> he also wonders whether the different departure and receiving policies may
> make matters worse for students who are left behind or who later leave KIPP
> schools. How would the KIPP model work if students who cannot handle the

rigorous KIPP demands could not move to conventional public schools? (Welner, 2010, n.p.)

The claimed "comeback" of embracing the "culture of poverty," then, is not something new or renewed, but something dark and sinister at the core of the social narratives driving the U.S. and many of its central institutions. We regard people living in poverty as the Other, and we define people living in poverty by the negatives, by those material goods they do not have.

And these Others are essentially ignored and silenced.

"The myth of a 'culture of poverty' distracts us from a dangerous culture that does exist—the culture of classism," argues Gorski (2008b, n.p.), but our commitment to deficit views of people living in poverty allows us to mask the failures of our class structures—and the dynamics that maintain those class distinctions. We now proclaim from the White House to the cinema to the TV and all across the country that our public schools are failing and that they are bloated with bad teachers. Yet, teachers account for only about 10 to 20% of student achievement, and the remaining majority of influence lies outside of school.

Children living and learning in poverty are overwhelmed by the conditions of their lives, but we ignore these facts just as we ignore that the U.S. tolerates one in four children living in poverty in the U.S. while many other nations have single digit poverty rates for children (and schools we praise as superior to our own). To argue about what constitutes a "culture of poverty," or whether or not that culture exists, is precious time wasted. Instead, we should be concerned about the systemic failures of our economic and political system that marginalizes and demonizes any and all people, including children, who find themselves living in poverty.

HUMAN AGENCY AND THE WEIGHT OF CLASS

"2010 wasn't a very good year for public education—or public anything, for that matter," lamented Klonsky (2010), adding:

> It was just about a year ago for example, that Education Secretary Arne Duncan began his "no excuses" campaign, announcing in the press that he had "no patience for teachers and schools" that tick off all the reasons why their poor or minority students can't score as high on standardized tests.
>
> Duncan has chosen to ignore poverty's downward effect on test scores and focus entirely on what he calls "bad teachers" and "failing schools." Recently confronted by educators teaching in some of the nation's highest-poverty areas about the need to do something about the living conditions of their students, Duncan cynically responded, "poverty is not destiny."

His "no excuses" mantra, essentially blaming poor students and their teachers for low test results, is now being echoed by many governors, urban mayors and school administrators like Springfield's Milton, all hoping their compliance will somehow be rewarded with federal dollars from Duncan to fill the holes in their shrinking school budgets. (n.p.)

Klonsky's characterization of the complex and powerful dynamic among politics, funding, education, and poverty captures directly both how a cultural ideology shapes education policy and how that same ideology distorts the stated democratic aims of universal public education.

As I have noted earlier, regardless of political partisanship, the ruling and corporate elite share a notebook of narratives that simultaneously recognizes poverty by ignoring it. In the contorted logic of political and corporate discourse, poverty is both a primary correlation with social and educational problems needing reform and a fact of existence those in privilege are not allowing those living in poverty to use as an excuse. This perverse manipulation of acknowledging the essential nature of human agency is one of the most disturbing aspects of the elite maintaining the status quo of their privilege by constantly celebrating individual freedom and empowerment.

What, then, should we take from these narratives about poverty and education? First, any discussion or characterization about a class of people should raise concerns. Class is a debatable concept—at best a set of tentative parameters based on evidence and at worst mere bigotry. Those people living in a class designated by whatever terminology ("upper," "lower," "labor," or "leisure") can be labeled by using careful data and classification, but the question must be *should* that labeling occur and *if* such labeling contributes anything valuable to individuals or the society at large. This same problem of labeling class is reflected in the labeling of children in school—labels that tend to stratify and isolate students in ways that parallel social stratifications.

Next, discussions of class often create the risk of self-fulfilling prophesies, as exposed in the work and popularity of Ruby Payne. Gorski (2008a), along with numerous scholars identified earlier, discusses the allure and harm embedded in Payne's claims about poverty, families in poverty, and students in poverty, cataloging

"eight elements of oppression" in her framework—the ways, according to existing critiques, that Payne's work contributes to classism, racism, and other inequities: (1) uncritical and self-serving "scholarship," (2) the elusive culture of poverty, (3) abounding stereotypes, (4) deficit theory, (5) invisibility of classism, (6) the "it's not about race" card, (7) peddling paternalism, and (8) compassionate conservatism. (p. 131)

As Gorski explains, Payne's claims work against the exact conditions and people she and those who purchase her workbook and workshops suggest they are seeking to help (itself a problematic stance of paternalism). But Dudley-Marling (2007) sees Payne's popularity in context:

> Ruby Payne portrays the lives of the poor as pathological, deficient in the cognitive, emotional, linguistic, and spiritual resources needed to escape poverty and move into the middle class. At a moment when "scientifically-based" research is a dominant theme of educational reform, Payne's work is without a research base. Yet, Payne's sensationalist caricatures of people living in poverty have achieved enormous popularity with teachers, administrators, and policy makers (Keller, 2006). (n.p.)

Since Payne's framework lacks scholarly credibility and promotes "classism, racism, and other inequities" (Gorski, 2008a, p. 131), that her work is popular and profitable reveals that many educators remain victims of their own unfounded assumptions about class—a truly damning fact.

Payne is wrong about class, but her popularity exposes hard and critical truths about cultural and educational beliefs and practices concerning children who happen to live in poverty through no fault of their own. Cultural and educational perspectives that focus on the flaws and deficits of individuals and that decontextualize those deficits from causes outside the control of the individual create a dehumanizing cycle of addressing both poverty and people living and learning in poverty: The person must be corrected, repaired, and provided that which the person lacks.

Haberman (1991) explains that deficit approaches to children in poverty, notably children of color in urban schools, reaches back at least into mid-twentieth century and characterizes a pedagogy of poverty:

> There are essentially four syllogisms that undergird the pedagogy of poverty. Their "logic" runs something like this.
>
> 1 Teaching is what teachers do. Learning is what students do. Therefore, students and teachers are engaged in different activities.
> 2 Teachers are in charge and responsible. Students are those who still need to develop appropriate behavior. Therefore, when students follow teachers' directions, appropriate behavior is being taught and learned.
> 3 Students represent a wide range of individual differences. Many students have handicapping conditions and lead debilitating home lives. Therefore, ranking of some sort is inevitable; some students will end up at the bottom of the class while others will finish at the top.
> 4 Basic skills are a prerequisite for learning and living. Students are not necessarily interested in basic skills. Therefore, directive pedagogy. (p. 291)

These qualities—authoritarian teachers, compliant students, transmissional instruction, skill and drill—outlined by Haberman represent the traditional stratification of students in schools where students receive different educations based on sorting structures that reflect the conditions of those children's lives and insure that social inequities are perpetuated and even exacerbated.

From well before the civil rights movement of the 1960s and then into the twenty-first century, a pedagogy of poverty has gripped public education, highlighted by the rise of Payne in the years after NCLB. As Haberman (1991) explained decades ago, "the pedagogy of poverty does not work" (p. 291) and

> the pedagogy of poverty is not a professional methodology at all. It is not supported by research, by theory, or by the best practice of superior urban teachers. It is actually certain ritualistic acts that, much like the ceremonies performed by religious functionaries, have come to be conducted for their intrinsic value rather than to foster learning. (p. 292)

Like Payne's deficit-based workbook approach to training children from poverty to conform to middle-class norms, the pedagogy of poverty, Haberman (1991) emphasizes, focuses almost exclusively on compliance and indoctrination—not academics, not challenging the intellect, not exploring the ethical, not pursuing human agency and empowerment. School for children labeled deficient is a social institution designed to monitor their cooperation, to reward their silence and compliance, and to insure that a labor class remains to support the leisure and privilege of the ruling elite.

Kohn (2011) recognizes that Haberman's criticism of the pedagogy of poverty found little traction, and "the result is that 'certain children' are left farther and farther behind. The rich get richer, while the poor get worksheets" (n.p.). As well, Kohn notes that the enduring commitment to deficit views of poverty, to ideologies focusing on outcomes and ignoring causation, and to mechanistic and bureaucratic policies insures only a widening of the equity gap as reflected in the narrow achievement gap (even when outliers succeed in raising some test scores for some students by teaching strictly to the tests):

> Unfortunately, that result is often at the expense of real learning, the sort that more privileged students enjoy, because the tests measure what matters least. Thus, it's possible for the accountability movement to *simultaneously narrow the test-score gap and widen the learning gap* [emphasis in original]. (Kohn, n. p.)

Human agency is a central element of being fully human. We should not debate whether people feel compelled to read, re-read, write, and re-write their own lives. But the neoliberal ideology driving the consumer culture of the U.S. depends on raising a small leisure class to its place of privilege on the labor of the vast majority of society who must be compelled to believe in a cultural narrative that has little basis in the evidence. The rugged individual makes for powerful stories, but it is a harsh template for children, who cannot choose the station of their lives, who have no direct political power (except as proxy consumers of their parent's capital), and who exist in a default position of subservience in all formal situations such as school.

Two powerful failures of logic sit beneath our deficit view of poverty, people of poverty, and children learning while living in poverty. First, those people under the weight of poverty are directly and indirectly blamed for their own circumstances, as if the people with the least capital and political power in the culture are creating the social realities of the entire country; this, of course, allows the ruling elite to be relieved of their primary roles as cause agents behind social inequity. The political and corporate elite at least tolerate increasing childhood poverty in the U.S. and at worst are actively creating it.

Second, the cultural deficit view of poverty is reflected in the deficit practice in the pedagogy of poverty that dominates the stratified public education system; students labeled deficient or failing are then subjected to the most scripted, least engaging, and ultimately least substantial curriculum, teaching, learning, and assessment—assuring that some measurable and some qualitative learning is in fact deficient when compared against children learning and living in privilege. Not to be ignored in this second dynamic is that many people and entities, such as Payne and the testing industry, benefit handsomely by the market sprung up through bureaucracy around addressing the achievement gap. Even poverty in the United States of consumerism creates wealth for those already living in the privilege of wealth, again on the lives and labor of those marginalized as lacking what it takes to succeed in a free society.

POVERTY AND TESTING IN EDUCATION: "THE PRESENT SCIENTIFICO-LEGAL COMPLEX"

Jim Taylor (2011) entered the poverty and education debate by asking Secretary Duncan and billionaire/education entrepreneur Gates a direct question: "I really don't understand you two, the U.S. Secretary of Education and the world's second richest man and noted philanthropist. How can you possibly say that public education can be reformed without eliminating poverty?" (n.p.). Taylor's discussion comes to an important element in the poverty/education debate when he addresses Gates: "Because without understanding the causes of problems, we can't find solutions," explains Taylor, adding. "You're obviously trying to solve public education's version of the classic 'chicken or egg' conundrum" (n.p.).

Here, recognizing the poverty/education debate as a chicken-or-egg problem is the crux of how this debate is missing the most important questions about poverty—and as a result, insuring that Duncan and Gates are winning the argument by perpetuating the argument. The essential questions about poverty and education should not focus on whether we should address poverty to improve education (where I stand, based on the evidence) or whether we should reform education as a mechanism to alleviate poverty (the tenant of the "no excuses" ideology promoted by Duncan and Gates); the essential question about poverty is: Who creates and allows poverty to exist in the wealthiest and most powerful country in recorded history?

As a basic point of logic, any organized entity—a society, a business, a school—has characteristics that are either created or tolerated by those in power controlling that organization. All entities are by their nature *conservative*—functioning to maintain the entity itself. In other words, institutions resist change, particularly radical change that threatens the hierarchy of power. Thus, if the power structure of the U.S. is stable while poverty exists, that power structure has little motivation to address poverty unless that poverty threatens the elite's position at the top.

In the U.S., then, poverty exists in the wider society and performs a corrosive influence in the education system (among all of our social institutions) because the ruling elite—political and corporate leaders—need poverty to maintain their elite status at the top of the hierarchy of power. While the perpetual narratives promoted by the political and corporate elite through the media elite have allowed this point of logic to be masked and ignored in American society, we must face the reality that people with power drive the realities of those without power. Yes, the cultural narratives driven by the elite suggest that people trapped in poverty are somehow in control of that poverty—creating it themselves due to their own sloth, somehow deserving their station in life, or failing to rise above that poverty (and this suggestion allows the source of poverty to be ignored) from their own failure to lift themselves up by their own bootstraps (the manifestation of the deficit perspective).

But that narrative has no basis in evidence—except that those without power do have control of that which creates the conditions, ironically, benefitting the elite. The powerful must allow those without power to have some autonomy—as parents with children—in order to create the illusion of autonomy to keep revolt at bay; this is why the political and corporate elite use the word "choice" and perpetuate the myth that all classes in America have the same access to choice.

How does poverty, then, benefit the powerful in the U.S.?

- U.S. cultural narratives depend on utopian elements of democracy, meritocracy, and individual freedom. Those ideals form the basis for most of the cultural narratives expressed by the political and corporate elite in the U.S. Poverty works as the *Other* in those narratives—that which we must all reject, that which we must strive to avoid. If the utopian goals, including eliminating poverty, is ever achieved, however, the tension between the working-/middle- class and those in poverty would be eliminated as well, exposing the artificial perch upon which the ruling elite sit. The necessity of poverty works both to keep us from attaining the utopian goals and to make the utopian goals attractive.

- Poverty contributes to the *crisis motif* that keeps the majority of any society distracted from the minority elite benefiting disproportionately from the labor of the majority. Crises large and small—from Nazis, Communists, and Terrorists to crime to teen pregnancy to the achievement gap and the drop-out crisis—create the perception that the average person cannot possibly keep these crises under control (crises that would plunge otherwise decent people into the abyss of poverty) and, thus, need the leadership of the elite. The majority of average people can only be carried to the promised land of utopian peace and equality by the sheer force of personality held by only a few; these ruling elite are the only defense against the perpetual crises threatening the ideals we hold sacred (see below for how we identify those elite).

- Along with utopian promises and the refrain of crisis, the ruling elite need the pervasive atmosphere of fear—whether real or fabricated—in order to occupy the time and energy of the majority (Foucault, 1984). Poverty becomes not just a condition to be feared, but also those people to be feared. The cultural narratives—in contrast to the evidence (Gorski, 2008b)—about poverty and people living in poverty connect poverty and crime, poverty and drug abuse, poverty and domestic violence, poverty and unattractiveness, and most of all, poverty and the failure of the individual to grasp the golden gift of personal freedom afforded by the United States.

Just as we rarely consider the sources of poverty—who controls the conditions of our society—we rarely examine the deficit perspective we are conditioned to associate with poverty and people living in poverty. Are the wealthy without crime? Without drug abuse? Without deceptions of all kinds? Of course not, but the consequences for these acts by someone living in privilege are dramatically different than the consequences for those trapped in poverty. The ruling elites have created a culture where we see the consequences of poverty, but mask the realities of privilege.

Winners always believe the rules of the game to be fair, and winners need losers in order to maintain the status of "winner." The U.S., then, is a democracy *only* as a masking narrative that maintains the necessary tension among classes—the majority working-/middle- class fearful of slipping into poverty, and so consumed by that fear that they are too busy and fearful to consider who controls their lives: "those who are stuck at a machine and supervised for the rest of their lives" (Foucault, 1984, p. 177).

In the narrow debate about poverty and education, we are being manipulated once again by the ruling elite, within which Duncan and Gates function, to focus on the chicken-or-egg problem of poverty/education so that we fail to examine the ruling elite creating and tolerating poverty for their own benefit. By perpetuating the debate they want, they are winning once again. And that success derives in large part from their successful propaganda campaign about the value of testing as a mechanism within education to end poverty.

THE MERITOCRACY MYTH, SCIENCE, AND THE RISE OF NEW GODS

Now that I have suggested shifting the discourse about poverty and education away from the chicken-or-egg problem to the role of sustaining and tolerating poverty for the benefit of the ruing elite, let's look at the central role testing plays in maintaining the status quo of power in the U.S. And let's build that consideration on a couple pillars of evidence.

First, despite decades committed to the science of objective, valid, and reliable standardized testing, outcomes from standardized tests remain most strongly correlated with the socioeconomic status of the students. As well, standardized tests also remain biased instruments (Thomas, 2011y). Next, more recently during the 30-year accountability era, the overwhelming evidence shows that standards, testing, and accountability do not produce the outcomes that proponents have claimed (Hout & Elliot, 2011). Thus, just as the poverty/education question should address who creates and allows poverty and why, the current and historical testing obsession should be challenged in terms of who is benefiting from our faith in testing and why—and how that testing obsession perpetuates, not alleviates, a stratified society.

The history of power, who sits at the top and why, is one of creating leverage for the few at the expense of the many. To achieve that, often those at the top have resorted to explicit and wide-scale violence as well as fostering the perception that anyone at the top has been chosen, often by the gods or God, to lead—power is taken or deserved. "God chose me" and "God told me" remain powerful in many cultures, but in a secular culture with an ambiguous attitude toward violence (keep the streets of certain neighborhoods *here* crime-free, but war in other countries is freedom fighting) such as the U.S., the ruling elite needed a secular god—thus, the rise of science, objectivity, and testing:

> A correlative history of the modern soul and of a new power to judge; a genealogy of the present scientifico-legal complex from which the power to punish derives its bases, justifications, and rules; from which it extends it effects and by which it masks its exorbitant singularity. (Foucault, 1984, p.170)

As I noted above, testing remains a reflection of the inequity gap in society (Thomas, 2011v) and the high-stakes testing movement has not reformed education or society, so the rising call for even more testing of students, testing based on a national curriculum and used to control teachers, must have a purpose other than the utopian claims by the political and corporate elite who are most invested in the rising testing-culture in the U.S. That purpose, as with the persistence of poverty, is to maintain the status quo of a hierarchy of power and to give that hierarchy the appearance of objectivity, of science. Standards, testing, and accountability are the new gods of the political and corporate elite.

Schools in the U.S. are designed primarily to coerce children to be compliant, to be docile (Thomas, 2011z); much of what we say and consider about education is related to discipline—classroom management is often central to teacher preparation and much of what happens during any school day:

> The exercise of discipline presupposes a mechanism that coerces by means of observation; an apparatus in which the techniques that make it possible to see induce effects of power in which, conversely, the means of coercion make those on whom they are applied clearly visible. (Foucault, 1984, p. 189)

In education reform, the surveillance of students, and now the surveillance of teachers, is not covert, but in plain view in the form of tests, allowing that surveillance to be disembodied from those students and teachers—and thus appearing to be impersonal—and examined as if objective and a reflection of merit.

Testing as surveillance in order to create compliance is central to maintaining hierarchies of power both within schools (where a premium is placed on the docility of students and teachers) and society, where well-trained and compliant voters and workers sustain the positions of those in power:

> The art of punishing, in the regime of disciplinary power, is aimed neither at expiation, nor precisely at repression.... It differentiates individuals from one another, in terms of the following overall rule: that the rule be made to function as a minimal threshold, as an average to be respected, or as an optimum toward which one must move. It measures in quantitative terms and hierarchizes in terms of value the abilities, the level, the "nature" of individuals... The perpetual penalty that traverses all points and supervises every instant in the disciplinary institution compares, differentiates, hierachizes, homogenizes, excludes. In short, it *normalizes*. (Foucault, 1984, p. 195)

The political and corporate elite in the U.S. have risen to their status of privilege within the "scientifico-legal complex" (Foucault, 1984, p. 170) that both created that elite and is then perpetuated by that elite. As I noted above, the winners always believe the rules of the game to be fair and will work to maintain the rules that have produced their privilege.

THE EXPANDED TEST CULTURE:
"THE AGE OF INFINITE EXAMINATION"

Foucault (1984) has recognized the central place for testing within the power dynamic that produces a hierarchy of authority that includes those in privilege and those trapped in poverty: "The examination combines the techniques of an observing hierarchy and those of normalizing judgment. It is a normalizing gaze, a surveillance that makes possible to qualify, to classify, and to punish" (p. 197). Thus, as the rise of corporate paradigms to replace democratic paradigms has occurred in the U.S. over the last century, we can observe a rise in the prominence of testing along with how those tests are used. From the early decades of the twentieth century, testing in the U.S. has gradually increased and expanded in its role for labeling and sorting students. In the twenty-first century, testing is now being wedged into a parallel use to control teachers.

Those in power persist in both cases—testing to control students and testing to control teachers—to claim that tests are a mechanism for achieving utopian goals of democracy, meritocracy, and individual freedom, but those claims are masks for implementing tests as the agent of powerful gods (science, objectivity, accountability) to justify the current hierarchy of power—not to change society or education: "The age of the 'examining' school marked the beginnings of a pedagogy that functions as science" (Foucault, 1984, p. 198). Foucault, in fact, identifies three ways that testing works to reinforce power dynamics, as opposed to providing data for education reform driven by a pursuit of social justice.

First, testing of individual students and using test data to identify individual teacher quality create a focus on the individual that reinforces discipline:

> In discipline, it is the subjects who have to be seen. Their visibility assures the hold of the power that is exercised over them. It is the fact of their being constantly seen ... that maintains the disciplined individual in his subjection. And the examination is the technique by which power ... holds them in a mechanism of objectification. (Foucault, 1984, p. 199)

This use of testing resonates in President Obama's first term as Secretary Duncan simultaneously criticizes the misuse of testing in No Child Left Behind and calls for an expansion of testing (more years of a student's education, more areas of content, and more directly tied to individual teachers), resulting in: "We are entering the age of infinite examination and of compulsory objectification" (Foucault, p. 200).

Next, testing has provided a central goal of sustaining the hierarchy of power—"the calculation of gaps between individuals, their distribution in a given 'population'" (Foucault, 1984, p. 202). Testing, in effect, does not provide data for addressing the equity/achievement gap, testing has *created* those gaps, labeled those gaps, and marginalized those below the codified level of standard. What tends to be ignored in the testing debate as it impacts those in poverty is that some people with authority determine what is taught, how that content is taught, what is tested, and how that testing is conducted. *In short, all testing is biased and ultimately arbitrary in the context of who has authority.*

And finally, once the gaps are created and labeled through the stratifying of students and teachers, "it is the individual as he[/she] may be described, judged, measured, compared with others, in his[/her] very individuality; and it is also the individual who has to be trained or corrected, classified, normalized, excluded, etc." (Foucault, 1984, p. 203). Within the perpetual education and reform debates, the topics of poverty and testing are central themes, but we too often are missing the key elements that should be addressed in the dynamic that exists between poverty and testing.

Yes, standardized tests remain primarily reflections of social inequity that those tests perpetuate, labeled as "achievement gaps." But the central evidence we should acknowledge is that the increased focus on testing coming from the political and corporate elite is proof that those in privilege are dedicated to maintaining poverty as central to their hierarchy of authority. Standards, testing, accountability, science, and objectivity are the new gods that the ruling class uses to keep the working-/middle-class in a state of "perpetual anxiety," fearing the crisis du jure and the specter of slipping into poverty—realities that insure the momentum of the status quo.

CONFRONTING POVERTY, DEFICIT PERSPECTIVES, AND SOCIAL JUSTICE

Another charge that comes from the same new reformers who want to accept "no excuses" for poverty is that those of us rejecting their reforms and their deficit views of poverty are actually rejecting reform and embracing the status quo—that we never offer any reforms of our own. Here, as I end this discussion, I want to offer an outline of the education reforms needed to address poverty by no longer ignoring it through deficit views of those living and learning in poverty. These recommendations for authentic and critical education reform in the name of social justice are grounded in the work of Haberman (1991) and Gorski (2008a), as well as the rich scholarship of critical pedagogy and critical literacy.

The essence of the education reforms I am proposing against the status quo of traditional public school and the pseudo-reforms of the new reformers is that universal public education must provide equal access for all students regardless of class, must support education (as well as all involved in the process) as a mechanism of social reform, and must embrace differentiated practices within that equal access. The reforms should include the following:

- Schools must cease practices that label and stratify students as well as create schools with inequitable offerings and resources. The traditional practices that must be ended include tracking, standardized testing, inequitable labeling of children in poverty as special needs, inequitable assigning of teachers, school choice policies, inequitable school funding linked to community economics, and the like.
- As I have noted earlier, we must speak in terms of the equity gap and must reduce or eliminate the role of standardized testing in our schools. Focusing on terms and outcomes that allow us to ignore the contexts of learning are destined to perpetuate, not confront and change, inequity.
- Students must be allowed and encouraged to examine and explore the realities of oppression. Public education has traditionally been driven by cultural narratives that are idealistic, not realistic. Students need and deserve realistic versions of living in a free society that has yet to reach the ideals that do matter to remaining a free people.

- Schools, administrators, teachers, and students must be viewed as change agents—not dispassionate cogs in a social machine. Change and compliance are antithetical to each other. If we genuinely want schools that reform our society, we must honor everyone in the teaching/learning process as empowered.

- Instruction must be student-centered, focusing on student engagement, student choice, active students, and student reflection. "Schooling is living," Haberman (1991) argues, "not preparation for living" (p. 293).

- Students must be invited to examine the rich and complex nature of human diversity—and not indoctrinated into classist and unfounded classifications. An appreciation and awareness of diversity must be interdisciplinary—not the domain of one area of content and transmitted as facts to students.

- Learning must be holistic, and not linear. To come to know and understand must be an act of discovery among teachers and students, not the mere transmission of delineated facts endorsed by the teacher and for the students. To understand the world as a whole allows a greater commitment to social justice and lessens the likelihood of falling victim to seeing oneself as distinct for *others* as marginalized or lesser.

- School must invite students to be agents of social justice as part of their learning. The school experience should provide all students with authoritative teachers who model and engage in social justice as a continual act of being and becoming.

- School must avoid being reduced to the merely academic and pursue the real world by engaging students in authentic behaviors and experiences found in the lives of the fields we teach. How do historians do history? How do scientists do science? How do writers write? These and questions like these should drive all classrooms—not workbooks, skills instruction, or test prep.

- Students must learn with a diverse cohort of learners—race, class, gender, ability, and any such designations that we can identify.

- Students must be allowed and required to revisit and revise their work. We must set aside time-based and single-shot views of learning and assessment.

- Technology must be acknowledged in schools, but placed within the context of its potential to both alleviate and exacerbate inequity. School must not pursue technology for technology's sake, and students need to be invited to develop a critical understanding of technology—not a blind embracing of technology as consumers.

- And finally, schools must be grounded in critical pedagogy, not positivistic and behavioral ideology. Social justice requires the confronting of assumptions and norms, not the arbitrary pooling of authority and indoctrination.

Universal public education in the U.S. has not failed, just as our grand experiment in democracy has not failed. The truth is that we have failed universal public education and democracy.

Instead of living toward the ideal of human agency found in learning and living for democracy and equity, we have allowed democracy and social justice to be a mask for the corrosive consequences of competition and consumerism, the lifeblood of a market economy that replaces human voice with human capital. When our political leaders champion education as the great equalizer, they have been mostly dishonest and deceptive, but on balance, they could be proven right if, ironically, their plans for education reform are rejected along with their deficit views of people living in poverty and children trapped in poverty not of their making.

If education is to change this world for the good of each person and the entire community as well as the human race, then teachers and students must teach and learn as empowered humans, as change agents, as fully human.

DEFICIT PERSPECTIVES OF POVERTY: ANNOTATED BIBLIOGRAPHIES

- Ahlquist, R., Gorski, P., & Montano, T., eds. (2011). *Assault on kids: How hyper-accountability, corporatization, deficit ideology, and Ruby Payne are destroying our schools.* New York: Peter Lang.

  This edited volume presents for sections: hyper-accountability, the privatization and corporatization of public schools, deficit ideology, and Ruby Payne. It is a powerful and essential work to examine the interplay of these dynamics as well as the flaws inherent in Payne's workshops/workbooks as they perpetuate deficit perspective of poverty and people living in poverty.
- Bohn, A. (2006, Winter). A framework for understanding Ruby Payne. *Rethinking Schools, 21*(2). Retrieved from http://www.rethinkingschools.org/archive/21_02/fram212.shtml

  Bohn shares coming to be aware of and then confronting the work of Payne, exposing the flaws in Payne's claims and concluding:

  > Instead of allowing ourselves to be misled about a culture of poverty, we need to critically examine the culture of denial that has become

> institutionalized in our society and has caused the study of poverty in the last 20 years to be more concerned with promoting a theory of individual culpability than with addressing institutionalized inequities. (n.p.)

- Bomer, R., Dworin, J. E., May, L., & Semingson, P. (2008). Miseducating teachers about the poor: A critical analysis of Ruby Payne's claims about poverty. *Teachers College Record, 110*(12), 2497-2531.

  Bomer et al., present an extensive analysis of Payne's framework and place her claims within a scholarly context that refutes the broad and specific claims made by Payne about people living in poverty, poverty, and appropriate pedagogy for children living in poverty. This piece identifies Payne's perspective as deficit thinking and rejects that perspective as valid or appropriate for education: "Her success indicts all of us in education, indeed most of the American public, as it reveals the degree to which we use the education system to protect our own sense of entitlement to privilege" (n.p.). This is an essential work for examining both deficit perspectives and Payne's corrosive framework.

- Bomer, R., Dworin, J. E., May, L., & Semingson, P. (2009, June 3). What's wrong with a deficit perspective? *Teachers College Record.* Retrieved June 12, 2009 from http://www.tcrecord.org

  Following Payne's rebuttal to Bomer et al. (2008), Bomer et al. address the inherent flaws in deficit thinking and note Payne's own misuse of research, including misrepresenting research and offering evidence that does not match her claims. Finally, Bomer et al. clarify Payne's argument that Bomer et al. are being deterministic or fatalistic in their arguments about poverty; in fact, Bomer et al. view Payne's work as "social determinism" itself: "Poverty and its effects should be meliorated, but that will not happen through the continual reproduction of ancient bigotries in explanations of the reasons for poverty" (n.p.).

- Dudley-Marling, C. (2007). Return of the deficit. *Journal of Educational Controversy, 2*(1). Retrieved June 29, 2009 from http://www.wce.wwu.edu/Resources/CEP/eJournal/v002n001/a004.shtml

  "The purpose of this paper is to interrogate the deficit model that undergirds the impoverished, 'proto-militaristic' curricula that dominate the educational experiences of students attending poor, urban schools (Kozol, 2005b)," explains Dudley-Marling (n.p.). This article places deficit thinking in the historical context of claims about a culture of poverty. Dudley-Marling discusses in detail the focus on language as a central element of deficit thinking about people and children coming from poverty. Dudley-Marling concludes by examining the negative consequences of a "deficit gaze" on people in poverty within a democratic goal for education. This is an essential work for understanding deficit thinking and the role of attitudes about language in that thinking.

- Dudley-Marling, C., & Lucas, K. (2009, May). Pathologizing the language and culture of poor children. *Language Arts, 86*(5), 362-370.

  This article directly confronts the foundational work of Hart and Risley [Hart, B., & Risley, T. R. (1995). *Meaningful differences in the everyday experiences of young American children*. Baltimore: Brookes] as it contributes to deficit views of language, particularly as related to teaching children living in poverty. The detailed critique of Hart and Risley leads to Dudley-Marling and Lucas offering an alternative to a deficit perspective built on respect for children and their backgrounds, a respect that honors what children bring to their learning instead of measuring them against norms and reducing them to deficits.

- Dworin, J. E., & Bomer, R. (2008, January). What we all (supposedly) know about the poor: A critical discourse analysis of Ruby Payne's "Framework." *English Education, 40*(2), 101-121.

  Dworin and Bomer build on the challenges made in Bomer et al. (2008) by examining Payne's claims about poverty through a Critical Discourse Analysis lens, revealing "how the author enlists readers' participation in deficit discourses about the poor" (p. 101). Dworin and Bomer present the flaws in Payne's claims, the use of her work in teacher professional development, and the oppressive nature of implementing Payne's recommendations, especially in literacy education.

- Gorski, P. (2006a, February 9). The Classist underpinnings of Ruby Payne's Framework. *Teachers College Record*. Retrieved June 24, 2007 from http://www.tcrecord.org

  Gorski offers one of the first and most important challenges to the rise of popularity of Payne's deficit-driven frameworks by deconstructing her work through critical social theory. Gorksi presents three critiques: "(1) Payne's framework fails to consider the class inequities that pervade U.S. schools; (2) Payne draws from a deficit perspective; and (3) Payne's values are fundamentally conservative (as in conserving the status quo), and not transformative, in nature" (n.p.). Gorski explains that Payne's work does not reflect research on class and poverty but speaks to a middle-class norm that is not transformative but destined to maintain the status quo.

- Gorski, P. (2008a). Peddling poverty for profit: Elements of oppression in Ruby Payne's Framework. *Equity & Excellence in Education, 41*(1), 130-148. http://www.edchange.org/publications/Peddling-Poverty-Payne.pdf

    Gorski continues to examine Payne's influence on addressing poverty in education, highlighting her profit motive and presenting eight elements of oppression found in her framework: "(1) uncritical and self-serving 'scholarship,' (2) the elusive culture of poverty, (3) abounding stereotypes, (4) deficit theory, (5) invisibility of classism, (6) the 'it's not about race' card, (7) peddling paternalism, and (8) compassionate conservatism" (p. 131). This piece is important as well for offering alternative to deficit perspectives in the closing section—alternatives that address the political nature of poverty and the failure of education to confront classism in society and in schools.

- Gorski, P. (2006b, July 19). Responding to Payne's Response. *Teachers College Record.* Retrieved June 12, 2009 from http://www.tcrecord.org

    Payne responded to Gorski in TCR, and Gorski briefly confronts her response here. Essentially, Gorski notes the decontextualized and conservative framing of Payne's arguments that use claims of "practical" to mask the classism inherent in her framework and the education system. Gorski ends by offering a few resources more credible than Payne.

- Gorski, P. (2006c, Winter). Savage unrealities: Classism and racism around Ruby Payne's Framework. *Rethinking Schools, 21*(2). http://www.edchange.org/publications/Savage_Unrealities.pdf

    Gorski opens by explaining that he first heard of Payne in the context of his own reading of Kozol's *Savage Inequalities,* leading him to believe Payne was offering teachers practical advice in the same context as Kozol. Then, Gorski explains, he discovered the flaws in Payne's arguments. This piece challenges Payne and classist perspectives, suggests how to more toward a more authentic view of poverty and teaching children from poverty, and offers an expanded lists of resources.

- Gorski, P. (2008b, April). The myth of the "Culture of Poverty." *Educational Leadership, 65*(7), 32-36. http://www.ascd.org/publications/educational-leadership/apr08/vol65/num07/The-Myth-of-the-Culture-of-Poverty.aspx

    Gorski presents and refutes four myths about a culture of poverty: "Poor people are unmotivated and have weak work ethics" (n.p.); "Poor parents are uninvolved in their children's learning, largely because they do not value education" (n.p.); "Poor people are linguistically deficient" (n.p.); and "Poor people tend to abuse drugs and alcohol" (n.p.). He then argues for a shift to understanding a culture of classism. He ends with 14 suggestions for addressing the inequity of opportunity children from poverty face instead of labeling children from poverty as flawed and using schools to "'fix' poor students."

- Howley, C. B., Howley, A. A., Howley, C. W., & Howley, M. D. (2006). *Saving the children of the poor in rural schools.* Paper presented at the Annual Meeting of the American Educational Research Association, San Francisco, California. Available at http://www.eric.ed.gov:80/ PDFS/ED495031.pdf

  Howley et al. studied six rural schools and uncovered that attitudes toward social class fell into three categories: (1) a paternalistic goal of saving children from poverty and introducing them into middle-class norms, (2) marginalizing and demonizing those in poverty, and (3) not identifying those living in poverty as the poor but as "common people." The research examines these dynamics and concludes that no credible perspective on poverty blames the people in poverty themselves, suggesting that economic examinations of poverty should prove most effective in addressing poverty in schools.

- Jones, S. (2006). *Girls, social class, and literacy: What teachers can do to make a difference.* Portsmouth, NH: Heinemann.

  Based on a 5-year study of eight girls from working-class backgrounds, Jones presents an extended consideration of the power of classism in the lives of girls. This is a practical book that focuses on changing how teachers view poverty, gender, and learning in lives of poverty. The discussion presents practical approaches to rethinking literacy pedagogy through critical literacy.

- Ng, J., & Rury, J. (2009, Winter). Problematizing Payne and understanding poverty: An analysis with data from the 2000 census. *Journal of Educational Controversy, 4*(1). Retrieved from http:// www.wce.wwu.edu/Resources/CEP/eJournal/v004n001/a001.shtml

  Ng and Rury present a wealth of data related to Payne's framework, children living in poverty, an analysis of the causes of poverty, and success and failure related to teaching children from poverty. The article ends by conceding that the authors share with Payne a concern for addressing children living and learning in poverty, but recommends that a number of scholars offer valid examinations of poverty not found in Payne's workbooks and workshops.

- Ng, J. C., & Rury, J. L. (2006b, July 18). Poverty and education: A critical analysis of the Ruby Payne phenomenon. *Teachers College Record*. Retrieved June 24, 2007 from http://www.tcrecord.org

  Ng and Rury outline Payne's claims about poverty and people living in poverty and conclude: "the reality of working with such students is often considerably more complicated than her scenarios may suggest, and poverty may not be as closely tied to morality and associated 'hidden rules' as she seems to believe" (n.p.). The authors admit Payne's workbook and presentation are powerful, primarily from being clear and simple, but add that her work is "largely unsubstantiated in current research literature" (n.p.). The piece ends by suggesting that educators address better the questions of poverty raised by looking closely at Payne.

- Osei-Kofi, N. (2005). Pathologizing the poor: A framework for understanding Ruby Payne's work. *Equity & Excellence in Education*, *38*, 367-375.

  Osei-Kofi critiques Payne's framework because issues of class and poverty are essential for education and the lives of children. Next, the author places Payne's work within the powerful "culture of poverty" ideology reaching back to mid-twentieth century. Osei-Kofi explains that people in poverty are objictified by Payne in order to appeal to the middle-class norms common among teachers and schools; further, the author challenges the premise of clear class-based "hidden rules." NCLB and ideologies that frame poverty and knowledge as capital help perpetuate Payne's influence, Osei-Kofi adds. The piece ends with a call to teachers as change agents that confront simplistic views of class and reducing knowledge and poverty to a capital paradigm.

- Sato, M., & Lensmire, T. J. (2009, January). Poverty and Payne: Supporting teachers to work with children of poverty. *Phi Delta Kappan*, *9*(5), 365-370.

  Sato and Lensmire open by recognizing that education is paying more attention to the weight of poverty on learning but that education relies far too often on deficit ideology to label and address those children in school. This article offers three approaches to reframing approaches to poverty personified by Payne's framework: "1) an emphasis on children's competency, 2) a focus on the teacher's cultural identity, and 3) a professional development model based in ongoing collaborative work among teachers" (n.p.).

- Starnes, B. A. (2008, June). On lilacs, tap-dancing, and children of poverty. *Phi Delta Kappan*, 779-780.

Starnes places the power of Payne's work to seduce well-meaning teachers in the context of her own life story. This piece rejects the calls to address poverty by conforming children in poverty to middle-class norms. Starnes exposes Payne's claims about people who are poor as stereotypes we should challenge, not perpetuate.

- Thomas, P. L. (2010b). The Payne of addressing race and poverty in public education: Utopian accountability and deficit assumptions of middle class America. *Souls, 12*(3), 262-283. Retrieved from http://bit.ly/kva8Mm

    This essay places the work of Payne and deficit views of poverty within the utopian goals and crisis discourse that dominates the accountability era over the past three decades.

- Thomas, P. L. (2009). Shifting from deficit to generative practices: Addressing impoverished and all students. *Teaching Children of Poverty, 1*(1). Retrieved September 13, 2009 from http://journals.sfu.ca/tcop/index.php/tcop/article/view/8/1

    The achievement gap and efforts to close the achievement gap have created even more stratified classes for children in poverty. The article identifies deficit practices to avoid and generative practices to embrace.

- Valencia, R. R. (2010). *Dismantling contemporary deficit thinking: Educational thought and practice*. New York: Routledge.

    Valencia's award-winning work (2011 AERA Outstanding Book Award) examines deficit thinking by confronting connecting intelligence and heredity; the culture of poverty promoted in Payne's work; at-risk labels for students; deficit thinking among educators, administrators, and scholars; and the failure of accountability as it contrasts democratic goals for schools.

CONCLUSION

"THERE IS NO SUCH THING AS A CULTURALLY DEPRIVED KID"

In 1963, Ralph Ellison (2003) delivered a speech to educators at a conference in Massachusetts. Ellison's address concerned "'these children,' the difficult thirty percent" (p. 546)—African American children dropping out of school. While Ellison experienced criticism from critical leaders in the civil rights movement at mid-twentieth century—an affinity for traditional and mainstream assumptions about being successful, possibly at the expense of people of color—Ellison's speech is unlike the new reformers' seemingly uncritical view of lowering the drop-out rate and closing the achievement gap. In fact, Ellison's words speak critically to us today.

Decades before Ruby Payne's framework reduced the discourse about poverty, class, and race to worksheets and lists (see Chapter 7), Ellison (2003) argued for both a complex and humane view of African American children—children often labeled and marginalized by the school system designed to offer them avenues out of their lives of inequity. In his early remarks, in fact, he chastised assumptions about "one monolithic culture…, one which is perfect, the best of all possible cultures, with the best of all people affirming its perfection" (p. 546). Ellison acknowledged for his audience of teaches my own caution about utopian education goals flawed by assumptions that we treat as truth. U.S. culture is in fact diverse, but any subgroup we care to identify is a collection of unique and diverse people.

Ellison (2003) also confronted the deficit thinking that is endemic in U.S. culture, its public schools, and the claims made by Payne. He explained:

> There is no such thing as a culturally deprived kid. That kid down in Alabama whose parents have no food, where the mill owner has dismantled the mills and moved out west and left them to forage in the garbage cans of Tuskegee, has nevertheless some awareness that he is part of a larger American scene, and he is being influenced by this scene.... How is his badly trained teacher going to view him and his possibilities as a future American adult? What I'm trying to say is that the problem seems to me to be one of really scrutinizing the goals of American education. (p. 547)

Educators must, then, see each student for what she or he brings to our classes—not assuming that since a child comes from poverty (or is classified by race or special needs), the child is lacking something teachers are obligated to provide. Further, Ellison also challenges us to consider that some, if not most, problems education faces may lie in the flaws with the system itself (often as a reflection of the wider society) and not inherent deficits in the children.

Speaking from his own experiences as an African American, Ellison (2003) rejected deficit thinking and monolithic views of any classification of people. He detailed that his perception of African Americans is nuanced because he "live[d] principally with" them (p. 547). But he moved beyond these points to call for how educators should view children of color and children living in poverty (both of whom today remain disproportionately represented in drop-out rates, low student achievement, and classifications as students with special needs): "Let's not play these kids cheap; let's find out what they have. What do they have that is a strength? What do they have that you can approach and build a bridge upon?" (p. 548). This generative stance (Thomas, 2009) is constructivistic in nature and enabling, humane.

A profound failure of deficit approaches to education and children living in poverty, as noted in the previous chapter, is measuring students against assumptions-as-norms that highlight human deficits. For example, Ellison (2003) argued against the conventional wisdom that characterizes African Americans in the South as language deficient (reflecting racial and regional biases); in fact, he claimed just the opposite, citing the work of William Faulkner and decrying the value of using tests to determine literacy. His argument expanded to include a belief that children living in poverty have strengths that are hidden by a system intent on seeing only their weaknesses—that casting a dark shadow on children is actually a culture pointing *over there* so no one looks closely at that society: "As we approach the dropouts, let us identify who *we* are and where we are. Let us also have a little bit of respect for what we were and from whence we came" (p. 550, emphasis in original).

The American nature, then, is to project both an *other* and a *self* that prove to be equally inaccurate. "There is a bit of the phony," Ellison (2003) believed, "built into every American" (p. 550). The American spirit struggles against the bedrock of tradition and the lure of change that are equally at the core of the American mythos: "We are tempted to become actors, and when we forget who we are and where we are from, our phony selves take command" (p. 550).

As Gladwell (2008) explores in *Outliers*, nearly everyone conforms unconsciously to the norms of her/his society. Ellison (2003) appeared to be voicing a similar concept in his speech that suggested any individual is at risk of psychological conflict when the true self comes in conflict with the norms of society: A dropout can see herself/himself only as a failure because this is the message society sends—dropouts are the problems, not the system from which the child drops out, not the society that creates the schools. The deficit ideology absolves social norms of culpability and places all blame on the (implicitly flawed) individual.

Instead of teachers trained to view poverty through worksheets and lists of characteristics of families living in poverty (so that student test scores can be improved and the achievement gap closed), Ellison (2003) called for humane teachers "who can convey to [students] an awareness that they do indeed come from somewhere, some place of human value, and that what they've learned there does count in the larger society" (p .551). *Human potentiality* of all children, regardless of race and regardless of economic oppression or privilege, is a basic commitment for any teacher, for any school, and for any culture claiming to value human freedom. Instead, we are now trapped in a culture of standards and testing that distracts us from those human potentialities, although Ellison (2003) would have none of that: "Therefore, I do not believe that the basic problem is a Negro problem, no matter what the statistics tell us" (p. 551).

Again, this speech is from 1963, but Ellison (2003) recognized a mechanistic system and society entrenched in deficit thinking and narrow forms of measurement that left our children "unprepared by their education to live in this world without extensive aid":

> We are missing the target, and all of our children are suffering as a result. To be ill-clothed, ill-housed and ill-fed is not the only way to suffer deprivation.... When a child has no sense of how he should fit into the society around him, he is culturally deprived, no matter how high his parents' income. When a child has no fruitful way of relating the cultural traditions and values of his parents to the diversity of cultural forces with which he must live in a pluralistic society, he is culturally deprived. When he has to spend a great part of his time in the care of a psychoanalyst, he is, again,

culturally deprived. Thus I would broaden the definition.... For one thing, many American children have not been trained to reject enough of the negative values which our society presses upon them. Nor have they been trained sufficiently to preserve those values which sustained their forefathers and which constitute an important part of their heritage. (p. 553)

Instead of accepting classist ideology that perpetuates that it is the duty of schools to conform all children to the norms of their society, Ellison (2003) acknowledged that "these dropouts ... are living critics of their environment, of our society and our educational system, and they are quite savage critics of some of their teachers" (p. 555). While Payne justifies her framework by providing anecdotal evidence (teachers raise their hands when she asks who is the first generation in their family to complete college), reducing any group of humans to a monolithic "framework," whether it be a race or *children living in poverty*, is ignoring the complexities of being human, and in educational settings, these practices are, as Ellison noted, self-fulfilling prophesies of failure. I think educators may do well to move forward with Ellison's final words in mind:

> I don't know what intelligence is. But this I do know, both from life and from literature: whenever you reduce human life to two plus two equals four, the human element within the human animal says, "I don't give a damn." You can work on that basis, but the kids cannot. If you can show me how I can cling to that which is real to me, while teaching me a way into the larger society, then I will not only drop my defenses and my hostility, but I will sing your praises and help you to make the desert bear fruit. (p. 555)

The purposes and role of education in a democracy as well as the agency of the teachers in that system are at the core of any discussion of class in the United States. To acknowledge poverty only to maintain that poverty is not an excuse for any person's status is essentially to ignore poverty. The American culture and its public education system will remain mired in classism and inequity as long as we cling to ideology and cultural narratives to the exclusion of evidence.

Idealizing the rugged individual and the power of education as a lever of change is a persistent flaw in the political discourse and ultimately the policy of the U.S. The great and disturbing irony is that as long as we hold education to utopian goals while ignoring poverty against the backdrop of "no excuses," that same public education system will never achieve the social reform it is charged to do.

Instead, we must confront the social causes of poverty—inequities and privileges built into a consumer culture that rejects social justice for the Social Darwinism of the free market—and embrace educators as change agents. These shifts in culture present us with a tremendous paradox since such change is likely to come only through education—and the rise of educators who embrace their roles as change agents against the threat of a repressive system committed to education as indoctrination.

NOTE

Drafting a Book on Poverty in the Twenty-First Century

This book is a hybrid work of sorts—the combination of commentaries and Op-Eds weaved into a larger scholarly work confronting how many different stakeholders in universal public education—politicians, corporate leaders, political appointees, the general public, administrators, teachers, and students—view poverty, people living in poverty, students learning in poverty, and teaching and learning. The commentaries and Op-Eds I published in traditional publications and through online media such as blogs add to the larger body of scholarly work both discourse aimed at a wide readership and interactive discussions impacted by online writing, prompting and allowing readers to post comments and engage me as a scholar in a living and evolving conversation.

While this book is primarily a work about U.S. poverty and education in the twentieth and twenty-first centuries, my work as a scholar is tied inextricably with my work as a writer; thus the work itself, like all of my work, is a commentary on discourse and writing. Just as assumptions about poverty and education impact and tint how we address both, assumptions, conventions, and norms about discourse control not only what is expressed but also how discourse is presented. One hybrid aspect of this book is the blending of discourse aimed at the general public and a scholarly audience. Too often, I believe, public discourse lacks the evidence-based elements necessary in scholarly work (citations and references that allow the readers to examine the validity of the claims made in the piece), while scholarly work tends to be expressed in language and media that create an insular discourse, scholars speaking to scholars in the language of scholarship.

Another element of the book that often creates tension when I submit work for publication is what I frame as quilting; I view scholarly discourse as a fabric weaved out of a community of voices. The use of citations and quoting sources to illuminate and reinforce claims are essential elements of presenting scholarly authority (in the Freirian sense of authoritative, not authoritarian), but many conventions of scholarly writing encourage burying the voice of the cited scholars within paraphrasing. I, instead, tend to highlight in quotes not only the claims of my citations, but also the voice itself—how the claim is framed by the source. This stylistic choice celebrates the collaborative and communal nature of making scholarly claims, although it comes with risk within the academic community that is often deeply conservative about discourse conventions while being more embracing of radical ideas and claims.

Making scholarly and public claims creates a tension for democratic ideals: What voice matters, and should all voices matter equally? Democratic ideals suggest that all voices must be honored, but rarely do we confront in our democracy the weight of each voice—does giving credibility to expert voices over inexpert voices betray democracy? To argue for social equity, human agency, and equitable schools, making a parallel argument that some voices are more valid than others appears hypocritical, but therein lies the paradox of critical scholarship genuinely committed to democracy and human agency.

My arguments and evidence, then, have been an organic act, informed by my scholarship and by interacting with readers within the new media world of online publications and discussing topics with readers. While this book becomes a fixed statement, it too is part of a living and breathing tapestry, a quilt offered as a place to begin and maintain a discussion that leads toward a more equitable education system that feeds a more equitable society. This is a confrontation of many types of poverty—the poverty of economics that imprisons people in a society driven by privilege, the poverty of access, the poverty of voice, the poverty of information ironically persisting in a world bombarded by media.

And I feel compelled to end with these words from Kurt Vonnegut (1991):

> I listen to the ethical pronouncements of the leaders of the so-called religious revival going on in this country, including those of our President, and am able to distill only two firm commandments from them. The first commandment is this: "Stop thinking." The second commandment is this:

"Obey." Only a person who has given up on the power of reason to improve life here on Earth, or a soldier in basic training, could accept either commandment gladly: "Stop thinking" and "Obey." (p. 158)

Inequity is the life-blood of privilege, and the privileged depend on the majority of the public to stop thinking and obey. Let's not.

REFERENCES

Adamson, P. (2005). Child poverty in rich countries 2005. Innocenti Report Card (6). United Nations Children's Fund Innocenti Research Centre. Florence, Italy. Retrieved August 17, 2011 from http://www.unicef-irc.org/publications/371

Adamson, P. (2007). Child poverty in perspective: An overview of child well-being in rich countries. Innocenti Report Card (7). Florence, Italy: United Nations Children's Fund Innocenti Research Centre. Retrieved August 17, 2011 from http://www.unicef-irc.org/publications/445

Aguerrebere, J. A. (2008, June 11). NBPTS statement on "Assessing accomplished teaching: Advanced-level certification programs": A report by the National Research Council of the National Academies. Arlington, VA: National Board for Professional Teaching Standards. Retrieved June 22, 2008 from http://www.nbpts.org/index.cfm?t=downloader.cfm&id=906

Ahlquist, R., Gorski, P., & Montano, T. (Eds.). (2011). *Assault on kids: How hyper-accountability, corporatization, deficit ideology, and Ruby Payne are destroying our schools*. New York, NY: Peter Lang.

Altman, A. (2009, October 20). Author Malcolm Gladwell. *Time*. Retrieved April 22, 2011 from http://www.time.com/time/arts/article/0,8599,1931100,00.html?xid=rss-arts

Armario, C., & Turner, D. (2010, December 21). SHOCKING: Nearly 1 In 4 high school graduates can't pass military entrance exam. *The Huffington Post*. Retrieved January 11, 2011 from http://www.huffingtonpost.com/2010/12/21/high-school-grads-fail-military-exam_n_799767.html

Au, W. (2010, Winter). Neither fair nor accurate: Research-based reasons why high-stakes tests should not be used to evaluate teachers. *Rethinking Schools*. Retrieved June 12, 2011 from http://www.rethinkingschools.org/archive/25_02/25_02_au.shtml

Auguste, B., Kihn, P., & Miller, M. (2010, September). Closing the talent gap: Attracting and retaining top-third graduates to careers in teaching. McKinsey and Company. Retrieved July 28, 2011 from http://www.mckinsey.com/clientservice/Social_Sector/our_practices/Education/Knowledge_Highlights/Closing_the_talent_gap.aspx

Ayers, W. (2001). *To teach: The journey of a teacher* (2nd ed.). New York, NY: Teachers College Press.

Baker, B. D. (2009a, August 31). Andrew Coulson should learn to read … private school study. Schoolfinance101 [Web log post]. Retrieved November 2, 2009, from http://schoolfinance101.wordpress.com/2009/08/31/andrew-coulson-should-learn-to-read-private-school-study/

Baker, B. D. (2009b). *Private schooling in the U.S.: Expenditures, supply, and policy implications*. Boulder, CO and Tempe, AZ: Education and the Public Interest Center & Education Policy Research Unit. Retrieved August 24, 2009, from http://epicpolicy.org/publication/private-schooling-US

Baker, B. D. (2011, May 9). More on NAEP poverty gaps & why state comparisons don't work. School Finance 101 [Web log post]. Retrieved May 28, 2011, from http://schoolfinance101.wordpress.com/2011/05/09/more-on-naep-poverty-gaps-why-state-comparisons-dont-work/

Baker, B., Ng, J., & Rury, J. (2006, June 7). Questioning a speaker's knowledge of poverty. *Education Week, 25*(39), 36. Retrieved January 11, 2012, from http://www.edweek.org/ew/articles/2006/06/07/39letter-2.h25.html

Baker, B. D., & Ferris, R. (2011). *Adding up the spending: Fiscal disparities and philanthropy among New York City charter schools*. Boulder, CO: National Education Policy Center. Retrieved April 26, 2011, from http://nepc.colorado.edu/publication/NYC-charter-disparities

Baker, E. L., Barton, P. E., Darling-Hammond, L., Haertel, E., Ladd, H. F., Linn, R. L. et al. (2010, August 20). Problems with the use of student test scores to evaluate teachers. EPI Briefing Paper #278. Washington DC: Economic Policy Institute. Retrieved June 12, 2011, from http://www.epi.org/publications/entry/bp278

Ballou, D., Teasley, B., & Zeidner, T. (2006, August). Comparison of charter schools and traditional public schools in Idaho. Nashville, TN: The National Center for the Study of Privatization in Education. Retrieved August 6, 2009, from http://www.ncspe.org/publications_files/OP135.pdf

Barkan, J. (2011, January 6). Got dough? Public school reform in the age of venture philanthropy. *truthout*. Retrieved January 10, 2011, from http://www.truth-out.org/got-dough-public-school-reform-age-venture-philanthropy66598

Barseghian, T. (2010, September 27). Teach.gov: Arne Duncan's call to arms. Mind/Shift. KQED. Retrieved June 12, 2011, from http://mindshift.kqed.org/2010/09/teach-gov-arne-duncans-call-to-arms/

Barton, P. E., & Coley, R. J. (2007, September). The family: America's smallest school. Princeton, NJ: Educational Testing Service, Policy Information Center. Retrieved December 27, 2007, from http://www.ets.org/Media/Education_Topics/pdf/5678_PERCReport_School.pdf

Barton, P. E., & Coley, R. J. (2009). Parsing the achievement gap II. Princeton, NJ: Educational Testing Service, Policy Information Center. Retrieved May 8, 2009, from http://www.ets.org/Media/Research/pdf/PICPARSINGII.pdf

Belfield, C. R. (2006, January). The evidence of education vouchers: An application to the Cleveland scholarship and tutoring program. Nashville, TN: The National Center for the Study of Privatization in Education. Retrieved August 6, 2009 from http://www.ncspe.org/readrel.php?set=pub&cat=127

Bell, C. A. (2005, October). All choices created equal?: How good parents select "failing" schools. Nashville, TN: The National Center for the Study of Privatization in Education. Retrieved August 6, 2009, from http://www.ncspe.org/readrel.php?set=pub&cat=120

Berdan, S. N., & Weiner, R. (2010, December 13). Why the PISA debates are misleading—and useful. *Huffington Post*. Retrieved March 8, 2011, from http://www.huffingtonpost.com/stacie-nevadomski-berdan/why-the-pisa-debates-are-_b_793589.html

Berliner, D. C. (2009). Poverty and potential: Out-of-school factors and school success. Boulder, CO and Tempe, AZ: Education and the Public Interest Center & Education Policy Research Unit. Retrieved August 25, 2009, from http://epicpolicy.org/publication/poverty-and-potential

Bessie, A. (2010a, October 15). The myth of the bad teacher. *truthout*. Retrieved January 10, 2011, from http://archive.truthout.org/the-myth-bad-teacher64223

Bessie, A. (2010b, December 29). To fix education: Fire teachers, hire holograms. *The Daily Censored*. Retrieved August 15, 2011, from http://dailycensored.com/2010/12/29/to-fix-education-fire-human-teachers-hire-holograms/

Bessie, A. (2011, January 22). Let's not "reform" public education. *truthout*. Retrieved March 7, 2011, from http://www.truth-out.org/lets-not-reform-public-education67006

Bifulco, R., Ladd, H. F., & Ross, S. (2008, September). Public school choice and integration: Evidence from Durham, North Carolina. Working Paper No. 109. Syracuse, NY: Center for Policy Research.

Board-certified teachers boost student scores. (2008, June 11). *USA Today*. Retrieved June 22, 2008 from http://www.usatoday.com/news/education/2008-06-11-certified-teachers_N.htm

Boaz, D. (1997). *Libertarianism: A primer*. New York, NY: The Free Press.

Bohn, A. (2006, Winter). A framework for understanding Ruby Payne. *Rethinking Schools, 21*(2). Retrieved from http://www.rethinkingschools.org/archive/21_02/fram212.shtml

Bomer, R., Dworin, J. E., May, L., & Semingson, P. (2008). Miseducating teachers about the poor: A critical analysis of Ruby Payne's claims about poverty. *Teachers College Record, 110*(12), 2497-2531.

Bomer, R., Dworin, J. E., May, L., & Semingson, P. (2009, June 3). What's wrong with a deficit perspective? *Teachers College Record*. Retrieved June 12, 2009 from http://www.tcrecord.org

Borsuk, A. J. (2007, October 24). Choice may not improve schools, study says: Report on MPS comes from longtime supporter of plan. *Milwaukee-Wisconsin Journal Sentinel*. Retrieved July 18, 2011, from http://www.jsonline.com/news/education/29319654.html

Bracey, G. W. (2003). April foolishness: The 20th anniversary of A Nation at Risk. *Phi Delta Kappan, 84*(8), 616-621.

Bracey, G. W. (2004). *Setting the record straight: Responses to misconceptions about public education in the U.S.* Portsmouth, NH: Heinemann.

Bracey, G. W. (2006). *Reading educational research: How to avoid getting statistically snookered*. Portsmouth, NH: Heinemann.

Bracey, G. W. (2007, June 11). Margaret Spellings: Small signs of progress, but, then, there she goes again into Orwell's realm. *Huffington Post*. Retrieved March 8, 2011 from http://www.huffingtonpost.com/gerald-bracey/margaret-spellings-small-_b_51619.html

Bracey, G. W. (2008, December 9). International Comparisons: More Fizzle than Fizz. *Huffington Post*. Retrieved January 10, 2011, from http://www.huffingtonpost.com/gerald-bracey/international-comparisons_b_149690.html

Braun, H., Jenkins, F., & Grigg, W. (2006, July). Comparing private schools and public schools using hierarchical linear modeling. Washington, DC: U.S. Department of Education. Retrieved December 28, 2008, from http://nces.ed.gov/pubsearch/pubsinfo.asp?pubid=2006461

Brooks, D. (2009, May 7). The Harlem miracle. *The New York Times*, A31. Retrieved August 17, 2011, from http://www.nytimes.com/2009/05/08/opinion/08brooks.html

Brooks, D. (2011, June 30). Smells like school spirit. *The New York Times*. Retrieved July 5, 2011 from http://www.nytimes.com/2011/07/01/opinion/01brooks.html

Bryant, J. (2011, June 9). The values of education get lost in the numbers. Washington, DC: Campaign for America's Future. Retrieved July 5, 2011, from http://www.ourfuture.org/blog-entry/2011062309/values-education-get-lost-numbers

Buddin, R., & Zimmer, R. (2005, September). Is charter school competition in California improving the performance of traditional public schools? Working paper prepared for the Smith Richardson Foundation. Santa Monica, CA: RAND. Retrieved October 5, 2008, from http://www.rand.org/pubs/working_papers/WR297.html

Callahan, R. E. (1962). *Education and the cult of efficiency: A study of the social forces that have shaped the administration of the public schools.* Chicago: The University of Chicago Press.

Camus, A. (1955). The myth of Sisyphus. In *The Myth of Sisyphus and other essays* (pp. 88-91). J. O'Brien (Trans.). New York, NY: Vintage Books.

Carlin, G. (2004). *When will Jesus bring the pork chops?* New York, NY: Hyperion.

Carr, M., & Ritter, G. (2007). Measuring the competitive effect of charter schools on student achievement in Ohio's traditional public schools. Retrieved October 5, 2008, from the National Center for the Study of Privatization in Education, http://www.ncspe.org/readrel.php?set=pub&cat=184

Center for Research on Education Outcomes (CREDO). (2009, June). Multiple choice: Charter school performance in 16 states. Stanford, CA: Center for Research on Education Outcomes. Retrieved November 2, 2009 from http://credo.stanford.edu/reports/MULTIPLE_CHOICE_CREDO.pdf

Chemsak, S. (2008, May). A comprehensive, non-partisan analysis of Arizona's charter school plan. Retrieved August 6, 2009, from the National Center for the Study of Privatization in Education, http://www.ncspe.org/readrel.php?set=pub&cat=197

Civil Rights Framework for Providing All Students an Opportunity to Learn through Reauthorization of the Elementary and Secondary Education Act. (2010, July 26). National Opportunity to Learn (OTL) Campaign. Cambridge, MA: The Schott Foundation for Public Education. Retrieved January 10, 2011 from http://www.otlcampaign.org/resources/civil-rights-framework-providing-all-students-opportunity-learn-through-reauthorization-el

Clawson, L. (2011, March 28). Investigation shows questionable test results under Michelle Rhee. *Daily Kos.* Retrieved April 22, 2011, from http://www.dailykos.com/story/2011/03/28/960859/-Investigation-shows-questionable-test-results-under-Michelle-Rhee

Cody, A. (2010, November 8). Schools in a banana Republic. Living in Dialogue [Web log post]. *Education Week.* Retrieved July 17, 2011, from http://blogs.edweek.org/teachers/living-in-dialogue/2010/11/schools_in_a_banana_republic.html

Cody, A. (2011a, March 15). The myth of the "superteacher." The Answer Sheet [Web log post]. *The Washington Post.* Retrieved May 29, 2011, from http://www.washingtonpost.com/blogs/answer-sheet/post/the-myth-of-the-superteacher/2011/03/14/ABfRM4V_blog.html

Cody, A. (2011b, April 10). The media discovers there is a debate over educational reform! Living in Dialogue [Web log post]. *Education Week.* Retrieved April 22, 2011, from http://blogs.edweek.org/teachers/living-in-dialogue/2011/04/the_media_discovers_there_is_a.html

Cohen, P. (2010, October 17). "Culture of poverty" makes a comeback. *The New York Times.* Retrieved July 13, 2011, from http://www.nytimes.com/2010/10/18/us/18poverty.html

Cohen-Zada, D., & Sander, W. (2007, May). Private school choice: The effects of religious affiliation and participation. Retrieved August 6, 2009, from http://www.ncspe.org/publications_files/OP140.pdf

Colbert, S. (2010). Episode 804. Guests Jake Tapper and Michelle Rhee. [Television series episode]. In *The Colbert Report.* New York, NY: Comedy Central. December 1, 2010.

Colbert, S. (2011). Episode 815. Guests Ron Paul, David Leonhardt, and Geoffrey Canada. [Television series episode]. In *The Colbert Report.* New York, NY: Comedy Central. January 4, 2011.

The College Board. (2002). Guidelines on the uses of College Board test scores and related data. Princeton, NJ: Author. Retrieved July 24, 2009, from http://www.collegeboard.com/prod_downloads/research/RDGuideUseCBTest020729.pdf

The College Board. (2005). College-bound seniors: Total group profile report. Princeton, NJ: Author. Retrieved August 27, 2009 from http://www.collegeboard.com/prod_downloads/about/news_info/cbsenior/yr2005/2005-college-bound-seniors.pdf

The College Board. (2010). SAT trends: Background on the SAT takers in the class of 2010. Princeton, NJ: Author. Retrieved August 17, 2011 from http://professionals.collegeboard.com/profdownload/2010-sat-trends.pdf

Coulson, A. J. (2009, July 15). The myth of Arne Duncan's "Chicago Miracle." Cato @ Liberty. Retrieved April 22, 2011, from http://www.cato-at-liberty.org/the-myth-of-arne-duncans-chicago-miracle/

Cowan, J., & Mancini, S. (2011, January 11). KIPP responds to criticism on attrition rates. The Answer Sheet [Web log post]. *The Washington Post*. Retrieved May 28, 2011. from http://voices.washingtonpost.com/answer-sheet/charter-schools/kipp-responds-to-criticism-on.html?wprss=answer-sheet

Crane, D., Kauffman, M., Curtis, M. (Writers), & Bright, K. S. (Director). (1995) The one where Heckles dies [Television series episode]. In M. Borkow, B. Borns, K. Bright, D. Crane, M. Kauffman, W. Knoller, M. McLoughlin, & T. Stevens (Producers), *Friends*. Burbank, CA: Warner Bros. Television.

Darling-Hammond, L. (2002, September 6). Research and rhetoric on teacher certification: A response to "Teacher Certification Reconsidered." *Education Policy Analysis Archives, 10*(36). Retrieved July 28, 2009 from http://epaa.asu.edu/epaa/v10n36.html

David, J. L. (2011, March). High-stakes testing narrows the curriculum. *Educational Leadership, 68*(6), 78-80.

DeBellis, R. J., & Zdanawicz, M. (2000, November). Bacteria battle back: Addressing antibiotic resistance. Boston: Massachusetts College of Pharmacy and Health Science. Retrieved September 13, 2009, from http://www.tufts.edu/med/apua/Educ/CME/BBB.pdf

d'Entremont, C., & Gulosino, C. (2008). Circles of influence: How neighborhood demographics and charter school locations influence student enrollments. Retrieved August 6, 2009, from http://www.ncspe.org/publications_files/OP160.pdf

Dewey, J. (1997). *Experience and education*. New York, NY: Free Press. (Original work published 1938)

DiCarlo, M. (2010, October 25). The real effect of teachers union contracts. The Answer Sheet [Web log post]. *The Washington Post*. Retrieved January 10, 2011, from http://voices.washingtonpost.com/answer-sheet/guest-bloggers/how-states-with-no-teacher-uni.html

DiCarlo, M. (2011, January 7). What 2010 education research really shows about reform. The Answer Sheet [Web log post]. *The Washington Post*. Retrieved June 26, 2011, from http://voices.washingtonpost.com/answer-sheet/guest-bloggers/what-2010-education-research-r.html

Dobbie, W., & Fryer, R. G., Jr. (2009). *Are high-quality schools enough to close the achievement gap? Evidence from a bold social experiment in Harlem*. Cambridge, MA: Harvard University. Retrieved June 5, 2009, from http://www.economics.harvard.edu/faculty/fryer/files/hcz%204.15.2009.pdf

Dodenhoff, D. (2007, October). Fixing the Milwaukee public schools: The limits of parent-driven reform. *Wisconsin Policy Research Institute Report, 20*(8). Retrieved August 6, 2009, from http://www.wpri.org/Reports/Volume 20/Vol20no8/Vol20no8p1.html

Doyel, G. (2011, June 3). Heat return to their smug ways and Mavs make them pay. CBSSports.com. Retrieved June 5, 2011, from http://www.cbssports.com/#!/nba/story/15192684/heat-return-to-their-smug-ways-and-mavs-make-them-pay

Dudley-Marling, C. (2007). Return of the deficit. *Journal of Educational Controversy, 2*(1). Retrieved from http://www.wce.wwu.edu/Resources/CEP/eJournal/v002n001/a004.shtml

Dudley-Marling, C., & Lucas, K. (2009, May). Pathologizing the language and culture of poor children. *Language Arts, 86*(5), 362-370.

Duncan, A. (2009, September 24). Reauthorization of ESEA: Why we can't wait. Washington DC: U.S. Department of Education. Retrieved March 8, 2011 from http://www.ed.gov/news/speeches/reauthorization-esea-why-we-cant-wait

Duncan, A. (2010a, July 27). Secretary Arne Duncan's remarks at the National Urban League Centennial Conference. Washington DC: U.S. Department of Education. Retrieved January 10, 2011 from http://www.ed.gov/news/speeches/secretary-arne-duncans-remarks-national-urban-league-centennial-conference

Duncan, A. (2010b, August 25). Secretary Arne Duncan's Remarks at the Statehouse Convention Center in Little Rock, Arkansas. Washington DC: U.S. Department of Education. Retrieved March 7, 2011, from http://www.ed.gov/news/speeches/secretary-arne-duncans-remarks-statehouse-convention-center-little-rock-arkansas

Duncan, A. (2010c, November 4). The vision of education reform in the United States: Secretary Arne Duncan's remarks to United Nations Educational, Scientific and Cultural Organization (UNESCO), Paris, France. Washington DC: U.S. Department of Education. Retrieved March 7, 2011 from http://www.ed.gov/news/speeches/vision-education-reform-united-states-secretary-arne-duncans-remarks-united-nations-ed

Duncan, A. (2010d, November 16). Secretary Arne Duncan's remarks to National Council for Accreditation of Teacher Education. Washington DC: U.S. Department of Education. Retrieved January 10, 2011, from http://www.ed.gov/news/speeches/secretary-arne-duncans-remarks-national-council-accreditation-teacher-education

Duncan, A. (2010e, December 7). Secretary Arne Duncan's remarks at OECD's release of the Program for International Student Assessment (PISA) 2009 results. Washington DC: U.S. Department of Education. Retrieved January 10, 2011, from http://www.ed.gov/news/speeches/secretary-arne-duncans-remarks-oecds-release-program-international-student-assessment-

Dworin, J. E., & Bomer, R. (2008, January). What we all (supposedly) know about the poor: A critical discourse analysis of Ruby Payne's "Framework." *English Education, 40*(2), 101-121.

Einstein, A. (1941). Science and religion II. *Science, Philosophy and Religion, A Symposium.* Retrieved January 11, 2011, from http://www.sacred-texts.com/aor/einstein/einsci.htm

Education: Standards for Noah's Ark? (1962, March 16). *Time.* Retrieved August 15, 2011 from http://www.time.com/time/magazine/article/0,9171,940666-1,00.html

Elacqua, G. (2005, May). An analysis of parental preferences and search behavior. The National Center for the Study of Privatization in Education. Retrieved August 6, 2009, from http://www.ncspe.org/publications_files/OP97_update.pdf

Elacqua, G. (2006, August). Enrollment practices in response to vouchers: Evidence from Chile. The National Center for the Study of Privatization in Education. Retrieved August 6, 2009, from http://www.ncspe.org/publications_files/OP125.pdf

Elacqua, G. (2009, July). For-profit schooling and the politics of education reform in Chile: When ideology trumps evidence. Universidad Diego Portales: Centro de Politicas Comparadas de Educacion. Retrieved August 19, 2009, from http://www.ncspe.org/publications_files/OP178.pdf

Elden, R. (2011, January 10). Five words and phrases that sound different to teachers. Rick Hess Straight Up [Web log post]. *Education Week.* Retrieved July 5, 2011, from http://blogs.edweek.org/edweek/rick_hess_straight_up/2011/01/five_words_and_phrases_that_sound_different_to_teachers.html

Ellison, R. (1952). *Invisible man* (30th anniversary ed.). New York, NY: Vintage Books.

Ellison, R. (2003). *The collected essays of Ralph Ellison.* J. F. Callahan (Ed.). New York, NY: The Modern Library.

Emerson, R. W. (2009). The American scholar. Ralph Waldo Emerson—Texts. (Original work published 1837). Retrieved January 10, 2011, from http://www.emersoncentral.com/amscholar.htm

Emerson, R. W. (2009). Self-reliance. Ralph Waldo Emerson—Texts. (Original work published 1841). Retrieved January 10, 2011, from http://www.emersoncentral.com/selfreliance.htm

Esposito, C. L., & Cobb, C. D. (2008). Estimating the school level effects of choice on academic achievement in Connecticut's magnet, technical and charter schools. Retrieved December 28, 2008, from http://www.ncspe.org/publications_files/OP156.pdf

Farmer, M. (2011, January 8). A fan's note (The sequel). *The Huffington Post*. Retrieved January 10, 2011, from http://www.huffington-post.com/matt-farmer/a-fans-notes-the-sequel_b_806238.html

Faulkner, W. (1990). *As I lay dying*. The corrected text. New York, NY: Vintage International. (Original work published 1930)

Faulkner, W. (1930). *A rose for Emily*. Retrieved January 11, 2011, from http://www.wwnorton.com/college/english/litweb05/workshops/fiction/faulkner1.asp

Felch, J., Song, J., & Smith, D. (2010, August 14). Who's teaching L.A.'s kids? *Los Angeles Times*. Retrieved June 26, 2011, from http://www.latimes.com/news/local/la-me-teachers-value-20100815,0,2695044.story

Finn, C., & Ryan, T. (2010, Fall). Authorizing charters. *Education Next, 10*(4). Retrieved May 28, 2011, from http://educationnext.org/authorizing-charters/

Flesch, R. (1955). *Why Johnny can't read—And what you can do about it*. New York, NY: William Morrow.

Forster, G. (2011, March). *A win-win solution: The empirical evidence on school vouchers* (2nd ed.). Indianapolis, IN: The Foundation for Educational Choice. Retrieved April 22, 2011, from http://www.edchoice.org/Research/Reports/A-Win-Win-Solution--The-Empirical-Evidence-on-School-Vouchers.aspx

Foucault, M. (1984). *The Foucault reader*. P. Rabinow (Ed.). New York, NY: Pantheon Books.

Frankenberg, E., Siegel-Hawley, G., & Wang, J. (2011). Choice without equity: Charter school segregation. *Educational Policy Analysis Archives, 19*(1). Retrieved April 26, 2011, from http://epaa.asu.edu/ojs/article/view/779

Freire, P. (1993). *Pedagogy of the oppressed*. New York, NY: Continuum.

Freire, P. (1998). *Pedagogy of freedom: Ethics, democracy, and civic courage*. P. Clarke (Trans.). Lanham, MD: Rowman and Littlefield.

Freire, P. (2005). *Teachers as cultural workers: Letters to those who dare to teach*. D. Macedo, D., Koike, & A., Oliveira (Trans.). Boulder, CO: Westview Press.

Friedman, T. L. (2010, November 20). Teaching for America. *The New York Times*. Retrieved August 15, 2011, from http://www.nytimes.com/2010/11/21/opinion/21friedman.html

Friedman Foundation for Educational Choice. (2011). *Mission & History*. Indianapolis, IN: Author.

Fuller, E. (2011, April 25). Characteristics of students enrolling in high-performing charter high schools. A "Fuller" Look at Education Issues [Web log post]. Retrieved April 26, 2011, from http://fullerlook.wordpress.com/2011/04/25/hp-charter-high-schools/

Fung, K. (2011, April 7). Bill Gates should hire a statistical advisor. Junk Charts [Web log post]. Retrieved April 22, 2011 from http://junk-charts.typepad.com/junk_charts/2011/04/bill-gates-should-hire-a-statistical-advisor.html

Gaiman, N. (2001, February 9). Letter to reviewers. Retrieved July 11, 2011, from http://www.neilgaiman.com/works/Books/American+Gods/in/184/

Garcia, D. (2011). Review of "Going Exponential: Growing the Charter School Sector's Best." Boulder, CO: National Education Policy Center. Retrieved April 26, 2011 from, http://nepc.colorado.edu/thinktank/review-going-exponential.

Gardner, H. (1996). *Leading minds: An anatomy of leadership*. New York, NY: Basic Books.

Gardner, W. (2010a, August 18). How not to win support for teachers unions. Walt Gardner's Reality Check [Web log post]. *Education Week*. Retrieved June 26, 2011, from http://blogs.edweek.org/edweek/walt_gardners_reality_check/2010/08/how_not_to_win_support_for_teachers_unions.html

Gardner, W. (2010b, September 20). Poverty rate and the achievement gap. Walt Gardner's Reality Check [Web log post]. *Education Week*. Retrieved July 8, 2011, from http://blogs.edweek.org/edweek/walt_gardners_reality_check/2010/09/poverty_rate_and_the_achievement_gap.html

Gardner, W. (2010c, October 11). Expecting too much from the best teachers. Walt Gardner's Reality Check [Web log post]. *Education Week*. Retrieved March 8, 2011, from http://blogs.edweek.org/edweek/walt_gardners_reality_check/2010/10/expecting_too_much_from_the_best_teachers.html

Gardner, W. (2010d, October 16). "Superman" offers mirage, not a miracle. *The Sacramento Bee*. Retrieved March 11, 2011, from http://www.sacbee.com/2010/10/16/3108075/superman-offers-mirage-not-a-miraclehorror.html

Gardner, W. (2010e, October 27). Stripping teachers of freedom of speech. Walt Gardner's Reality Check [Web log post]. *Education Week*. Retrieved June 26, 2011, from http://blogs.edweek.org/edweek/walt_gardners_reality_check/2010/10/freedom_of_speech_for_teachers_does_not_exist.html

Gardner, W. (2011, June 8). Principals as management, teachers as labor. Walt Gardner's Reality Check [Web log post]. *Education Week*. Retrieved June 12, 2011, from http://blogs.edweek.org/edweek/walt_gardners_reality_check/2011/06/principals_as_management_teachers_as_labor.html#comments

Gates, B. (2011, February 28). How teacher development could revolutionize our schools. *The Washington Post*. Retrieved April 22, 2011 from http://www.washingtonpost.com/wp-dyn/content/article/2011/02/27/AR2011022702876.html

Get adjusted. (1947, December 15). *Time*. Retrieved April 2, 2008, from http://www.time.com/time/magazine/article/0,9171,934231,00.html

Gewertz, C. (2010, September 13). Few changes on SAT posted by class of 2010. *Education Week, 30*(4). Retrieved March 7, 2011, from http://www.edweek.org/ew/articles/2010/09/13/04sat.h30.html

Gibbons, S., Machin, S., & Silva, O. (2006, July). Choice, competition, and pupil achievement. Retrieved December 28, 2008, from http://www.ncspe.org/publications_files/OP129.pdf

Gillum, J., & Bello, M. (2011, March 30). When standardized test scores soared in D.C., were the gains real? *USA Today*. Retrieved April 22, 2011, from http://www.usatoday.com/news/education/2011-03-28-1Aschooltesting28_CV_N.htm

Ginsberg, A. E. (2010, Summer). Waiting for Superman: He's "adequate" and near proficient! *Journal of Education Controversy, 5*(2). Retrieved March 11, 2011, from http://www.wce.wwu.edu/Resources/CEP/eJournal/v005n002/a008.shtml

Giroux, H. (2010a, October 5). When generosity hurts: Bill Gates, public school teachers and the politics of humiliation. *truthout*. Retrieved March 8, 2011, from http://archive.truthout.org/when-generosity-hurts-bill-gates-public-school-teachers-and-politics-humiliation63868

Giroux, H. (2010b, November 23). Lessons to be learned from Paulo Freire as education is being taken over by the mega rich. *truthout*. Retrieved January 10, 2011 from http://archive.truthout.org/lessons-be-learned-from-paulo-freire-education-is-being-taken-over-mega-rich65363

Giroux, H. (2011a, January 4). In the twilight of the social state: Rethinking Walter Benjamin's angel of history. *truthout*. Retrieved January 11, 2011, from http://www.truth-out.org/in-twilight-social-state-rethinking-walter-benjamins-angel-history66544#19

Giroux, H. (2011b, July 11). Trickle-down cruelty and the politics of austerity. *truthout*. Retrieved January 11, 2011, from http://www.truth-out.org/trickle-down-cruelty-and-politics-austerity/1310134880#8

Gladwell, M. (2008). *Outliers: The story of success*. New York, NY: Little, Brown, and Company.

Goldhaber, D. (2010, December 1). When the stakes are high, can we rely on value-added? Center for American Progress. Retrieved June 12, 2011, from http://zedc3test.techprogress.org/issues/2010/12/vam.html

Goldstein, D. (2011, June 2). Integration and the "no excuses" charter school movement. *The Washington Post*. Retrieved June 5, 2011, from http://www.washingtonpost.com/blogs/ezra-klein/post/integration-and-the-no-excuses-charter-school-movement/2011/06/02/AGmKLRHH_blog.html

Goodman, J. F. (2011, May 25). When students are silenced. *Education Week*, *30*(32), 20-22. Retrieved June 5, 2011, from http://www.edweek.org/ew/articles/2011/05/25/32goodman.h30.html

Goodman, A., & Gregg, P. (2010, March 29). Poorer children's educational attainment: how important are attitudes and behaviour? Joseph Rowntree Foundation. York, North Yorkshire, UK. Retrieved April 22, 2011, from http://www.jrf.org.uk/publications/educational-attainment-poor-children

Gorski, P. (2006a, February 9). The Classist underpinnings of Ruby Payne's Framework. *Teachers College Record*. Retrieved June 24, 2007, from http://www.tcrecord.org

Gorski, P. (2006b, July 19). Responding to Payne's Response. *Teachers College Record*. Retrieved June 12, 2009, from http://www.tcrecord.org

Gorski, P. (2006c, Winter). Savage unrealities: Classism and racism around Ruby Payne's Framework. *Rethinking Schools*, *21*(2). Retrieved August 17, 2011, from http://www.edchange.org/publications/Savage_Unrealities.pdf

Gorski, P. (2008a). Peddling poverty for profit: Elements of oppression in Ruby Payne's Framework. *Equity & Excellence in Education*, *41*(1), 130-148. Retrieved from http://www.edchange.org/publications/Peddling-Poverty-Payne.pdf

Gorski, P. (2008b, April). The myth of the "Culture of Poverty." *Educational Leadership*, *65*(7), 32-36. Retrieved August 17, 2011, from http://www.ascd.org/publications/educational-leadership/apr08/vol65/num07/The-Myth-of-the-Culture-of-Poverty.aspx

Grether, M. (2010). Quality education in Chicago: For members only? [Web log comment]. Retrieved from http://www.huffingtonpost.com/social/Michael_Grether/quality-education-in-chic_b_805531_73209566.html

Guisbond, L., & King, J., (Eds.). (2011, June 12). Flawed Massachusetts teacher evaluation proposal risks further damage to teaching and learning. Jamaica Plain, MA: Massachusetts Working Group on Teacher Evaluation of the National Center for Fair & Open Testing. Retrieved June 27, 2011, from http://fairtest.org/flawed-ma-teacher-evaluation-proposal-report-home

Haberman, M. (1991, December). The pedagogy of poverty versus good teaching. *Phi Delta Kappan*, 290-294. Retrieved July 13, 2011, from https://www.ithaca.edu/compass/pdf/pedagogy.pdf

Haimson, L. (2010, December 28). Fact-checking "Waiting for Super-man": False data and fraudulent claims. NYC Public School Parents [Web log post]. Retrieved March 11, 2011, from http://nycpublicschoolparents.blogspot.com/2010/12/fact-checking-waiting-for-superman.html

Hakel, M. D., Koenig, J. A., & Elliott, S. W. (Eds.). (2008). Assessing accomplished teaching: Advanced-level certification programs. Washington, DC: The National Academies Press. Retrieved July 21, 2009, from http://www.nap.edu/catalog.php?record_id=12224#toc

Hanushek, E. (2010, December). The economic value of higher teacher quality. Working paper 56. Washington, DC: Calder, The Urban Institute.

Heilig, J. V., & Jez, S. J. (2010). Teach For America: A review of the evidence. Boulder, CO and Tempe, AZ: Education and the Public Interest Center & Education Policy Research Unit. Retrieved June 26, 2011, from http://epicpolicy.org/publication/teach-for-america

Heitin, L. (2010, October 15). Study explores "talent gap" in teaching. Teacher. Education Week. Retrieved July 28, 2011, from http://www.edweek.org/tm/articles/2010/10/15/mckinsey.html

Hemphill, F. C., Vanneman, A., & Rahman, T. (2011, June). Achievement gaps: How Hispanic and white students in public schools perform in mathematics and reading on the National Assessment of Educational Progress. Institute of Education Science, National Center for Education Statistics. Washington DC: U.S. Department of Education. Retrieved July 7, 2011, from http://nces.ed.gov/nationsreportcard/pubs/studies/2011459.asp

Hess, R. (2010, July 30). It's a bird, it's a plane, it's... Supersecretary! Rick Hess Straight Up [blog]. Education Week. Retrieved July 5, 2011, from http://blogs.edweek.org/edweek/rick_hess_straight_up/2010/07/duncans_limitless_authority.html

Hess, R. (2011, June 9). Moe v. Meier on teacher unions. Rick Hess Straight Up [Web log post]. Education Week. Retrieved July 5, 2011, from http://blogs.edweek.org/edweek/rick_hess_straight_up/2011/06/moe_v_meier_on_teacher_unions.html

Hicks, G. (1963). The engineers take over. The Vonnegut Web. Retrieved January 11, 2011, from http://www.vonnegutweb.com/playerpiano/pp_nytimes.html

Hirsch, D. (2007, September). Experiences of poverty and educational disadvantage. York, North Yorkshire, UK: Joseph Rowntree Foundation. Retrieved December 27, 2007, from http://www.jrf.org.uk/knowledge/findings/socialpolicy/2123.asp

Hirsch, E. D. (2009, March 22). Reading test dummies. *New York Times*. Retrieved March 8, 2011 from http://www.nytimes.com/2009/03/23/opinion/23hirsch.html

Hoff, D. J. (2007, September 25). NAEP scores rise; NCLB gets credit. NCLB: Act II [Web log post]. *Education Week*. Retrieved March 8, 2011 from http://blogs.edweek.org/edweek/NCLB-ActII/2007/09/naep_scores_rise_nclb_gets_cre.html

Holton, G. (2003, April 25). An insider's view of "A Nation at Risk" and why it still matters. *The Chronicle Review, 49*(33), B13.

Horn, J. (2009, June 3). Duncan's Chicago miracle turns mirage. Schools Matter [Web log post]. Retrieved April 22, 2011, from http://www.schoolsmatter.info/2009/06/duncans-chicago-miracle-turns-mirage.html

Horn, J. (2010a, August 28). Rhee's hard data or "single data points" depends on whose value is being added. Schools Matter [Web log post]. Retrieved March 7, 2011, from http://www.schoolsmatter.info/2010/08/rhees-hard-data-or-single-data-points.html

Horn, J. (2010b, November 22). U.S. education reformers' cartoon version of Finland's teacher education system. Schools Matter [Web log post]. Retrieved March 8, 2011, from http://www.schoolsmatter.info/2010/11/u-s-education-reformers-cartoon-version.html

Horn, J. (2011, May 23). Bill Gate's call boy, Rick Hess: "Everybody's implicated." Schools Matter [Web log post]. Retrieved July 5, 2011, from http://www.schoolsmatter.info/2011/05/gatess-call-boy-rick-hess-everybodys.html

Hout, M., & Elliott, S. W. (2011). *Incentives and test-based accountability in education*. Washington DC: The National Academies Press. Retrieved June 23, 2011, from http://www.nap.edu/catalog.php?record_id=12521

How to fix our schools: A manifesto by Joel Klein, Michelle Rhee and other education leaders. (2010, October 10). *The Washington Post*. Retrieved March 8, 2011, from http://www.washingtonpost.com/wp-dyn/content/article/2010/10/07/AR2010100705078.html

Howley, C. B., Howley, A. A., Howley, C. W., & Howley, M. D. (2006). Saving the children of the poor in rural schools. Paper presented at the Annual Meeting of the American Educational Research Association, San Francisco, California. Retrieved from http://www.eric.ed.gov:80/PDFS/ED495031.pdf

Howley, C. B., Howley, A. A., & Huber, D. S. (2005). Prescriptions for rural mathematics instruction: Analysis of the rhetorical literature. *Journal of Research in Rural Education, 20*(7), 1-16.

Hu, W. (2010, September 6). In a new role, teachers move to run schools. *The New York Times*. Retrieved May 28, 2011, from http://www.nytimes.com/2010/09/07/education/07teachers.html

Hudson, D. L., Jr. (2010, October 25). Teachers lack First Amendment right on curriculum. First Amendment Center. Retrieved May 29, 2011 from http://www.firstamendmentcenter.org/teacher-lacks-first-amendment-right-on-curriculum

Imberman, S. A. (2007, November 20). The effect of charter schools on non-charter students: An instrumental variables approach. Retrieved August 5, 2009 from http://www.ncspe.org/publications_files/OP149.pdf

Institute on Race and Poverty. (2008). Failed promises: Assessing charter schools in Twin Cities. Minneapolis, MN: Author. Retrieved August 6, 2009, from http://www.irpumn.org/uls/resources/projects/2_Charter_Report_Final.pdf

Jacoby, S. (2004). *Freethinkers: A history of American secularism*. New York, NY: Henry Holt and Company.

Jefferson, T. (1900). *The Jeffersonian cyclopedia*. New York, NY: Funk and Wagnalls Company. Retrieved December 29, 2010, from http://guides.lib.virginia.edu/content.php?pid=77323&sid=573588

Jones, S. (2006). *Girls, social class, and literacy: What teachers can do to make a difference*. Portsmouth, NH: Heinemann.

Jones, B. (2011, January 10). Dr. King and the achievement gap. *Huffington Post*. Retrieved July 13, 2011, from http://www.huffingtonpost.com/brian-jones/dr-king-and-the-achieveme_b_806392.html

Kahlenberg, R. D. (2011a, January 4). Myths and realities about KIPP. The Answer Sheet [Web log post]. *The Washington Post*. Retrieved May 28, 2011, from http://voices.washingtonpost.com/answer-sheet/charter-schools/myths-and-realities-about-kipp.html

Kahlenberg, R. D. (2011b, January 10). More questions about KIPP. The Answer Sheet [Web log post]. *The Washington Post*. Retrieved May 28, 2011, from http://voices.washingtonpost.com/answer-sheet/charter-schools/more-on-kipp.html

Keohane, J. (2010, July 11). How facts backfire. *The Boston Globe*. Retrieved January 11, 2011 from http://www.boston.com/bostonglobe/ideas/articles/2010/07/11/how_facts_backfire/

Kincheloe, J. L, & Weil, D. (2001). *Standards and schooling in the United States: Vols. 1-3*. Denver, CO: ABC-CLIO.

King, M. L., Jr. (1967). Final words of advice. *Wealth and Want*. Retrieved February 11, 2011, from http://www.wealthandwant.com/docs/King_Where.htm

Kingsolver, B. (1995). Somebody's baby. *High tide in Tucson: Essays from now or never* (pp. 99-107). New York, NY: Harper Perennial.

Klein, S. P., Hamilton, L. S., McCaffrey, D. F., & Stecher, B. M. (2000). What do test scores in Texas tell us? Issue Paper, Rand Education. Santa Monica CA: Rand Corporation. Retrieved August 20, 2009, from http://www.rand.org/pubs/issue_papers/IP202/index.html

Kliebard, H. M. (1995). *The struggle for the American curriculum: 1893-1958.* New York, NY: Routledge.

Klonsky, M. (2010, December 29). The year they began calling poverty and homelessness an "excuse." *Huffington Post.* Retrieved July 13, 2011, from http://www.huffingtonpost.com/michael-klonsky-phd/ the-year-they-begain-call_b_801931.html

Klonsky, M. (2011, May 26). The new Social-Darwinism charter schools for those with "highest potential" [Web log post]. Boulder, CO: National Education Policy Center. Retrieved May 28, 2011, from http://nepc.colorado.edu/blog/new-social-darwinism-charter-schools-those-highest-potential

Knowledge is Power Program. (2011). Five Pillars of KIPP. New York, NY: Author. Retrieved from http://www.kipp.org/about-kipp

Kobrin, J. L., Patterson, B. F., Shaw, E. J., Mattern, K. D., & Barbuti, S. M. (2008). Validity of the SAT for predicting first-year college grade point average. College Board Research Report No. 2008-5. New York, NY: The College Board. Retrieved August 12, 2008 from http:// professionals.collegeboard.com/profdownload/ Validity_of_the_SAT_for_Predicting_First_Year_College_Grade_Point _Average.pdf

Kohn, A. (2003a, September 17). The folly of merit pay. *Education Week.* Retrieved July 7, 2011, from http://www.alfiekohn.org/teaching/ edweek/meritpay.htm

Kohn, A. (2003b, Spring). Professors who profess: Making a difference as scholar-activists. *Kappa Delta Pi Record.* Retrieved July 3, 2011, from http://www.alfiekohn.org/teaching/professing.htm

Kohn, A. (2004, November). Challenging students... And how to have more of them. *Phi Delta Kappan.* Retrieved November 15, 2008, from http://www.al?ekohn.org/teaching/challenging.htm

Kohn, A. (2008a, Spring). Progressive education: Why it's hard to beat, but also hard to find. *Independent School.* http://www.alfiekohn.org/ teaching/progressive.htm

Kohn, A. (2008b, November) Why self-discipline is overrated: The (troubling) theory and practice of control from within. *Phi Delta Kappan,* *90*(3), 168-176. Retrieved August 20, 2009, from http:// www.alfiekohn.org/teaching/selfdiscipline.htm

Kohn, A. (2010a, October 18). How to sell conservatism: Lesson 1—Pretend you're a reformer. *The Huffington Post.* Retrieved January 10,

2011, from http://www.huffingtonpost.com/alfie-kohn/how-to-sell-conservatism-_b_767040.html

Kohn, A. (2010b, November 18). "Ready to learn" equals easier to educate. *The Huffington Post.* Retrieved January 10, 2011, from http://www.huffingtonpost.com/alfie-kohn/ready-to-learn-easier-to-_b_785362.html

Kohn, A. (2011, April 27). Poor teaching for poor children... in the name of reform. *Education Week.* Retrieved July 13, 2011, from http://www.alfiekohn.org/teaching/edweek/poor.htm

Kovacs, P. (2008, Winter). The educator roundtable: Working to create a world where teachers *can* school as if democracy matters. *Journal of Educational Controversy, 3*(1). Retrieved April 16, 2011, from http://www.wce.wwu.edu/resources/cep/ejournal/v003n001/a011.shtml

Krashen, S. (2001). More smoke and mirrors: A critique of the National Reading Panel (NRP) report on fluency. *Phi Delta Kappan, 83*(2), 118-122.

Krashen, S. (2006, October 2). Did Reading First work? *The Pulse.* Retrieved August 20, 2009, from http://www.districtadministration.com/pulse/commentpost.aspx?news=no&postid=17349

Krashen, S. (2007). NCLB: No impact on state fourth grade reading test scores. *The Pulse.* Retrieved September 7, 2009, from http://www.districtadministration.com/pulse/commentpost.aspx?news=no&postid=19497

Krashen, S. (2008, Spring) Bogus claims about Reading First. *Rethinking Schools Online, 22*(3). Retrieved August 20, 2009, from http://www.rethinkingschools.org/archive/22_03/bogu223.shtml

Krashen, S. (2010, October 8). The Manifesto got it all wrong. Schools Matter [Web log post]. Retrieved March 8, 2011, from http://www.schoolsmatter.info/2010/10/manifesto-got-it-all-wrong.html

Krashen, S. (2011, January 2). The freedom in education act. Susan Ohanian.org. Retrieved January 11, 2011, from http://susanohanian.org/outrage_fetch.php?id=840

Ladd, H. F., Fiske, E. B., & Ruijs, N. (2009, September). Parental choice in the Netherlands: Growing concerns about segregation. Retrieved November 21, 2009, from http://www.ncspe.org/publications_files/OP%20182.pdf

Lai, F. (2007, April). The effect of winning a first-choice school entry lottery on student performance: Evidence from a natural experiment. Retrieved August 6, 2009 from, http://www.ncspe.org/publications_files/OP139.pdf

Land, K. C. (2010, June 8). 2010 child well-being index (CWI). New York, NY: Foundation for Child Development. Retrieved August 15, 2011, from http://www.fcd-us.org/resources/2010-child-well-being-index-cwi

Landsberg, M. (2009, May 31). Spitting in the eye of mainstream education. *Los Angeles Times* online. Retrieved June 29, 2009, from http://www.latimes.com/news/education/la-me-charter31-2009may31,0,6482403.story

Larkin, J. (2011, February 18). 14 Democratic senators flee Wisconsin, teachers strike for second day in a row. *Ballot News*. Retrieved June 27, 2011, from http://ballotnews.org/2011/02/18/14-democratic-senators-flee-wisconsin-teachers-strike-for-second-day-in-a-row/

Learning about teaching: Initial findings from the measures of effective teaching project. (n.d.). METProject Research Paper. Seattle, Washington: Bill and Melinda Gates Foundation. Retrieved June 13, 2011 from, http://www.metproject.org/downloads/Preliminary_Findings-Research_Paper.pdf

Legend, J. (2010, October 4). Wake up! We know how to fix our schools. *Huffington Post*. Retrieved April 16, 2011, from http://www.huffingtonpost.com/john-legend/wake-up-we-know-how-to-fi_b_748608.html

Leonhardt, D. (2011, June 7). The German example. *The New York Times*. Retrieved July 5, 2011, from http://www.nytimes.com/2011/06/08/business/economy/08leonhardt.html

Levy, R. (2011a, January 9). Mr. President, we want your children's education, too. *truthout*. Retrieved January 11, 2011, from http://archive.truthout.org/mr-president-we-want-your-childrens-education-too66425

Levy, R. (2011b, May 28). Teach For America: From service group to industry. All Things Education [Web log post]. Retrieved June 26, 2011, from http://allthingsedu.blogspot.com/2011/05/teach-for-america-from-service-group-to.html

Lewin, T. (2011, January 8). Study finds family connections give big advantage in college admissions. *The New York Times*. Retrieved March 7, 2011, from http://www.nytimes.com/2011/01/09/education/09legacies.html

Lightbourn, G. (2007). The truth about choice in the public schools. Thiensville, WI: Wisconsin Policy Research Institute, Inc. Retrieved September 7, 2009, from http://www.wpri.org/Commentary/2007/10.07/Li10.29.07/Li10.29.07.html

Lubienski, C. (2009). Review of "A Win-Win Solution: The Empirical Evidence on How Vouchers Affect Public Schools." Boulder, CO: National Education Policy Center. Retrieved April 22, 2011, from http://nepc.colorado.edu/thinktank/review-win-win-solution

Lubienski, C., & Lubienski, S. T. (2006). Charter, private, public schools and academic achievement: New evidence from the NAEP mathematics data. Retrieved December 28, 2008, from http://www.ncspe.org/readrel.php?set=pub&cat=126

Lubienski, C., & Weitzel, P. (2008). The effects of vouchers and private schools in improving academic achievement: A critique of advocacy research. *Brigham Young University Law Review* (2), 447-485. Retrieved April 26, 2011, from http://lawreview.byu.edu/archives/2008/2/91LUBIENSKI.FIN.pdf

Lyons, D. (2010, December, 20). Bill Gates and Randi Weingarten. *Newsweek*. Retrieved January 11, 2011, from http://www.newsweek.com/2010/12/20/gates-and-weingarten-fixing-our-nation-s-schools.html

Lyons, G. (2011, April 6). Michelle Rhee: Education reform huckster. *Salon*. Retrieved April 22, 2011, from http://www.salon.com/news/politics/war_room/2011/04/06/michelle_rhee_lyons

Maher, B. (2010a). Episode 180. Interview with Richard Tillman. [Television series episode]. In *Real time with Bill Maher*. New York, NY: HBO. September 24, 2010. Retrieved from http://www.youtube.com/watch?v=Iwsy8FEL0ls

Maher, B. (2010b). Episode 193. Guests John Legend, Markos Moulitsas, Dana Loesch, and Dan Neil. [Television series episode]. In *Real time with Bill Maher*. New York, NY: HBO. October 15, 2010.

Marshak, D. (2010, February 19). Why did the Gates small-high-schools program fail?: Well, actually it didn't. *Education Week, 29*(22). Retrieved April 22, 2011, from http://www.edweek.org/ew/articles/2010/02/17/22marshak.h29.html

Martin, M. T. (2010, December 22). Waiting for superfraud. Kennewick School District Citizens [Web log post]. Retrieved from http://ksdcitizens.org/2010/12/22/waiting-for-superfraud/

Mathis, W. J. (2010). *The "Common Core" Standards Initiative: An Effective Reform Tool?* Boulder, CO and Tempe, AZ: Education and the Public Interest Center & Education Policy Research Unit. Retrieved March 8, 2011, from http://epicpolicy.org/publication/common-core-standards

Mathis, W. J. (2011, May 17). Refusing to confront reality: The great harm in pretending schools can close the poverty gap [Web log post]. National Education Policy Center. Retrieved May 28, 2011, from http://nepc.colorado.edu/blog/refusing-confront-reality-great-harm-pretending-schools-can-close-poverty-gap

Matthews, J. (2011, March 25). Vouchers work, but so what? Class Struggle. *The Washington Post*. Retrieved April 22, 2011 from http://www.washingtonpost.com/blogs/class-struggle/post/vouchers-work-but-so-what/2011/03/24/ABNNgrPB_blog.html

McKenzie, J. (2007, January). Good doubt and bad doubt. *The Question Mark, 3*(4). Retrieved April 22, 2011, from http://questioning.org/jan07/doubt.html

Michie, G. (2011, January 9). How to be taken seriously as a reformer (don't be an educator). The Answer Sheet (Web log post). *The Washington Post*. Retrieved January 10, 2011, from http://voices.washingtonpost.com/answer-sheet/guest-bloggers/how-to-be-taken-seriously-as-a.html

Miller, A. (1954). *The crucible*. New York, NY: Bantam Books.

Miracleschools. (2011). [Wiki]. San Francisco, CA: Tangient LLC. Retrieved July 5, 2011, from http://miracleschools.wikispaces.com/

Miron, G. (2011). Review of "Charter Schools: A Report on Rethinking the Federal Role in Education." Boulder, CO: National Education Policy Center. Retrieved April 26, 2011, from http://nepc.colorado.edu/thinktank/review-charter-federal.

Miron, G., & Urschel, J. L. (2010). *Equal or fair? A study of revenues and expenditure in American charter schools*. Boulder, CO and Tempe, AZ: Education and the Public Interest Center & Education Policy Research Unit. Retrieved April 26, 2011, from http://epicpolicy.org/publication/charter-school-finance

Miron, G., Urschel, J. L., Mathis, W, J., & Tornquist, E. (2010). *Schools without Diversity: Education management organizations, charter schools and the demographic stratification of the American school system*. Boulder, CO and Tempe, AZ: Education and the Public Interest Center & Education Policy Research Unit. Retrieved April 26, 2011, from http://epicpolicy.org/publication/schools-without-diversity

Miron, G., Urschel, J. L., & Saxton, N. (2011, March). What makes KIPP work?: A study of student characteristics, attrition, and school finance. Teachers College, Columbia University. Retrieved April 26, 2011, from http://www.ncspe.org/readrel.php?set=pub&cat=253

Molnar, A. (2001, April 11). The media and educational research: What we know vs. what the public hears. Milwaukee, WI: Center for Education Research, Analysis, and Innovation. Retrieved July 18, 2009, from http://epsl.asu.edu/epru/documents/cerai-01-14.htm

Moore, A., & Gibbons, D. (1986, 1987). *Watchmen*. New York, NY: DC Comics.

The National Council of the Churches of Christ in the USA. (2010). New York, NY. Retrieved August 16, 2011, from http://www.ncccusa.org/elmc/pastoralletter.pdf

National Opportunity to Learn Campaign. (2010). Civil rights framework for providing all students an opportunity to learn through reauthorization of the Elementary and Secondary Education Act. Retrieved 16 August 2011, from http://www.otlcampaign.org/resources/

civil-rights-framework-providing-all-students-opportunity-learn-through-reauthorization-el

Newport, F. (2010, December 17). Four in 10 Americans believe in strict creationism. Washington, DC: Gallup. Retrieved January 11, 2011, from http://www.gallup.com/poll/145286/Four-Americans-Believe-Strict-Creationism.aspx

Ng, J., & Rury, J. (2006a, July 20). Responding to Payne's response. *Teachers College Record*. Retrieved from www.tcrecord.org ID# 12610

Ng, J., & Rury, J. (2006b, July 18). Poverty and education: A critical analysis of the Ruby Payne phenomenon. *Teachers College Record*. Retrieved June 24, 2007, from http://www.tcrecord.org

Ng, J., & Rury, J. (2009, Winter). Problematizing Payne and understanding poverty: An analysis with data from the 2000 census. *Journal of Educational Controversy*, 4(1). Retrieved from http://www.wce.wwu.edu/Resources/CEP/eJournal/v004n001/a001.shtml

Ni, Y. (2007, September). The impact of charter schools on the efficiency of traditional public schools: Evidence from Michigan. Retrieved December 28, 2008, from http://www.ncspe.org/publications_files/OP145.pdf

Noah, T. (2010, September 3). The United States of inequality. *Slate*. Retrieved January 10, 2011, from http://www.slate.com/id/2266025/entry/2266026

Ong, S., Nakase, J., Moran, G. J., Karras, D. J., Kuehnart, M. J., & Talan, D. A. (2007, September). Antibiotic use for emergency department patients with upper respiratory infections: Prescribing practices, patient expectations, and patient satisfaction. *Annals of Emergency Medicine, 50*(3), 213-220.

Orwell, G. (1946). Politics and the English language. The Complete Works of George Orwell. Retrieved March 7, 2011, from http://www.george-orwell.org/Politics_and_the_English_Language/0.html

Osei-Kofi, N. (2005). Pathologizing the poor: A framework for understanding Ruby Payne's work. *Equity & Excellence in Education*, (38), 367-375.

Otterman, S. (2010, October 12). Lauded Harlem schools have their own problems. *The New York Times*. Retrieved May 28, 2011, from http://www.nytimes.com/2010/10/13/education/13harlem.html

Owen, J. (2006, August 10). Evolution less accepted in U.S. than other western countries, study finds. *National Geographic*. Retrieved January 11, 2011, from http://news.nationalgeographic.com/news/2006/08/060810-evolution.html

Pallas, A. (2009a, December 7). Just how gullible is Anderson Cooper? *Gotham Schools* [Web log post]. Retrieved March 22, 2010, from http://gothamschools.org/2009/12/07/just-how-gullible-is-anderson-cooper/

Pallas, A. (2009b, May 8). Just how gullible is David Brooks? *Gotham Schools* [Web log post]. Retrieved May 8, 2009, from http://gotham-schools.org/2009/05/08/just-how-gullible-is-david-brooks/

Pallas, A. (2009c, May 4). Wishful thinking. *Gotham Schools* [Web log post]. Retrieved March 8, 2011, from http://gothamschools.org/2009/05/04/wishful-thinking/comment-page-1/

Pareene, A. (2011, April 21). *Time* puts Michelle Rhee on a list, ignores her critics and scandals. *Salon*. Retrieved April 22, 2011, from http://www.salon.com/news/politics/war_room/2011/04/21/rhee_time

Peske, H. G., & Haycock, K. (2006, June). Teaching inequality: How poor and minority students are shortchanged on teacher quality. Washington DC: The Education Trust, Inc. Retrieved September 7, 2009, from http://www2.edtrust.org/NR/rdonlyres/010DBD9F-CED8-4D2B-9E0D-91B446746ED3/0/TQReportJune2006.pdf

Petrilli, M. J. (2011, June 10). A school reformer gets real. The Answer Sheet [Web log post]. *The Washington Post*. Retrieved July 5, 2011, from http://www.washingtonpost.com/blogs/answer-sheet/post/a-school-reformer-gets-real/2011/06/09/AGcNWvNH_blog.html

Pontari, B. A., & Rasmussen, P. R. (2009). Competition reconsidered: A perspective from psychology. In W. B. Worthen, A. S. Henderson, P. R. Rasmussen, & T. L. Benson (Eds.), *Competition: A multidisciplinary analysis* (pp. 47-59). Boston: Sense.

Poor, J. (2011, February 18). Michele Bachmann weighs in on Wisconsin teacher sick-out strike: "It's a dereliction of duty." *The Daily Caller*. Retrieved June 27, 2011, from http://dailycaller.com/2011/02/18/michele-bachmann-weighs-in-on-wisconsin-teacher-sick-out-strike-its-a-dereliction-of-duty/

Popham, W. J. (2001). *The Truth about testing: An educator's call to action*. Alexandria, VA: Association for Supervision and Curriculum Development.

Popham, W. J. (2003). *Test better, teach better: The instructional role of assessment*. Alexandria, VA: Association for Supervision and Curriculum Development.

Quintero, E. (2011, August 16). Merit pay: The end of innocence? Shanker Blog [Web log post]. Retrieved August 16, 2011, from http://shankerblog.org/?p=3410

Ramsay, C., Kull, S., Lewis, E., & Subias, S. (2010, December 10). Misinformation and the 2010 Election: A Study of the US Electorate. College Park, MD: University of Maryland. Retrieved from http://www.worldpublicopinion.org/pipa/pdf/dec10/Misinformation_Dec10_rpt.pdf

Randi Weingarten says students in strong union states perform better academically. (2010, September 2). PolitiFact.com. Retrieved April 22,

2011, from http://www.politifact.com/truth-o-meter/statements/2010/
sep/02/randi-weingarten/randi-weingarten-says-students-strong-
union-states/

Ravitch, D. (2009a, May 4). Data suggests NCLB slows student progress.
Common Core [Web log post]. Retrieved March 8, 2011, from http://
blog.commoncore.org/2009/05/04/ravitch-blogs-here-on-
naep-results-data-suggests-nclb-slows-student-progress/

Ravitch, D. (2009b, May 12). What the "Harlem Miracle" really teaches.
Bridging Differences [Web log post]. *Education Week*. Retrieved
December 27, 2009, from http://blogs.edweek.org/edweek/
Bridging-Differences/2009/05/what_the_harlem_miracle_really.html

Ravitch, D. (2010a). *The death and life of the great American school system:
How testing and choice are undermining education*. New York, NY: Basic
Books.

Ravitch, D. (2010b, October 26). Demonizing public education. Bridging
Differences [Web log post]. *Education Week*. Retrieved March 11, 2011,
from http://blogs.edweek.org/edweek/Bridging-Differences/2010/10/
dear_deborah_i_reviewed_waitin.html

Ravitch, D. (2010c, November 11). The myth of charter schools. *The New
York Review of Books*. Retrieved March 11, 2011, from http://
www.nybooks.com/articles/archives/2010/nov/11/myth-
charter-schools/

Ravitch, D. (2010d, November 23). 12th grade NAEP scores are meaning-
less. Bridging Differences [Web log post]. *Education Week*. Retrieved
July 6, 2011, from http://blogs.edweek.org/edweek/Bridging-
Differences/2010/11/12th_grade_naep_scores_are_mea.html

Ravitch, D. (2011a, February 15). Ravitch: The problem with Teach for
America. The Answer Sheet [Web log post]. *The Washington Post*.
Retrieved June 26, 2011, from http://voices.washingtonpost.com/
answer-sheet/diane-ravitch/ravitch-the-problem-with-teach.html

Ravitch, D. (2011b, April 5). Ignoring lessons of phony "Texas miracle."
The Answer Sheet [Web log post]. *The Washington Post*. Retrieved April
22, 2011, from http://www.washingtonpost.com/blogs/answer-sheet/
post/ravitch-ignoring-lessons-of-phony-texas-miracle/2011/04/05/
AFRENljC_blog.html

Ravitch, D. (2011c, May 31). Waiting for a school miracle. *The New York
Times*. Retrieved July 3, 2011, from http://www.nytimes.com/2011/06/
01/opinion/01ravitch.html

Ravitch, D. (2011d, June 12). A standardized path to school ruin. *St.
Petersburg Times*. Retrieved June 12, 2011, from http://www
.tampabay.com/news/perspective/a-standardized-path-to-school-ruin/
1174500

The real facts about Waiting for Superman. (2010, September 29). Jamaica Plain, MA: FairTest: The National Center for Fair and Open Testing. Retrieved March 11, 2011, from http://www.fairtest.org/real-facts-about-waiting-superman

Reardon, S. F. (2009). Review of "How New York City's charter schools affect achievement." Boulder, CO and Tempe, AZ: Education and the Public Interest Center & Education Policy Research Unit. Retrieved July 5, 2011, from http://epicpolicy.org/thinktank/review-How-New-York-City-Charter

Reed, P. (1995). "Player piano" overview. *The Vonnegut Web*. Retrieved January 11, 2011, from http://www.vonnegutweb.com/playerpiano/pp_peterjreed.html

Report of the Committee of Ten on Secondary School Studies. (1894). National Education Association. Retrieved September 25, 2009, from http://www.archive.org/stream/reportofcomtens00natirich/reportofcomtens00natirich_djvu.txt

Rich, A. (2001). *Arts of the possible: Essays and conversations*. New York, NY: W. W. Norton and Company.

Rickover, H. G. (1962). *Swiss schools and ours: Why theirs are better.* New York, NY: Little, Brown and Co.

Rickover, H. G. (1963). *American education, a national failure; the problem of our schools and what we can learn from England.* New York, NY: Dutton.

Riddile, M. (2010, December 15). PISA: It's poverty not stupid. The Principal Difference [Web log post]. Retrieved January 11, 2011, from http://nasspblogs.org/principaldifference/2010/12/pisa_its_poverty_not_stupid_1.html

Rose, M. (2011, January 5). Resolutions someone should make for 2011. The Answer Sheet [Web log post]. *The Washington Post*. Retrieved April 22, 2011, from http://voices.washingtonpost.com/answer-sheet/guest-bloggers/some-2011-resolutions-someone.html

Rothstein, J. (2011). Review of "Learning about teaching: Initial findings from the measures of effective teaching project." Boulder, CO: National Education Policy Center. Retrieved June 12, 2011, from http://nepc.colorado.edu/thinktank/review-learning-about-teaching.

Rothstein, R. (2010, October 14). How to fix our schools. Issue Brief 286. Washington DC: Economic Policy Institute. Retrieved January 10, 2011, from http://www.epi.org/publications/entry/ib286

Rothstein, R. (2011, March 11). How Bill Gates misinterprets ed facts. The Answer Sheet [Web log post]. *The Washington Post*. Retrieved March 11, 2011, from http://voices.washingtonpost.com/answer-sheet/school-turnaroundsreform/fact-challenged-education-poli.html

Rouse, C. E., & Barrow, L. (2008, August 6). School vouchers and student achievement: Recent evidence, remaining questions. The National

Center for the Study of Privatization in Education. Retrieved August 6, 2009, from http://www.ncspe.org/publications_files/OP163.pdf

Roy, J. (2010). Review of "How School Choice Can Create Jobs for South Carolina." Boulder, CO and Tempe, AZ: Education and the Public Interest Center & Education Policy Research Unit. Retrieved April 22, 2011, from http://epicpolicy.org/thinktank/Review-How-School-Choice

Sahlberg, P. (2010, December 27). Learning from Finland. *Boston.com*. Retrieved April 21, 2011, from http://articles.boston.com/2010-12-27/column/29316733_1_finland-teachers-or-schools-public-schools

Santelices, M. V., & Wilson, M. (2010, Spring). Unfair treatment? The case of Freedle, the SAT, and the standardization approach to differential item functioning. *Harvard Educational Review, 80*(1), 106-133.

Sato, M., & Lensmire, T. J. (2009, January). Poverty and Payne: Supporting teachers to work with children of poverty. *Phi Delta Kappan, 9*(5), 365-370.

Sawchuk, S. (2011). EWA research brief: What studies say about teacher effectiveness. Washington DC: Education Writers Association. Retrieved July 7, 2011, from http://www.ewa.org/site/PageServer?pagename=research_teacher_effectiveness

Schmidt, R., & Thomas, P. L. (2009). *21st century literacy: If we are scripted, are we literate?* Heidelberg, Germany: Springer.

Schorn, D. (2006, May 14). The Harlem Children's Zone: How one man's vision to revitalize Harlem starts with children. *60 Minutes*. Retrieved May 28, 2011, from http://www.cbsnews.com/stories/2006/05/11/60minutes/main1611936.shtml

Schulken, M. (2010, August 30). Researcher: Rural schools lose Race to Top. *Rural Education* [Web log post]. *Education Week* Retrieved March 7, 2011, from http://blogs.edweek.org/edweek/rural_education/2010/08/researcher_rural_schools_lose_race_to_the_top.html

Sears, J. T., Marshall, J. D., & Otis-Wilborn, A. (1994). *When best doesn't equal good: Education reform and teacher recruitment, a longitudinal study.* New York, NY: Teachers College Press.

Seelye, K. Q. (2010, November 29). Celebrating secession without the slaves. *The New York Times*. Retrieved January 11, 2011, from http://www.nytimes.com/2010/11/30/us/30confed.html?_r=1

Shakespeare, W. (1970). *Hamlet Prince of Denmark*. W. Farnham (Ed.). New York, NY: Penguin Books.

Shulman, R. (2009, August 2). Harlem program singled out as model. *The Washington Post*. Retrieved from http://www.washingtonpost.com/wp-dyn/content/article/2009/08/01/AR2009080102297.html

Sirota, D. (2010, September 12). The neoliberal bait-and-switch—the Great Education Myth. *The Seattle Times*. Retrieved February 10, 2011,

from http://seattletimes.nwsource.com/html/opinion/
2012865372_sirota13.html

Skeels, R. D. (2011a, June 12). NCTQ's LAUSD report's highly questionable veracity shows Bill Gates' pervasiveness and perniciousness.
Schools Matter [Web log post]. Retrieved July 3, 2011, from http://
www.schoolsmatter.info/2011/06/nctqs-lausd-reports-highly-question-
able.html

Skeels, R. D. (2011b, August 11). Elmo isn't Gramsci for kids and the
mythical soft bigotry of low expectations. *The Daily Censored*. Retrieved
August 16, 2011, from http://dailycensored.com/2011/08/11
/elmo-isnt-gramsci-for-kids-and-the-mythical-soft-bigotry-of-low-
expectations-debunked/

Smollin, M. (2011, January 6). Public servants and private schools: Where
top politicians send their kids. *Take Part*. Retrieved January 11, 2011,
from   http://www.takepart.com/news/2011/01/05/where-the-political-
whos-who-send-their-kids-to-school-

Snider, J. (2010, December 13). Lessons from Finland's education system.
Huffington Post. Retrieved March 8, 2011, from http://www
.huffingtonpost.com/justin-snider/finland-education-
system_b_794644.html

Snider, J. (2011, January 5). New book takes aim at ed reformers and status quo defenders. *Huffington Post*. Retrieved January 10, 2011, from
http://www.huffingtonpost.com/justin-snider/new-book-takes-aim-at-
ed-_b_804773.html

Sparks, S. D. (2011, June 23). Study finds gaps remain large for Hispanic
students. *Education Week, 30*(36). Retrieved July 7, 2011, from http://
www.edweek.org/ew/articles/2011/06/23/36hispanic.h30.html

Spelke, E. S. (2005, December). Sex differences in intrinsic aptitude for
mathematics and science? *American Psychologist, 60*(9), 950-958.

Spellings, M. (2011, February 22). It's an outrage. *Huffington Post*.
Retrieved June 27, 2011, from http://www.huffingtonpost.com/
margaret-spellings/its-an-outrage_b_826525.html

Stagnant, falling college admissions test scores reflect NCLB failure.
(2010, May 21). Jamaica Plain, MA: FairTest.org. Retrieved July 6,
2011, from http://www.fairtest.org/stagnant-falling-college-
admissions-scores

The standards. (2010). Common core state standards initiative: Preparing
America's students for college and career. Retrieved March 8, 2011,
from http://www.corestandards.org/the-standards

Starnes, B. A. (2008, June). On lilacs, tap-dancing, and children of poverty. *Phi Delta Kappan, 89*(1), 779-780.

Strauss, V. (2011a, January 3). America's disdain for its children. The
Answer Sheet [Web log post]. *The Washington Post*. Retrieved March

11, 2011, from http://voices.washingtonpost.com/answer-sheet/charter-schools/americas-disdain-for-its-child.html#more

Strauss, V. (2011b, March 10). Gates spends millions to sway public on ed reform. The Answer Sheet [Web log post]. *The Washington Post.* Retrieved March 11, 2011, from http://voices.washingtonpost.com/answer-sheet/gates-spends-millions-to-sway.html

Sweet, L. (2010, July 29). Obama National Urban League speech excerpts. The Scoop from Washington. *Chicago Sun-Times.* Retrieved January 10, 2011, from http://blogs.suntimes.com/sweet/2010/07/obama_national_urban_league_sp.html

Szabo, L. (2010, June 8). More than 1 in 5 kids live in poverty. *USA Today.* Retrieved March 7, 2011, from http://www.usatoday.com/news/health/2010-06-08-1Achild08_ST_N.htm

Taylor, J. (2009, December 22). Educating entrepreneurs will create prosperity. *The Greenville News.*

Taylor, J. (2011, August 1). The cluttered mind uncluttered. The Power of Prime [Web log post]. *Psychology Today.* Retrieved August 17, 2011, from http://www.psychologytoday.com/blog/the-power-prime/201108/education-arne-and-bills-misguided-adventure-open-letter

Thomas, P. L. (2009). Shifting from deficit to generative practices: Addressing impoverished and all students. *Teaching Children of Poverty, 1*(1). Retrieved September 13, 2009, from http://journals.sfu.ca/tcop/index.php/tcop/article/view/8/1

Thomas, P. L. (2010a). *Parental choice?: A critical reconsideration of choice and the debate about choice.* Charlotte, NC: Information Age Publishing.

Thomas, P. L. (2010b). The Payne of addressing race and poverty in public education: Utopian accountability and deficit assumptions of middle class America. *Souls, 12*(3), 262-283.

Thomas, P. L. (2010c, August 11). Why common standards won't work. *Education Week, 29*(37), 33-34.

Thomas, P. L. (2010d, August 14). Rugged individualism and our pursuit of education. *OpEdNews.com.* Retrieved from http://www.opednews.com/articles/Rugged-Individualism-and-O-by-Paul-Thomas-100813-901.html

Thomas, P. L. (2010e, August 17). Reconsidering education "miracles." *OpEdNews.com.* Retrieved from http://www.opednews.com/articles/Reconsidering-Education-M-by-P-L-Thomas-100816-438.html

Thomas, P. L. (2010f, August 21). Brave words? No, but startling occasion(s). *OpEdNews.com.* Retrieved from http://www.opednews.com/articles/Brave-Words-No-But-Star-by-P-L-Thomas-100821-426.html

Thomas, P. L. (2010g, August 27). Bitter lessons from chasing better tests. *OpEdNews.com.* Retrieved from http://www.opednews.com/articles/Bitter-Lessons-from-Chasin-by-P-L-Thomas-100826-630.html

Thomas, P. L. (2010h, September 6). Political reform must precede educational reform—Words matter. *OpEdNews.com*. Retrieved from http://www.opednews.com/articles/Political-Reform-Must-Prec-by-P-L-Thomas-100905-271.html

Thomas, P. L. (2010i, September 10). "The truth is always hard to swallow"—And other ironies. *OpEdNews.com*. Retrieved from http://www.opednews.com/articles/The-Truth-Is-Always-Hard-by-P-L-Thomas-100910-993.html

Thomas, P. L. (2010j, September 21). 2020 vision for No Child Left in Poverty. *OpEdNews.com*. Retrieved from http://www.opednews.com/articles/2020-Vision-for-No-Child-L-by-P-L-Thomas-100920-367.html

Thomas, P. L. (2010k, September 28). The great charter compromise: Masking corporate commitments in educational reform. *OpEdNews.com*. Retrieved from http://www.opednews.com/articles/The-Great-Charter-Compromi-by-P-L-Thomas-100927-363.html

Thomas, P. L. (2010l, October 6). Stop focusing on SAT. *The State*.

Thomas, P. L. (2010m, October 10). A tale of two films. *OpEdNews.com*. Retrieved from http://www.opednews.com/articles/A-Tale-of-Two-Films-by-Paul-Thomas-101010-109.html

Thomas, P. L. (2010n, October 16). "Don't ask, don't tell": There's a reason Captain America wears a mask. *OpEdNews.com*. Retrieved from http://www.opednews.com/articles/Don-t-Ask-Don-t-Tell-T-by-Paul-Thomas-101014-950.html

Thomas, P. L. (2010o, October 19). Legend of the fall: Snapshots of what's wrong in the education debate. *The Daily Censored*. Retrieved from http://dailycensored.com/2010/10/19/legend-of-the-fall-snapshots-of-whats-wrong-in-the-education-debate/

Thomas, P. L. (2010p, October 23). The (shifting) truth about charter schools. *OpEdNews.com*. Retrieved from http://www.opednews.com/articles/The-Shifting-Truth-about-by-Paul-Thomas-101021-188.html

Thomas, P. L. (2010q, October 24). The politicians who cried "crisis." *truthout*. Retrieved from http://www.truth-out.org/the-politicians-who-cried-crisis64359

Thomas, P. L. (2010r, November 3). Our debate culture—Someone wins, but never the Truth. *The Daily Censored*. Retrieved from http://dailycensored.com/2010/11/03/our-debate-culture%E2%80%94someone-wins-but-never-the-truth/

Thomas, P. L. (2010s, November 14). The teaching profession as a service industry. *The Daily Censored*. Retrieved from http://dailycensored.com/2010/11/14/the-teaching-profession-as-a-service-industry/

Thomas, P. L. (2010t, November 16). The corporate takeover of American schools. *Guardian.co.uk*. Retrieved from http://www

.guardian.co.uk/commentisfree/cifamerica/2010/nov/15/
education-schools

Thomas, P. L. (2010u, November 28). Our faith in a "culture of poverty" never left. *The Daily Censored*. Retrieved from http:// dailycensored.com/2010/11/28/our-faith-in-a-culture-of-poverty-never-left/

Thomas, P. L. (2010v, December 2). The education celebrity tour: Legend of the fall, pt. II. *The Daily Censored*. Retrieved from http:// dailycensored.com/2010/12/02/the-education-celebrity-tour-legend-of-the-fall-pt-ii/

Thomas, P. L. (2010w, December 6). The truth about failure in US schools. *Guardian.co.uk*. Retrieved from http://www.guardian.co.uk/ commentisfree/cifamerica/2010/dec/05/schools-education

Thomas, P. L. (2010x, December 16). Finnish envy. *OpEdNews.com*. Retrieved from http://www.opednews.com/articles/Finnish-Envy-by-Paul-Thomas-101214-873.html

Thomas, P. L. (2010y, December 17). Fire teachers, reappoint Rhee: Legend of the fall, pt. III. *The Daily Censored*. Retrieved from http:// dailycensored.com/2010/12/17/fire-teachers-reappoint-rhee-legend-of-the-fall-pt-iii/

Thomas, P. L. (2010z, December 26). Statistics obscuring real education challenge. *The State*. Retrieved from http://www.thestate.com/2010/12/ 26/1618366/thomas-statistics-obscuring-real.html

Thomas, P. L. (2010aa, December 28). Wrong questions = wrong answers: Legends of the fall, pt. IV. *The Daily Censored*. Retrieved from http:// dailycensored.com/2010/12/28/wrong-questions-wrong-answers-legend-of-the-fall-pt-iv/

Thomas, P. L. (2011a, January 3). Calculating the Corporate States of America: Revisiting Vonnegut's *Player Piano*. *OpEdNews*. Retrieved from   http://www.opednews.com/articles/Calculating-the-Corporate-by-Paul-Thomas-110103-130.html

Thomas, P. L. (2011b, January 8). Defending the status quo?—False dichotomies and the education reform debate. *OpEdNews*. Retrieved from   http://www.opednews.com/articles/Defending-the-Status-Quo--by-Paul-Thomas-110107-766.html

Thomas, P. L. (2011c, January 8). Spend energy on S.C. students, not on more tests. *The Greenville News*. Retrieved from http://www.greenville-online.com/article/20110108/OPINION/301080011/Paul-Thomas-Spend-energy-on-S-C-students-not-on-more-tests

Thomas, P. L. (2011d, January 10). Supermen or kryptonite?—Legend of the fall, pt. V. *The Daily Censored*. Retrieved from http:// dailycensored.com/2011/01/10/superman-or-kryptonite%E2%80%94legend-of-the-fall-pt-v/

Thomas, P. L. (2011e, January 12). 21st century segregation: Inverting King's dream. *The Daily Censored*. Retrieved from http:// dailycensored.com/2011/01/12/21st-century-segregation-inverting-kings-dream/

Thomas, P. L. (2011f, January 23). "Top level kids" and accountability—A radical response. *The Daily Censored*. Retrieved from http:// dailycensored.com/2011/01/23/top-level-kids-and-accountability%E2%80%94a-radical-response/

Thomas, P. L. (2011g, January 26). Belief culture: "We don't need no education." *truthout*. Retrieved from http://www.truth-out.org/ belief-culture-we-dont-need-no-education67154

Thomas, P. L. (2011h, February 4). The agenda behind teacher union-bashing. *Guardian.co.uk*. Retrieved from http://www.guardian.co.uk/ commentisfree/cifamerica/2011/feb/04/usdomesticpolicy-schools

Thomas, P. L. (2011i, March 1). Ironic lessons in education reform from Bill Gates. *OpEdNews.com*. Retrieved from http://www.opednews.com/ articles/Ironic-Lessons-in-Educatio-by-Paul-Thomas-110301-979.htm. Reposted at The Answer Sheet [Web log post]. *The Washington Post*, March 3, 2011, The Bill Gates problem in school reform.

Thomas, P. L. (2011j, March 13). "A question of power": Of accountability and teaching by numbers. *OpEdNews.com*. Retrieved from http:// www.opednews.com/articles/A-Question-of-Power--Of-by-Paul-Thomas-110311-481.html

Thomas, P. L. (2011k, March 27). Journalists, media fail education reform debate. *OpEdNews.com*. Retrieved from http://www.opednews.com/ articles/Journalists-Media-Fail-Ed-by-Paul-Thomas-110326-816.html

Thomas, P. L. (2011l, April 5). A case against standards. The Answer Sheet [Web log post]. *The Washington Post*. Retrieved from http:// www.washingtonpost.com/blogs/answer-sheet/post/2011/04/04/ AFgXSFgC_blog.html

Thomas, P. L. (2011m, April 6). Meritocracy myth v. the advantages of privilege (A tale of hubris). *The Daily Censored*. Retrieved from http:// dailycensored.com/2011/04/06/meritocracy-myth-v-the-advantages-of-privilege-a-tale-of-hubris/

Thomas, P. L. (2011n, April 11). Accountability? Start at the top. *OpEd-News.com*. Retrieved from http://www.opednews.com/articles/ Accountability-Start-at-t-by-Paul-Thomas-110411-375.html

Thomas, P. L. (2011o, April 22). Why advocacy and market forces fail education reform. *truthout*. Retrieved from http://www.truthout.org/ why-advocacy-and-market-forces-fail-education-reform

Thomas, P. L. (2011p, April 27). Shifting talking points among school choice advocates. *Daily Kos*. Retrieved from http://www.dailykos.com/

story/2011/04/27/970578/-Shifting-Talking-Points-among-School-Choice-Advocates

Thomas, P. L. (2011q, May 27). How do teachers matter? Not as change agents but as learning opportunities. *The Daily Censored*. Retrieved from   http://dailycensored.com/2011/05/27/how-do-teachers-matter-not-as-cause-agents-but-as-learning-opportunities/

Thomas, P. L. (2011r, May 30). Avoiding the poverty issue. Room for Debate. *The New York Times*.

Thomas, P. L. (2011s, June 3). NBA finals and "No Excuses" charters. *Daily Kos*. Reposted at The Answer Sheet [Web log post]. *The Washington Post*. NBA finals and 'no excuses' charter schools. Retrieved from http://www.washingtonpost.com/blogs/answer-sheet/post/nba-finals-and-no-excuses-charter-schools/2011/06/03/AGslHqIH_blog.html

Thomas, P. L. (2011t, June 7). Poverty and education: Questions raised, questions ignored. *Daily Kos*. Retrieved from http://www.dailykos.com/story/2011/06/07/982488/-Poverty-and-Education:-Questions-Raised,-Questions-Ignored

Thomas, P. L. (2011u, June 10). Public discourse about public discourse: Talking education reform. *Daily Kos*. [Web log post]. Retrieved from http://www.schoolsmatter.info/2011/06/public-discourse-about-public-discourse.html

Thomas, P. L. (2011v, June 26). Why the achievement gap matters and will remain. *Daily Kos*. Retrieved from http://www.dailykos.com/story/2011/06/26/988812/-Why-the-Achievement-Gap-Matters-and-Will-Remain

Thomas, P. L. (2011w, July 1). Smells like … another strawman argument. *Daily Kos*. Retrieved from http://www.dailykos.com/story/2011/07/01/990467/-Smells-Like--Another-Strawman-Argument

Thomas, P. L. (2011x, July 7). Test-based accountability and international comparisons—Lessons ignored. *The Daily Censored*. Retrieved from http://dailycensored.com/2011/07/07/test-based-accountability-and-international-comparisons%E2%80%94lessons-ignored/

Thomas, P. L. (2011y, July 21). Cheating? How about the cheated. *Daily Kos*. Retrieved from http://www.schoolsmatter.info/2011/07/cheating-how-about-cheated.html

Thomas, P. L. (2011z, July 27). The power and failure of coercion. *Daily Kos*. Retrieved from http://www.dailykos.com/story/2011/07/27/999397/-The-Power-and-Failure-of-Coercion

Thomas, P. L. (2011aa, August 8). Poverty and testing in education: "The present scientifico-legal complex." *The Daily Censored*. Retrieved from http://dailycensored.com/2011/08/08/poverty-and-testing-in-education-%E2%80%9Cthe-present-scientifico-legal-complex%E2%80%9D/

Thoreau, H. D. (1863). Life without principle. The Thoreau Reader. Retrieved August 17, 2011 from http://thoreau.eserver.org/lifewout.html

Tough, P. (2011, July 7). No, seriously: No excuses. *The New York Times*. Retrieved July 8, 2011, from http://www.nytimes.com/2011/07/10/magazine/reforming-the-school-reformers.html?pagewanted=1&_r=1

Traub, J. (2000, January 16). What no school can do. *New York Times Magazine*. Retrieved August 17, 2011, from http://local.provplan.org/pp170/materials/what%20no%20school%20can%20do.htm

Tucker, M. S. (2011, May 24). Standing on the shoulders of giants: An American agenda for education reform. Washington DC: National Center on Education and the Economy. Retrieved July 7, 2011, from http://www.ncee.org/wp-content/uploads/2011/05/Standing-on-the-Shoulders-of-Giants-An-American-Agenda-for-Education-Reform.pdf

Twain, M. (2000). *The autobiography of Mark Twain* (C. Neider, Ed). New York; Harper Collins.

U. S. Department of Education. (2010). A blueprint for reform: The reauthorization of the Elementary and Secondary Education Act. Retrieved May 28, 2011 from http://www2.ed.gov/policy/elsec/leg/blueprint/publication_pg5.html

Valencia, R. R. (2010). *Dismantling contemporary deficit thinking: Educational thought and practice*. New York, NY: Routledge.

Viadero, D., & Honawar, V. (2008, June 11). National-board teachers found to be effective. *Education Week, 27*(42). Retrieved November 4, 2009, from http://www.edweek.org/ew/articles/2008/06/11/42nrc_web.h27.html

Vonnegut, K. (1952). *Player piano*. New York, NY: Dell.

Vonnegut, K. (1991). *Fates worse than death: An autobiographical collage*. New York, NY: Berkley Books.

Walsh, M. (2010, October 21). Court: No teacher speech rights on curriculum. School Law [Web log post]. *Education Week*. Retrieved May 29, 2011, from http://blogs.edweek.org/edweek/school_law/2010/10/court_no_free_speech_rights_fo.html

Watson, L., & Ryan, C. (2009, June). Choice, vouchers and the consequences for public high schools: Lessons from Australia. Retrieved November 6, 2009, from http://www.ncspe.org/publications_files/OP181.pdf

Weiderspan, J. P., & Danziger, S. K. (2009). Review: *A framework for understanding poverty*. *Social Work, 54*(4), 376.

Welner, K. (2010, June 22). New KIPP study underestimates attrition effects. Boulder, CO: National Education Policy Center. Retrieved July 13, 2011, from http://nepc.colorado.edu/newsletter/2010/06/new-kipp-study-underestimates-attrition-effects-0

Welner, K. G., Hinchey, P. H., Molnar, A., & Weltzman, D., Eds. (2010). *Think tank research quality: Lessons for policy makers, the media, and the public.* Charlotte, NC: Information Age Publishing.

Wenglinsky, H. (2007, October). Are private high schools better academically than public high schools? The National Center for the Study of Privatization in Education. Retrieved December 28, 2008, from http://www.cep-dc.org/index.cfm?fuseaction=document_ext.showDocumentByID&nodeID=1&DocumentID=226

White, J. (2005, May 4). Army withheld details about Tillman's death. *The Washington Post.* Retrieved March 8, 2011, from http://www.washingtonpost.com/wp-dyn/content/article/2005/05/03/AR2005050301502.html

Whitehurst, G. J., & Croft, M. (2010, July 20). The Harlem Children's Zone, Promise Neighborhoods, and the broader, bolder approach to education. Washington, DC: Brown Center on Education Policy at Brookings. Retrieved March 30, 2011, from http://www.brookings.edu/reports/2010/0720_hcz_whitehurst.aspx

Whitman, D. (2008, Fall). An appeal to authority. *Education Next, 8*(4). Retrieved June 29, 2009 from http://educationnext.org/an-appeal-to-authority/

Why Johnny Can't Read. (1955, March 14). *Time.* Retrieved March 8, 2011, from http://www.time.com/time/magazine/article/0,9171,807107,00.html

Winerip, M. (2011, April 17). In public school efforts, a common background: Private education. *The New York Times.* Retrieved April 21, 2011, from http://www.nytimes.com/2011/04/18/education/18winerip.html

Witte, J. F., Carlson, D. E., & Lavery, L. (2008, July). Moving on: Why students move between districts under open enrollment. The National Center for the Study of Privatization in Education. Retrieved August 6, 2009, from http://www.ncspe.org/readrel.php?set=pub&cat=211

Wolf, P., Gutmann, B., Puma, M., Kisida, B., Rizzo, L., Eissa, N. et al. (2009, March). Evaluation of the DC Opportunity Scholarship Program: Final Report. Washington, DC: U.S. Department of Education, Institute of Education Sciences, National Center for Education Evaluation and Regional Assistance. Retrieved August 6, 2009, from http://ies.ed.gov/ncee/pubs/20104018/index.asp

Wylie, C. (2006). What is the reality of school competition? The National Center for the Study of Privatization in Education. Retrieved October 5, 2008, from http://www.ncspe.org/publications_files/OP126.pdf

Yeigh, M., Cunningham, A., & Shagoury, R. (2011, Summer). Testing what matters least: What we learned when we took the Praxis Reading Specialist Test. *Rethinking Schools*. Retrieved June 9, 2011, from http://rethinkingschools.org/archive/25_04/25_04_yeigh.shtml

Yettick, H. (2009). *The research that reaches the public: Who produces the educational research mentioned in the news media?* Boulder, CO and Tempe, AZ: Education and the Public Interest Center & Education Policy Research Unit. Retrieved August 5, 2009, from http://epicpolicy.org/publication/research-that-reaches

Zhao, Y. (2010, December 10). A true wake-up call for Arne Duncan: The real reason behind Chinese students top PISA performance. Yong Zhao [Web log post]. Retrieved January 11, 2011, from http://zhaolearning.com/2010/12/10/a-true-wake-up-call-for-arne-duncan-the-real-reason-behind-chinese-students-top-pisa-performance/

Zimmer, R., & Buddin, R. (2005, July). Charter school performance in urban districts: Are they closing the achievement gap? Working paper prepared for the Smith Richardson Foundation. Santa Monica, CA: RAND.

Zinn, H. (1994). *You can't be neutral on a moving train: A personal history of our times*. Boston: Beacon Press.

Zinn, H. (2003). *A people's history of the United States: 1492-present*. New York, NY: Harper Perennial.

ABOUT THE AUTHORS

P. L. Thomas, Associate Professor of Education (Furman University, Greenville SC), taught high school English in rural South Carolina before moving to teacher education. He is a column editor for *English Journal* (National Council of Teachers of English) and series editor for *Critical Literacy Teaching Series: Challenging Authors and Genres* (Sense Publishers), in which he authored the first volume—*Challenging Genres: Comics and Graphic Novels* (2010). He has served on major committees with NCTE and co-edits *The South Carolina English Teacher* for SCCTE. Recent books include *Parental Choice?: A Critical Reconsideration of Choice and the Debate about Choice* (Information Age Publishing, 2010) and *21st Century Literacy: If We Are Scripted, Are We Literate?* (Springer, 2009), co-authored with Renita Schmidt.

He has also published books on Barbara Kingsolver, Kurt Vonnegut, Margaret Atwood, and Ralph Ellison. His scholarly work includes dozens of works in major journals—*English Journal, English Education, Souls, Notes on American Literature, Journal of Educational Controversy, Journal of Teaching Writing*, and others. His commentaries have been included in The Answer Sheet (*Washington Post*), Room for Debate (*The New York Times*), *The Guardian* (UK), *truthout, Education Week, The Daily Censored, OpEdNews, The State* (Columbia, SC), and *The Greenville News* (Greenville, SC). His work can be followed at http://wrestlingwithwriting.blogspot.com/ and @plthomasEdD on twitter.

PREFACE AUTHOR BIO

Adam Bessie is an assistant professor of English at Diablo Valley College, a community college in the San Francisco Bay Area. He is a contributor to the award-winning Project Censored book series, a staff writer for its online counterpart, *Daily Censored,* and has appeared on KPFA Berkeley's Project Censored Radio, which is syndicated nationally. Bessie is also regular contributor to Truthout, and has been published in the *Washington Post's* "Answer Sheet." He lives in Oakland, California, with his wife, a public high school social studies teacher, and his son.

CPSIA information can be obtained at www.ICGtesting.com
Printed in the USA
LVOW070112211212

312721LV00002B/59/P